T0272465

A NEW
PHILOSOPHY
OF OPERA

A NEW PHILOSOPHY OF OPERA

YUVAL SHARON

Liveright Publishing Corporation

A Division of W. W. Norton & Company
Independent Publishers Since 1923

For information about permission to reproduce selections from this book,
write to Permissions, Liveright Publishing Corporation, a division of
W. W. Norton & Company, Inc., 500 Fifth Avenue, New York, NY 10110

For information about special discounts for bulk purchases, please contact
W. W. Norton Special Sales at specialsales@wwnorton.com or 800-233-4830

Manufacturing by Lakeside Book Company
Book design by Beth Steidle
Production manager: Julia Druskin

ISBN 978-1-63149-686-8

Liveright Publishing Corporation, 500 Fifth Avenue, New York, N.Y. 10110
www.wwnorton.com

W. W. Norton & Company Ltd., 15 Carlisle Street, London W1D 3BS

10 9 8 7 6 5 4 3 2 1

We are not so rich that we can do
without tradition. Let one with new
ears listen to it in a new way.
        —WALTER KAUFMANN, introduction to his
        English translation of Martin Buber's *I and Thou*

CONTENTS

The PLAYLIST referenced throughout *A New Philosophy of Opera* can be accessed at the book's webpage:

A NEW
PHILOSOPHY
OF OPERA

OVERTURE

AN ART FORM WITHOUT A FUTURE

LET'S IMAGINE A NEAR FUTURE—FORTY, MAYBE FIFTY years from now—in which the art form of opera ceases to exist.

In that future, our opulent opera houses would be transformed into experiential shopping malls, or perhaps expensive condominiums. Better yet: innovative live-shop combinations. Opera recordings don't necessary vanish; they just don't make the cut for an upgrade to however people consume music in the future. Music scores survive, but without performance opportunities they become dusty documents buried deep in academic libraries. The notes now seem more like hieroglyphic symbols than the language of music.

On the surface, little might seem to distinguish that future from our present. But I imagine that artists in an opera-free future would start feeling restless in their isolation from each other. Without opera, the most ingenious composers would probably turn less to symphony orchestras (assuming that symphonic works somehow managed to survive) and get involved in the latest forms of media, all of which need music. The other artists who make up opera—the poet, the director, the singers, the dancers, the instrumentalists, and the conductor—would all likely follow lonelier pursuits. Without opera, there would be no mechanism in place for artists to undertake ludicrously large-scale collaborations.

Yet I also like to imagine these future artists coming together to dream about a new art form that transcends each of their limited spheres of influence. Maybe they will have heard about a lost art form that defied all categorization but its own, and be inspired to re-create it on their own terms. What they create may not look or sound or feel like what we would call *opera* today . . . and yet, opera would be reborn.

Preoccupation with opera as a dying art never feels entirely unjustified, because this art form actually demands death in order to fulfill its true imperative: *to be reborn*.

Rebirth is opera's true power, manifested through the act of performance. Every time an opera appears on the stage, it's not simply replayed but resuscitated, renewed, reshaped. The dead-or-dying attitude results in historical reenactment, as if opera were a statue embalming an ideology. But an opera of rebirth is a shape-shifter: protean, not predictable. It resists getting pinned down and instead demands re-view and revision. Opera creates a circle where others see a line, with the past and the future inseparable and articulating each other. It's easy to claim opera is dying in the linear experience of time. It's much more difficult to recognize opera's cyclical identity as an art of resurrection.

In that future, where opera houses are converted into shopping malls, what would a reborn opera look like? What would emerge from the unruly and barely explicable impulse to collectively create?

// // // // //

A PHILOSOPHY OF OPERA—A FAITH in what it is and a vision for what it can be—animates everything I do as an opera director. This book attempts to articulate that vision in both practical and theoretical ways.

Mine is a philosophy without a system—because opera is an art form that is most exciting when it is unpredictable and unsystematic. While systems of philosophy attempt to classify, I think a philosophy of opera should constantly *de-classify*. Any definition of opera is a tricky and ultimately unsatisfying proposition that quickly produces its own exception:

An opera is a story told in music → Yes, but then what about Philip Glass's *Einstein on the Beach* and other operas without a narrative?

An opera is through-composed with singing from beginning to end. → Yes, but then what about *The Magic Flute*, the original versions of *Carmen* or *Faust,* and other operas with quite a bit of spoken dialogue? What, then, about a work like *Perfect Lives* by Robert Ashley, which has no singing at all? And what are mega-musicals like *Les Misérables* and *The Phantom of the Opera,* which are also through-composed?

All operas feature unamplified voices. → Yes, but then what about operas from the last thirty years or so, composed specifically for amplified voices? And would this mean opera must be eternally stuck in a time before microphones?

Opera's essential condition dodges any attempt to reduce it to a singularity—whether one singular voice or one singular meaning. So I will resist hard-and-fast definitions; they will ultimately keep opera trapped as what it currently is instead of making room for what may yet come.

The lack of definition doesn't scare an ideal opera lover. And I do have an ideal audience in mind, both for this book and for my productions. These spectators come to the theater in search of *imagination.* They realize that each performance is a new opportunity for venturing somewhere new and for expanding their minds. They relish the opportunity to view the world from a different perspective and to hear new voices that bring out something unique even from the oldest scores. Confronted by the unexpected, they don't fall into confusion or fight against it furiously; they lean in, curious, eager to know what will transpire over the course of the performance. They may eventually decide that they disagreed with what they saw. But the consideration of another perspective and the opportunity to think differently are ultimately the primary reason they bought a ticket in the first place. The risk is its own reward.

The casual reader should not feel embarrassed if this sounds foreign. Imagination can often be a luxurious extra rather than a given in an art form that for many is solely about re-creation. Yet there is no shortage of historical evidence for an audience's desire for novelty, at least according to the *Oxford Handbook of the Operatic Canon*. While that title may imply a love of everything rigid and classifiable in opera, the editors suggest instead that "for the majority of its 400-year history, opera was brought into the public domain through a lively marketplace in which novelty was the immediate, and often the only measure of value." When opera was most popular, the emphasis was always on the new. Seventeenth-century commercial theaters in Venice offered seasons in which only 15 percent of the repertoire consisted of repeated works, and "the score itself rarely survived the season for which it had been written." Until the nineteenth century and the appearance of Gioachino Rossini, Italy's musical culture was "commercial, craftsmanlike, collaborative, and ephemeral . . . centered on the here and now of production." Opera differed from city to city, rather than fitting a national concept, and the differences are more drastic when you compare countries.

But no matter where opera was produced, the emphasis was resolutely on either new works or existing works (no more than forty years old) that were given a fresh approach. London in the eighteenth century, for example, saw an overwhelming public demand for work "recently written on the continent and shipped over; newly written for London by the Opera House composer; older works newly dressed up with additions and alterations; or more elaborate structures, with old and new arias used in an established text, usually referred to as *pasticcios*." By the end of the century, the demand for novelty waned as a collection of masterpieces took shape.

> The final development of the "canon"—a group of works whose "greatness" was agreed on and from which a season's offerings might be drawn—was a disaster for the writing and staging of London opera. The audience, which had previously wanted drama and music in the latest styles by the newest composers, was given an "artistic" excuse to become gradually more and more conservative, a shift of taste and attitude that on one hand permanently stultified the repertory and on the other narrowed the horizons of the audience's ambition.

This snapshot of conservative audiences in late eighteenth-century London should sound familiar to twenty-first century audiences of opera in America.

Thinking cyclically rather than cynically, believing in opera as the art form of rebirth, we might prepare the ground for something more imaginative to emerge.

That process could begin right now.

Let's start thinking of opera as evolutionary rather than decaying. Let's consider the experience of going to the opera as a way of thinking and feeling that will benefit us outside the theater. Let's start viewing opera as an engine for empathy and awe, and decide to attend a performance with an explorer's mindset. That means opening ourselves up to the unfamiliar. What would happen if we approached opera on those terms, actively developing our curiosity about things we can't fathom but long to know?

Let's stop thinking about opera as a classification and instead identify both its field of possibilities and its repertoire of clichéd postures:

Opera wants to seem a sovereign, but it's actually a wanderer.

It behaves like a sage, when it's actually a rascal.

It fancies itself a fortress, although it's nothing but an organization of air.

All diamantine, frozen views of opera, widely on display most anywhere you look, are what need to stop "dying" and actually die—

Die, so that opera can be reborn.

/ / / / /

FOR AN ART FORM OF rebirth, the most potent path forward into
the future lies in its origins.

It was in a comfortable room that the Florentine gentlemen first
met, at the court of Count Giovanni de' Bardi in 1573. They were
humanists from different fields of study who shared a passion for exploring ancient and new forms of music and drama. Music, they believed,
had become corrupt and extravagant in their society. The fashion for
polyphony—where two or more equally prominent melodies are performed simultaneously—rendered poetic texts inaudible and ineffec-
tive. To truly evoke emotions and psychological truth, a leaner, more
spare musical style would be needed—perhaps taking on the clarity
and directness that distinguished the great comedies and tragedies of
ancient Athens.

They looked back to antiquity to forge something new.

This group provoked rivalry and inspiration around Italy, and some
thirty years later earned the name "Camerata," for the comfortable
"chamber" that served as their meeting place.

Whenever I read about the aspirations of those Florentine gentlemen of the Camerata, I can't help but wonder what they would make of
the peculiar art form that survived them by over 400 years. How would
they regard the institutions and professionalism that have made its
preservation a matter of routine? Would they consider that a "dialogue
between ancient and modern" was still taking place, or would they see a
stalemate of predictability?

I hark back to this original meeting of minds any time I encourage
people to give opera a chance. Try imagining the motley group of artists: a
composer, a poet, a group of musicians, some talented singers, and crafts-
people capable of creating elaborate visions (carpenters and painters to

build sets, a talented tailor with a flair for fantasy to make the costumes, and so on). Their gatherings were likely a glorious chaos, with no real designation for what it was they were founding. And rather than a faithful reproduction of classical antiquity, their Frankenstein monster—cobbled together from the talents of various and sometimes competing artisans—became a new art form, resisting any effort to catalogue it.

When this background is taken into account, the first operas always end up sounding less like the prototype for the highly systematized genre we know today and more like the sixteenth-century forerunner of happenings and performance art. Over the course of four centuries, this bizarre species morphed and adapted to the contemporaneous moment, evolving through geography, politics, fashion, and technology. If future artists do one day collaborate to revive the dead art form of what was once opera, everything they need to know can be found at its beginning.

// // // // //

THE OLDEST SURVIVING OPERA SCORE that's still frequently performed today is a collaboration between the composer Claudio Monteverdi and the poet Alessandro Striggio. *L'Orfeo*, their setting of the Orpheus myth, premiered during the 1607 Carnival season in Mantua. It was not called an opera, since the genre's name wasn't yet fixed. It was described as a *favola in musica*, or a fable told through music.

The first person we meet in this sung drama is the living embodiment of music ("La musica"), who introduces herself: "I am Music, who can calm each troubled heart and kindle the most frigid minds— sometimes with anger, sometimes with love" (SEE PLAYLIST). Even if La musica only appears in the brief Prologue, music itself is central to the depictions of celebration (the raucous wedding dances of shepherds and nymphs, Orpheus's joy at the prospect of a happy marriage to Eurydice) and mourning (the sad narration of Silvia, or "the Messenger," who describes Eurydice's death by snakebite, and the moving lament of two anonymous shepherds). In descending to the underworld to vie for his lost love, Orpheus uses his captivating singing voice to charm and lull to sleep the stone-cold ferryman who keeps watch over the river of the dead. And when Orpheus fails at the unprecedented task of releasing his fiancée from death (by breaking the one restriction placed on him, looking back at her), music becomes a final, lonely lament that moves the god Apollo to descend from his divine perch in the sky. As the god of music, Apollo makes a fitting father for the singer Orpheus, and his appearance acts as a bookend to a work that began with music's embodiment.

Historians speculate that early opera needed to justify the strange reality of characters singing rather than speaking. Contemporary audiences, who have grown accustomed to naturalism in most narrative art, can certainly relate to this concern; the idea of dialogue conveyed through song still strikes many as ridiculous. For the creators of early opera, the master singer Orpheus validated the new form of storytelling: he is always performing, praying, praising, or lamenting in ways that ground music in an understandable narrative reality. We know of two settings of the Orpheus story prior to Monteverdi, and there have been over seventy others since 1607. So the mythological Orpheus is not just a character in a drama: he became the father of a genre where song serves as the necessary expression of individuality.

The overall character of Monteverdi's music is declamatory, with the contour of the sung line closely following the text. Polyphony is mostly avoided so the poetry can come through clearly. The effect can feel like a play with music as the engine. Later operas would designate this type of dramatic setting *recitative,* or dramatic recitation, separate from musical set pieces that became known as *arias.* Arias are still what most audiences look forward to the most when attending an opera; they are the "big moments" for a solo performer, and may have become familiar from recordings, commercials, or performances at weddings. An aria can be an oasis within a narrative. You can fall in love with one without knowing the broader context of the opera it's part of—the plot or the language it's written in—as the melody carries so much of the emotional content. Recitative, on the other hand, is harder to appreciate if you can't follow the text, since the twists and turns, the rhymes and rhythms, of the language are precisely what the music and the performer are charged to articulate. Next to an aria, an accompanying recitative can usually feel like a dry offset, the "necessary evil" of contextualization—ideally, something quickly dispatched.

When Monteverdi wrote *Orfeo,* no such division between recitative and aria existed. Though the work features a few self-conscious songs in strophic patterns, only one moment in the opera could be considered a precursor of the aria: Orpheus's plea to the ferryman, known by his first words, "Possente spirito." Far from dry text-setting, Monteverdi's score is full of micro-melodies within the resonant language of the poetry. Even if they rarely blossom into aria-like musical moments, those fleeting melodies create a moment-by-moment fascination that can make for stirring drama. In Monteverdi's recitative-like style, enormous license is given to the performers. It becomes their responsibility to bring out the emotions and interiority of a character. *Orfeo* may be short on arias, but it teems with soliloquies that can feel Shakespearean. (*Hamlet* predates *Orfeo* by only seven years.)

Of the many theatrical works Monteverdi composed, only two besides *L'Orfeo* survive, both written for commercial theaters in Venice: *The Return of Ulysses to His Homeland* (1640) and *The Coronation of Poppea* (1643). Part of what makes these works fascinating is how little we know about how they were performed. Even the printed score leaves out such vital information as precise instrumentation, and no designs for the original production remain. Crucial instructions were not written down but transmitted verbally in rehearsal, built directly on the voices of the performers.

So at the dawn of opera, a composer's score was more of an instruction manual for particular performers, barely more than suggestion, and not created for posterity or future interpreters. And just as Monteverdi's performers were charged to bring the music and the characters to life, contemporary interpreters are offered that same sense of freedom and possibility. The singer who embodies Orpheus today is allowed to make choices suited to his instrument and his temperament, rather than repeating the discoveries of his predecessors. Ideally, the results feel extemporaneous and fresh, born in the moment rather than fixed through routine. Because the individual personality of the interpreter infuses the piece with soul, no two performances are ever alike.

Our current operatic landscape is vastly different from those heady early days: the spontaneity at the heart of Monteverdi's work has become calcified, and the institutions administering opera seem driven mostly by a desire for efficient, predictable reproductions. But each time Monteverdi is performed, necessitating the agency of performers and audience alike, contemporary audiences can reset their expectations. Reimagining opera as it used to be can constantly remind us of what opera may still become.

The future is always already there, in our past.

// // // // //

LET'S BEGIN BY IMAGINING THAT opera was born from the same spirit of inquiry that fuels speculative scientists—the posture I imagine the Camerata took, and the one that will motivate those imagined future artists who inherit an opera-less world. In both cases, opera is not a thing but a mechanism for a meeting of minds, spilling beyond every convention. Opera becomes the co-articulation of a singular expression, containing multitudes of messiness and mania. Not the confirmation or the illustration of accepted values, but an ambiguous search for what is unclassifiable and unspeakable. An unruly and unstable genre that unifies many personalities and embraces an encyclopedia of idiosyncrasies. Not a statement but a poem, one that might begin like this:

What art form could adequately
    mirror in miniature
        humanity
            in its peripatetic absurdity
                fugitive destiny
                    and extravagant illusion?

1

"DON'T YOU GET IT?"

A FIRST TIME AT THE OPERA

THE CRUCIAL MOMENT IN RICHARD WAGNER'S LAST opera, *Parsifal* (1882), is an anticipatory one: an elderly, long-winded knight brings a young boy without a name into a secret gathering. It's the sacred convocation of the knights of the Holy Grail. Their king, a wounded, tormented man, is forced to undergo a painful ritual of uncovering the relic. The knights feast on the sight of the chalice, gathering strength and summoning inspiration just from the sight of the holy object. Then they shuffle off to await the next unveiling.

The elderly knight believes the nameless boy possesses some special quality that may benefit the knights' community. Perhaps this boy, granted access to the mysterious ritual, will recognize a higher calling and bring forth some healing through the promise of continuity. The world around the boy seems to melt around him in a way he doesn't understand: "I'm hardly moving at all, and yet I've gone so far." The knight responds with a riddle: "Here time becomes space." Along with the boy, the audience is taken into the ritual space, accompanied by hallucinatory sounds that collapse all conventional dimensions (SEE PLAYLIST).

Some thirty minutes later, the ritual is over and the boy is left behind, dumbfounded. The elderly knight scolds him: "Don't you know what you just saw?" The boy tries to replicate what he experienced with a gesture, but it's a mimicry without feeling and without knowledge. Imagine the knight's disappointment, realizing that this boy who seemed special didn't understand a thing.

Anyone who has attended the opera as a young person intuitively understands this scene.

If we replace the mysterious ritual of the unveiling of the Grail with a night at the opera house, we have one of the best evocations of what it feels like to see your first opera. There you were, living your best childhood, which probably didn't involve sitting in a dark theater for hours at a time (like the young boy in *Parsifal*, who is a carefree hunter before stumbling upon the knight). An older and usually grouchier person consents to do something that will be "good for you." They take you to the opera—and what could be more of a holy grail in our culture than opera?

What transpires is a barely decipherable ceremony that makes you feel like the only one who never received instructions. Everyone else seems to know exactly what to do: when to clap and, more important, when not to clap; what to look for and what to appreciate; which aspects, strange as they seem, are not to be questioned. If at the end you didn't understand a thing, then you are nothing but a fool—although, of course, the failed visit invites other admonishments, such as "Do you have any idea how much these tickets cost?" Or "Do you know how lucky you are to be able to enjoy something like this?" (And if your first opera coincidentally happens to be *Parsifal*, then you're really out of luck, because Act I runs two hours with two more acts to go.)

The boy (whose name happens to be Parsifal) is made to feel at fault—just as first-time audience members must be when failing to respond to the pageantry unfolding before them. But who is truly responsible for this lack of connection? Could something be wrong with the ritual itself?

Is it the opera or the way it's presented that fails to elicit so little stirring in newcomers? Maybe, like in *Parsifal*, neither the young person's ignorance nor the inherent power of the ritual is to blame, but rather the way the ritual unfolds: the knights' blind obedience to habit dimming the light of the ideals they claim to uphold, to the point of snuffing it out entirely.

Samuel Beckett called habit "the great deadener," and nowhere is that more palpable than in the opera house, where responsible clockwork is prioritized over inspiration. It's all too common to enter an opera house and see a work born of intense inspiration that's been lobotomized by routine. That routine offers safety to people who have learned to limit their imaginative scope; it becomes a form of protection from the very holiness we claim to have desired when we bought a ticket. That holiness is the sacred convocation of artist and spectator sharing common time, common space, and that common realm where time becomes space. But most nights at the opera suffer the dull edge of routine in unimaginative and woefully under-rehearsed productions, offering an experience not dissimilar from the mumbled participation and general distraction of so many religious communities.

A first-time operagoer, surrounded with the promise of a religious experience, may find themselves left cold, forced to concede, "It must be me; I must not be ___(A)___ enough to understand this." It would take a lightning bolt of enlightenment for them to voluntarily return to a space that made them feel so ___(B)___.

A		B
smart	→	stupid
privileged	→	disadvantaged
sophisticated	→	illiterate
rich	→	poor
old	→	immature
awake	→	sleepy

Just as Parsifal is chastised for "not getting" what he was so fortunate to witness, everything about the ritual of opera can make an initiate feel deeply unsettled about their participation. It's no small discomfort;

in the wrong circumstances, the experience can awaken an existential uneasiness, striking at the heart of your identity—how you view yourself and your position in society.

// // // // //

IN THE 1990 FILM *PRETTY WOMAN*, a rich gentleman (Richard Gere) takes his escort (Julia Roberts) to a night at the opera—Giuseppe Verdi's *La traviata* (1853), the story of a nineteenth-century prostitute who dies just as she finds true love. Before the opera begins, the gentleman gives her the kind of pompous advice you would expect the elder knight to offer Parsifal: "People's reactions to opera the first time they see it is very dramatic; they either love it or they hate it. If they love it, they will always love it. If they don't, they may learn to appreciate it, but it will never become part of their soul."

Sure enough, as *La traviata* comes to a close, the escort is moved to tears by the death of her operatic double. Unlike Parsifal, who stands speechless and uncomprehending, the uninitiated "pretty woman" sheds tears for the heroine; she is revealed to intuitively understand the ritual unfolding before her. "She must have a heart of gold," the film implies, "and is worthy of transcending her station. Praise be to the rich man who did this for her!"

I hate this scene for so many reasons, not only because most opera companies' marketing departments reference it to try and hook new operagoers ("See the opera that made Julia Roberts cry!"). I hate it mostly because opera functions in this film as a symbol for luxury and refinement—like the fine dining and the pearls Richard Gere offered her in previous scenes. Opera becomes a trial of domestication, deployed to tame a fiercely independent character into the rich man's Pygmalion model of a respectable woman. I wish the scene conveyed what a more charitable viewer of the film might claim: that opera requires no education or "social conditioning" for it to speak powerfully and directly to anyone with an open mind and open heart. But the transactional context of the two characters' relationship reduces opera to a stand-in for expensive excellence in the film's capitalist love story.

As it turns out, *La traviata* was also my first opera: my dad took the twelve-year-old me to a production in Germany while he was working there. Unfortunately, no tears came to my eyes to prove I was a deep-feeling human. I was more like Parsifal watching the Grail ritual, mostly oscillating between boredom and incomprehension. At the time, no supertitles over the stage presented simultaneous translations of what was being sung; you were expected to *already know everything* about the work, as well as understand Italian. Nothing onstage captured my imagination or engagement. Singers came and went with a minimum of movement or true dramatic connection. Whoever coined the term "park and bark" for the standard operatic performance style—where singers enter, take one fixed position, and shout-sing until they exit—might have cited this performance as an example. In short, the evening sputtered along, with each scene unfolding exactly as everyone (except me) seemed to expect.

If the gentleman's platitude from *Pretty Woman* is to be taken as a truism, then loving opera is beyond me and I can only hope to appreciate it. But what if I had witnessed a truly invigorating and extraordinary production, instead of the tried-and-tired *Traviata* that happened to be my first experience? If that occasion had been my last encounter with opera, I would surely have never given opera another thought. Instead, I had the great fortune of having additional opportunities to experience works quite different from that production of *Traviata*. My second opera, at the Lyric Opera of Chicago, was Wagner's *Siegfried* (1871). With an extended scene featuring the title character forging a sword (to music that I would call "proto-metal" if that weren't such a bad pun) and the slaying of a dragon, this work was much easier for the thirteen-year-old me to digest. The opera also demanded a certain amount of theatricality to realize its creator's fantastical universe, and although I may not remember many details, I certainly remember feeling much more curious about the art form afterward.

Not too many years later, at the same theater, the world premiere of Anthony and Thulani Davis's *Amistad* (1997) dumbfounded me with the shocking fact that operas were *still being written*—a revelation for a young person who had understood the opera house primarily as a museum for old works. Now what appeared to be a contemporary art form began to fascinate me. In college, I elected to take an opera class to learn if dissecting these works like literature would help me appreciate them. When my professor, Mary Ann Smart, played a transcendent moment from Meredith Monk's *ATLAS* (1991), I experienced the intense flash of revelation that Parsifal experiences later in Wagner's opera. Suddenly, hearing Monk's voice—a singular musical imagination that felt both futuristic and ancient—I completely understood opera and its extraordinary potential.

My connection to opera as a genre was anything but instant or intuitive; far from "love at first sight," it took false starts and unexpected byways—not to mention a fair amount of privilege—that led me to discover that opera was indeed in my soul.

// // // // //

BUT BACK TO *PARSIFAL*: The young boy turns out to be the hero of the story, but not before undergoing arduous trials and endless self-flagellation for his initial lack of understanding. The discovery of his name and a cosmic kiss in Act II awaken a sudden and deep understanding of what he had witnessed among the Grail knights in Act I. In the third act, he must find his way back to them after years of senseless wandering. But when he returns, he is not only a fully enlightened participant in their ritual, he has come to take the place of their ailing king.

How many opera lovers wish this could be the story of everyone who first encounters opera: that any initial alienness nevertheless leaves a lasting—even if primarily unconscious—trace that begins a process of self-discovery and ultimately acceptance into the fold. And that a restless teenager who doesn't understand a thing of what's happening onstage becomes, one day, the chairperson of that same opera company's board of directors.

Such a transformation is beautifully illustrated by Wagner in Parsifal's vocal line. At the start of the evening, he crashes into the opera with short and jumpy phrases. During the ritual, he is forced to stay silent as the knights of the Grail do their inexplicable thing. In Act II, the sudden flash of illumination sends him into propulsive, open-hearted wailing. In his final aria, Parsifal's voice is magisterial, staying in a controlled range that gives him the appearance of authority, centered and steady. His voice is practically subsumed into the sonic dominance of the orchestra, which carries the melodic lines. You could say that Wagner shows how his character has grown through the way his vocal lines develop; or, you could just as easily argue, Wagner reveals how Parsifal has become indoctrinated into the ways of this religious cult, as his character-full music in Acts I and II flattens out into character-less anonymity. The ambiguity of music, which can't be reduced to a single meaning, allows Parsifal's identity to simultaneously mature and deaden.

If you wanted to read this opera—Wagner's last—as the story of Parsifal's domestication to a preexisting ideology, you would have the opposite of the kind of hero populating his earlier operas. Senta, Tannhäuser, Elsa, Siegmund, Brünnhilde, and Walther all resist social norms to stake a claim for their independence and an alternative way of living. Why, at the end of his life, did Wagner shift away from stories about nonconformists and revolutionaries, rejected by their shortsighted communities, toward stories of wild spirits who learn obedience and subservience? (The wildest character in *Parsifal,* Kundry, sings only one line in Act III: "I serve ... I serve ...") What happened? Is it the fate of all radical artists to become conservative as they grow old and settle into the familiarity of their celebrity? In the case of opera, it certainly seems the fate of the most radical works, which may have burst onto the scene as rebels, but which have become tamed through years of domestication at the opera house.

I think this is why I've come to really dislike the ending of *Parsifal.* The vision of the "wild child" assimilating into a rule-bound brotherhood feels less like the restoring of order and more like the loss of individuality, the promise of continuity at the expense of the revolutionary. Opera's problems can't be as easily solved as Wagner envisions in *Parsifal,* by replacing an ailing king and restoring "business as usual." Instead, we should shake off the dead layers suffocating the spirit and question everything that has settled into routine. The Grail may have contained holiness once, but now it's a poor substitute for true spirit. The next leaders must find the right way to smash it to pieces while keeping their community intact—not as an act of destruction but as an act of liberation. The true heirs to the throne would remind the community that the worship of an object has resulted in an empty ossification of something truly meaningful.

What the knights in *Parsifal* hold as holy has calcified into history—the Grail and a missing spear have become fetishized objects, capable of replacing food and water as sustenance for a closed-off community. This commodification is part of what makes *Parsifal* such an apt metaphor for the problems of the opera house, where the spirits of works are preserved in antiquated images and unexamined iconography. With the almost Dadaistic subtitle "ein Bühnenweihfestspiel" ("a festival to consecrate the stage"), *Parsifal* remains the only opera Wagner wrote specifically for the one-of-a-kind acoustics of the Bayreuther Festspielhaus, a theater custom-built as a home for his sprawling, epic cycle *The Ring of the Nibelung* (*Der Ring des Nibelungen*, 1876). In every way, *Parsifal* serves as a summation of the composer's extraordinary artistry—but enshrined within it is a deep-seated impulse toward conservation and objectification. Bayreuth began as an independent escape from the decadent demands of the opera industrial complex of the day; but by the time Wagner completed *Parsifal*, the theater had become a monument to his own heroic achievements.

No wonder *Parsifal*'s narrative centers on relics that become substitutes for real experience; that's the attitude toward opera the piece itself and the Festspielhaus sanctify. Imagine if a jazz lover started displacing his feelings for John Coltrane's *A Love Supreme* onto the actual vinyl it was embedded in. The Coltrane fan passes the album on lovingly to the next generation—but if they don't own a record player, they might see merely a round, black, shiny thing. The object becomes the new endpoint. Fast forward a few generations, to an increasingly dispirited relationship with the unplayed object, the music itself completely silenced. This is the direction opera is currently taking: the music is a fixed entity, the result of slavish repetitions of past practice.

But music is the ultimate resistance to reification. It rejects becoming objectified, no matter how desperately recordings try to convince us otherwise. Recordings encourage the subconscious substitution of a sound object for the music itself, and while I treasure them as testaments of great artistry, they have cultivated a kind of listening that easily leads to conservatism. For the last century, we have possessed the ability to sever the voice from the body: we can play and replay and replay a piece of vocal music until we've learned to anticipate what will happen rather than actually listen. Now there are standards and exemplars that singers are judged against, and what was once an interpretation has become a reference point. Singers and conductors in particular face the impossible task of living up to the recordings of great artists of the past. Do they try to replicate the stylistic conventions and interpretations of past masters? Or do they risk the displeasure of the expectant audience by bringing their own individuality to bear?

This is the choice facing any interpreter of a classic work, be it director, conductor, or singer. We can choose to either reinforce a studied and traditionalist view of the piece—as preservation—or we can attempt to liberate the spirit of the music, to present it in a way that's completely of the moment. We either display our mastery of past performance practice to the acceptance of an audience who have come to understand the work on those terms, or we can illuminate something about the work that has never been perceived before. The traditional view is reinforced by the recording catalogue; the other way gets at the heart of music's true nature. Music exists in the air only as long as the vibrations hang. It belongs to the present moment even as it slips through our fingers; nothing about a live performance can be a rote repetition of how it was done before. Music doesn't demand we sing along to a predictable melody or anticipate a well-studied path. Instead, it provokes the listener to be fully embodied in the present—an idea that is at least challenging, if not antithetical, to classical music's notion of studied grail-keeping.

// // // // //

HOW DO WE BREAK THE conditioning that inevitably leads to the stultifying ritual Parsifal finds so alien? The German philosopher Theodor Adorno offered a solution, involving the radio: he encouraged producers not to play uninterrupted performances of symphonies on the air but to broadcast live rehearsals instead, complete with mistakes and the conductor's interruptions. As unsatisfying as this may sound to the listener, the proposal is an ingenious way to open up the process of music-making, defy the sense of a hermetic and predictable musical structure, and preserve the primacy of a live performance. The listener couldn't just float along with an inevitable flow but would confront the provisional and the potential inherent to any iteration of that piece. Each aspect of the performance becomes a choice rather than a foregone conclusion.

Years after I first read Adorno's idea, I worked in the notion of interruption to my concept for Giacomo Puccini's *La bohème* for Detroit Opera. *Bohème* (1896) is frequently cited as a "perfect first opera" for its irresistible music, lovable characters, and relatable story of young love. (It's also often considered a "perfect date night," which probably follows the questionable *Pretty Woman* logic of opera serving as a litmus test for emotional life and refinement.) For the casual operagoer, opera is almost synonymous with Puccini's name, which may have something to do with his emergence at the same time as recordings. When phonographic records were first being produced, the tenor Enrico Caruso, a famous interpreter of Puccini's music, engaged audiences with operatic music within the comfort of their own homes. Some have even argued that Puccini's relatively short arias, most lasting between two and four minutes, were written in response to the length of time allowed on one phonographic side. Even if that's untrue, Puccini's works seem purpose-built for operatic fetishization. To disrupt that thinking, I imagined turning Puccini on his head: starting with Act IV and ending with Act I.

Reordering the traditional arc of *Bohème* was actually an idea that had emerged a decade earlier, from a conversation with the great set designer John Conklin. John liked to provoke his students with thought experiments that often seemed impossible to achieve in the theater. In the case of *Bohème,* with his characteristically devilish smile, he would ask his students, "Why not start with the end?" His primary justification was musical, as Act IV and Act I are sonic analogues of each other: beginning with a nearly identical gesture and opening onto the same dramatic situation of two artists struggling with blocks to their creativity. As the acts continue, their dramatic structure unfolds in identical ways. Both hinge on a key sequence in which Mimì, Rodolfo's downstairs neighbor, comes upstairs to light her candle. She loses her key in the darkness, which Rodolfo finds but withholds to allow him to make a romantic overture. The same action effectively "repeats" at the center of both acts—in Act I's present tense and as a memory in Act IV, with the music, naturally, creating a bridge between these two discrete moments in time. The apotheosis of both acts—the ecstatic unison of their voices in love and Rodolfo's anguished cries of Mimì's name upon her death—also form the two climactic moments of the score. The piece itself suggests a circularity, and the episodic and impressionistic nature of the opera as a whole lends itself to a nonlinear approach— what Arnold Schoenberg and Anton Webern would explore as musical "retrograde," or the type of narrative strategy that may have formerly been reserved for experimental fiction, like Julio Cortázar's *Hopscotch*, but has become an increasingly popular way of telling stories in the era of episodic television.

I left my conversation with John with the retrograde possibility of *Bohème* working through my thoughts. Here is where the potential of operatic recordings really came to my aid: I made a playlist of the opera in that reverse order and gave it a try. Listening through the piece out of sequence made me instantly fall in love with the possibilities of performing the opera in this way. Suddenly the *modernity* of the score— its breathless pace, its brevity, its almost quantum vision of time in the chaotically overlapping scenes in Act II—came to the fore. I found myself moved to tears, not like Julia Roberts's character at a sick woman's demise but by the purity and fearlessness of the hope of new love emerging, despite the looming catastrophe.

Pulling this off would necessitate some kind of guide for the audience. At first I imagined supertitles could help: a headline over the stage after Mimì's death that would read, "Three months earlier." But then, mulling over Adorno's notion of interruption, I imagined an ambiguous character who would appear and speak in the language of the audience. This character, whom we eventually called the Wanderer (originally played by the legendary tenor George Shirley), did more than narrate or explain the concept. At key moments the music stopped cold, and the Wanderer asked the audience to consider another direction the story could have taken. This happened at crucial and uncanny moments in the score where Puccini's music comes to a stop: decisive fermatas, strangely unnatural "joints" that seem uncharacteristic of his effortless musical flow. These strange and unsettling dramatic moments are usually rushed past and barely register to an audience. They feel like an uncomfortable silence in a big auditorium, as if the orchestra needed a moment for a page turn. It was at such moments that the Wanderer paused the action and posed a question: "What would have happened if Rodolfo had gone back inside?" Or "What would have happened if Musetta had stayed silent?" These Adorno-ian interruptions would not just jolt an audience out of autopilot listening habits; they would serve dramatically to emphasize choice and agency at crucial times in the narrative.

When I pitched this concept for *Bohème* to artistic directors at various companies, not surprisingly, I experienced different iterations of a door slamming in my face. (The politest rejection: "It's a brilliant idea, but not for us.") *Bohème,* for most houses, was not a site for experimentation; audiences wanted their romantic idea of the work served back to them. Producers would readily admit that Puccini's classic was an anchor for their programming, one that reliably sold tickets and was simple enough to be performed with little to no rehearsal time. Presenting *Bohème* in a season offsets the risks of more challenging fare. This has become the way almost every opera company operates: leave the classics (or, as they are often questionably labeled, "war horses") alone. It may make for sensible business, but what about Puccini's opera? (Or *Carmen,* or *La traviata*?) Is *Bohème* doomed to inadequately rehearsed and uninvestigated performances? And if a routinized performance serves as a person's first experience of opera, won't they be justified in reacting like Parsifal to the rote reproduction of ritual?

But upon my appointment as Artistic Director of Detroit Opera in 2020, I had the opportunity to realize the concept two years later—and the timing was perfect. Because Covid-19 had shut down the theater for two years, its reopening offered a critical moment of both return and progress. We had to "come back" to something that had been miss-ing during the pandemic, but we also had to show that the "normal" most people were hoping to experience would never return. For me, the perfect performance analogy for this circumstance was the reverse-chronology approach.

As word started to spread about this production, several critics (without having seen it) derided the idea as giving the opera an audience-friendly "happy end." Surely the more successful way of pandering to the audience would be to leave the piece alone, as all the producers who rejected the concept would attest. Instead, as the world was emerging from a time of death and destruction, the time was right to foreground (or start with) death, move against the stream of time, and remember what it was that makes life worth living. A singer in the Detroit Opera chorus told me with a quiver in her voice that the reverse chronology resembled the process of reconstructing a narrative in trauma therapy. In the wake of the global trauma of Covid, our *Bohème* invited the audi-ence to meditate on memory and the different routes life might take.

Given this new way of experiencing the work, I wanted the rest of the production not to seem too unfamiliar. From a picture or video of this *Bohème*, you might be fooled into thinking it was a straightforward telling of the opera. The costumes by Jessica Jahn evoked the story's orig-inal epoch, and John Conklin's set was simple, facilitating the opportu-nity to perform the entire piece without a break. (Most performances of *Bohème* run close to three hours owing to lengthy and elaborate changes of scenery; without those, the time can be reduced to about 100 min-utes.) Naturally, the idea of transplanting the story to some other time period or place, making the production visually unique and distancing ourselves even more radically from Puccini's original, was seductive. But I wanted to say that this, too, is *Bohème*—even in reverse order, this ver-sion has always existed in the opera itself.

"But did it work?" you might ask. Every audience member will respond differently, yet the numbers at least tell a success story: over half of the audience members were attending Detroit Opera for the first time. Opera Philadelphia saw the same statistic when the production played there a year later.

An aficionado's familiarity with Puccini was not a privilege in this case but often a disadvantage; without fail, the attendees who liked it the least were the ones clinging most to their own preconceptions and expectations. But opera lovers with an open mind relished the rare opportunity to feel like they were at *Bohème*'s world premiere. In either case, everyone in the audience was on the same level. There was no privileged perspective; you simply had to be present with this version as it unfolded.

Every opera performance should strive to achieve a similar kind of unveiling—not of a grail-like object, but rather of *the naked power of the moment*. Opera becomes an embodiment of pure presence, with artists and audiences partaking in the miracle of a momentary coordination, an instant that can never be repeated. Or, as composer John Cage perfectly put it, "Each now is the time, the space."

If opera can reclaim the spirit of intuition and momentary grace that music captures, it will be able to dust off its deadening layers of object-worship and reignite the essence and importance of true ritual. Then it won't matter if audiences are young or old, first-timers or seasoned fans; they will enter a charged space. And consciously or subconsciously, they will understand.

TIME-CURVE: HISTORIES OF OPERA

Let's visualize operatic history (and maybe also all history) as a cyclical phenomenon, traversing byways and curves and transcending the tyranny of "the arrow of time"—the perception that chronology conditions a true nature of reality. Opera enacts an experience of anti-chronological time better than any other art form; its examination of time is one of its superpowers.

Laying out histories of European opera in a nonlinear way allows fascinating patterns to emerge. Rather than a vision of history first articulated by the nineteenth-century German philosopher Georg W. F. Hegel who imagined constant and unerring progress from one epoch to another toward some final utopia—the circular process reveals a constant back-and-forth, a shuttling between institutionalization and reform. We discover how much of what we have considered innovative owes its appearance to impulses from previous centuries.

So rather than moving step-by-step from past to future, a time-curve implies no forward or backward motion, favoring recursive activity that can move in any direction. The greatest operas ultimately transcend forward- or backward-looking visions: they radiate in all directions in time.

ORIGIN STORIES

"Opera" is the European name for something that exists in every human culture: a multisensory ritual of togetherness. For its "invention" in Western countries, opera needed the example of Greco-Roman antiquity to center its own identity: a classical lineage would foster a sense of linear development on our perception of human experience. But what would have happened if those operatic pioneers knew of the musical spectacles in African, Egyptian, Chinese, or Native American cultures? What would opera as a genre have sounded like then?

458 BCE

In an open-air auditorium, an all-male ensemble performs the tragic story of the House of Atreus in a three-part drama that became known as *The Oresteia*. Even prisoners are freed from their cells to ensure that *all* Athenians are assembled to reflect on their past and their current society. Theater, civic identity, and nature began as symbiotic, reflected in the auditorium's democratic seating arrangement and the exposure to the elements. Historians would later imagine that actors declaimed their lines at a pitch resembling singing— the better for unamplified voices to carry clearly.

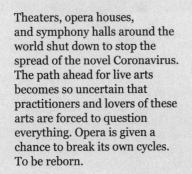

Theaters, opera houses, and symphony halls around the world shut down to stop the spread of the novel Coronavirus. The path ahead for live arts becomes so uncertain that practitioners and lovers of these arts are forced to question everything. Opera is given a chance to break its own cycles. To be reborn.

March
2020
CE

430
BCE

Nearly thirty years after the *Oresteia*, Athens suffers a five-year epidemic that leads to more than 100,000 deaths and likely precipitates Athens' defeat in a war against Sparta.

2008

British composer Harrison Birtwistle's *Minotaur* premieres—his third opera on Greek legend since his 1986 opera *The Mask of Orpheus*. In a singular musical language, Birtwistle reminds contemporary audiences of the same thing Homer's audience knew when listening to the retelling of familiar stories: originality is to be found less in *what* is told than in *how* you tell it.

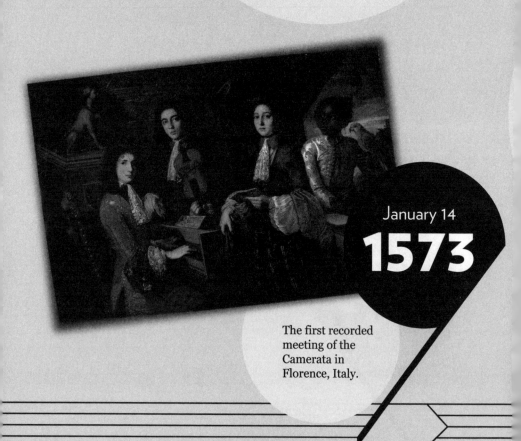

January 14
1573

The first recorded meeting of the Camerata in Florence, Italy.

AN OPEN DEFINITION

"Opera" wasn't identified as an autonomous genre until 1639. The Italian word translates to mean "a work," a rather prosaic ambivalence that gets at the heart of opera's hybrid identity. The notion that a collaborative work can be created that defies all preexisting genres, "in between" all other categories, has always struck me as inherently modern—fitting the early twenty-first century just as well as the late sixteenth century.

1597

Vincenzo Galilei, a prominent member of the Camerata, publishes *Dialogues on Ancient and Modern Music*, a detailed, mathematical analysis of the "corrupt" forms of contemporary music and how much his society would benefit from a revival of ancient modes of music. Galilei approaches music with a scientific rigor, not just in his writing but in sonic experiments with strings and tubes of all kinds. The father of Galileo solidifies at the earliest stages of opera that the searching spirit of science inspires this new inquiry into the nature of music and drama.

1581

Emerging from the Camerata, Jacopo Peri, a Florentine composer and keyboardist, and the poet Ottavio Rinnunci collaborate on a musical-dramatic performance based on the myth of Daphne. The private performance at the Palazzo Corsi of their undefinable creation, *Dafne*, leads the two men to collaborate again on a setting of the Orpheus myth: *Euridice*, the first work of its kind to be publicly performed.

2006

The Metropolitan Opera launches their "Live in HD" initiative, broadcasting live performances simultaneously to movie theaters around the globe.

EPHEMERALITY

The fact that every opera once had a world premiere is easy to forget. That's because the best ones do not follow a straight line but radiate in all directions, encompassing past, present, and future, and giving the impression that they have always existed.

The earliest operas were written for specific occasions, like weddings and coronations. The words and music were mostly considered fleeting and transitory, leading to most of these first experiments in opera to be forever lost. Four-hundred-plus years after Peri and Rinnunci, operatic creators strive for quite the opposite: *immortality*. Today's creators consider ephemerality a failure; they grapple instead with the monumental burdens of trajectory, history, and belonging to a canon. Is this a "development" for the art form, or an obstacle to its true creative spirit?

WHAT IS *L'ORFEO?*

Maybe Peri's musical setting of the Orpheus story is stronger and more imaginative than Monteverdi's. But we will never know: the forces of history have worked to preserve *L'Orfeo* and let *Euridice* disappear. Those forces have passed down the judgment that even if Monteverdi's opera isn't the first, it's still perhaps the best.

But what actually is Monteverdi's *L'Orfeo*? Is it the written score? Is it only the first performance of it in Mantua? Or is it the living performance of the work, which exists only as long as it happens in time and space—not any earlier and not any longer? Perhaps it forms a perfect microcosm of what it means to exist at all: an emptiness that can nevertheless contain so much beauty, profundity, insight, and possibility?

Claudio Monteverdi's *L'Orfeo* premieres in Mantua, Italy; many still refer to it as "the first opera."

See PLAYLIST

1607

A commercial production of Puccini's *La bohème* opens on Broadway and runs for 228 performances.

New York

2002

Parma, Italy

1618

To stage his elaborate stage spectacles and to celebrate his son's wedding to Margherita Medici, Duke Ranucci Farnese erects a theater in Parma with a proscenium arch. This architectural innovation masks elaborate stage machinery from the public and asks them to look through a picture frame. The separation of spectator and performer, of life and representation, initiates a new way of considering theatrical representation, which has impacted theater ever since.

1619

It's a deeply unfunny irony of history that the height of Europe's humanistic "rebirth" (or *Renaissance*) brings forth twin siblings: opera and the trans-Atlantic slave trade. Grand opera and "New World" colonialism become the foundational gemini of a nascent self-identity.

Opera takes hold of the popular imagination just as contact is made with lands and peoples unknown to the Europeans. In its grandiosity and spectacle, opera carries the imprint of colonialist chauvinism, parading artistic brilliance as a justification of cultural superiority.

Houston,
Texas

1991

Meredith Monk's
ATLAS premieres at
Houston Grand Opera.
See PLAYLIST

Venice

1637

Until now, pre-opera prototypes were seen only by
aristocratic audiences. But in 1637, the privately owned
Teatro San Cassiano in Venice offers the first opera to the
public at a ticket price of four lire. In the next four
decades, eight other theaters in Venice begin offering
opera as popular entertainment. In contrast to the courtly
entertainment in Mantua and Florence and the
quasi-scientific experiments of the Camerata, opera is
now easily accessible to a mass audience. The rivalry
among Venetian theaters inspires more and more
competition for spectacular sets and brilliant, illusionistic
scene changes; design and production values become an
integral part of an opera's aesthetic and appeal.

A POPULIST VS.
ELITIST ENTERTAINMENT

Both court theaters and public theaters flourish in the
seventeenth and eighteenth centuries. It didn't take long for
the central tension of opera as an elitist art form—reserved
for a private, aristocratic audience—or as a popular art
form—accessible to any paying member of the public—
to establish itself; uncertainty as to who opera is "for"
becomes increasingly burdensome as the centuries pass.

2

THE FUTURE IN OUR PAST

The past is an appeal; it is an appeal toward the future
which sometimes can save it only by destroying it.

—SIMONE DE BEAUVOIR,
Ethics of Ambiguity

IF A TIME-CURVE LETS US VISUALIZE OPERA'S CONSTANT
rebirth, perhaps a fitting analogue for its opposite is the childhood
game of a domino rally. This happened to be my favorite activity as
a kid: laboriously setting up a labyrinth of domino after domino in
perilous proximity to each other, forming a daredevil pattern that
would spread throughout our kitchen. After the build-up of excitement, there was such satisfaction in knocking down the first domino
and following the chain reaction along its serpentine course—hours
and hours of work for a brief moment of ephemeral beauty and the joy
of perfect functioning.

In many ways, directing opera resembles that painstaking preparation for a fleeting moment of transcendence, when all the planning functions like clockwork. The curtain going up is the equivalent of the first domino falling: the production is off and running and unstoppable, even if any slight miscalculation might derail it. The most accurate description I've ever heard about opera remains Terry Pratchett's perspicacious observation that "opera happens because a large number of things amazingly fail to go wrong."

The domino rally appears to be a harmless explication of Newton's first law of motion, but that long line of dominoes also resembles the conventional myth of history most of us learned in school. Textbooks want to portray our past as a linear path where cause-and-effect moves in one unstoppable motion toward the more enlightened present. No matter how many philosophers since Hegel have repudiated this idea of unidirectional progress, guided not by people with a vested interest in their own dominance but by an invisible hand, most schools still stand by it: one domino toppling another, that one another, and that one another, in an elegant, linear pattern. But once they've fallen, you're left with a dispirited mess, the ruins of a once beautiful architecture that, like Humpty Dumpty, can never be put together again. The past becomes a rubble still bearing the traces of its inevitable, doom-laden design.

The ruins of causality are what the Greek playwright Aeschylus shows us in beautiful miniature in his trilogy *Oresteia*—the most operatic of the ancient tragedies. Its three-part structure, telling a story of vengeance from one generation to another, illustrates the bitter truth that violence only begets more violence. The chain reaction of harm— from Agamemnon's murder of his daughter Iphigenia to his wife Clytemnestra's revenge-murder of Agamemnon and their son Orestes's revenge-murder of his mother—is a kind of domino rally, but the stacking up of actions justified by a past act of violence never reaches a final blow. Each act takes on more and more weight from the past, like an ever-lengthening fetter. Only divine intervention—in the form of Athena, who descends from the heavens as the classic example of the Greek theatrical concept of *deus ex machina*—can stop the violence. The furies of vengeance become, through a goddess's command, visions of benevolent justice.

From the Greeks to the dominoes, nothing would seem more natural than thinking of our own pasts as enormous burdens of dead activity that propel us inexorably forward. The most ingenious equivalent to this experience in opera is the final installment in Wagner's four-opera *Ring of the Nibelung*. In the beginning, Wagner depicts a world that's still innocent. Each character or object or idea is represented by a clear, identifiable musical motif that rings out like an individual stone in a mosaic. But as murder, incest, rape, acts of greed, and other heinous events pile onto one another, the motifs begin to overlap, conflate, conflict, splinter, and reconfigure—the musical equivalent of a new generation overburdened by its cataclysmic history and murky memory.

Like the Greeks witnessing Aeschylus's multipart tragedy, Wagner's audience witnesses a compounding corruption that merges with their own experience of many hours in the theater. Is the music becoming denser and harder to parse, or is your head just pounding from listening to so much Wagner night after night? By the final act of *Götterdämmerung* (*Twilight of the Gods*), the last opera in the cycle, the only way out of this dreadful accumulation is complete destruction, brought about by Brünnhilde, the Athena-like Valkyrie and favorite daughter of the creator god Wotan. The corruption is *so* bad in Wagner's vision of the world that it's not enough for Brünnhilde to simply announce a fresh start of forgiveness: she needs to immolate herself and the entire world with her. (To solidify the confusion between fantasy and real life, Wagner originally suggested that the *Ring* cycle should conclude with the theater itself burning down.)

Why, then, should we resist this vision of history, as Wagner and Aeschylus depict it? Aren't there ample instances of seemingly intractable problems—racism, colonialism, partisanship, the climate crisis—to offer us evidence of how past wrongdoings only accumulate until we reach a breaking point, until we must worry that only a violent act of destruction and/or a complete reset can save us?

I think there are plenty of reasons to fight this narrative—or at least to weaken the appearance of its inevitability. For one, the illusion of the *deus ex machina* has outlasted its metaphoric value to human culture. Employing a "hard cut" in a cycle of violence is now naïve and misleading; in the absence of helpful gods and left to our own devices, we have known traumas to last for centuries. And we see that forgiveness and reconciliation create a painful, ongoing cycle all their own. Athena's appearance becomes the dream of a "quick fix"—a salvation not only quixotic but potentially harmful, because the miraculous appearance minimizes the need for individual human agency. We can no longer leave grace and forgiveness in the hands of saviors who come to the rescue right when all hope runs out.

That doesn't mean we should stop performing the *Oresteia, Götterdämmerung,* or any other work enacting last-minute deliverance. But how we depict those acts of salvation is critical in creating a bridge of proximity between ancient humanity and our own. And for every performance of Monteverdi's *L'Orfeo*, where Apollo descends to put an end to Orpheus's sad stalemate, I hope a new opera is performed, which offers audiences another way to think about individual responsibility in the face of overwhelming consequences.

But there's a bigger issue worth challenging, and that is the assumption that the past is an objective, fixed entity—a burden and a mess, like the floor of fallen dominoes. History, in this view, is a massive iceberg, and we are running in place on its slippery peak. Why does our culture default to this view? In her recent study *Ancient Bones,* the German paleontologist Madeleine Böhme claims that the assumed theory of human life beginning in Africa has been discredited by the discovery of more ancient human remains in China and elsewhere. With this new information, the story we have told about ourselves needs to be rewritten, and our perception of human history must broaden. In his sprawling 1913 novel *In Search of Lost Time*, Marcel Proust's narrator comments on Baron de Charlus's inexplicably strange behavior around him and other young men. Much later in the story, the narrator peers over a wall to witness Charlus having sex with another man. His past behavior is illuminated, and all the narrator's recollections need to be revised with present understanding. "My eyes had been opened by a transformation in Charlus as complete and as immediate as if he had been touched by a magician's wand," he concludes. "Everything that hitherto had seemed to my mind incoherent became intelligible, appeared self-evident." In seismic ways, such as with Böhme's discoveries, or in personal ways, like Proust's reformation of memories, the constant shaping and reshaping of the past is an essential part of our growth.

History is not a dead continent—a heap of dominoes—but a living conversation partner changing alongside us. The past is just as multi-directional as the paths into the future, and art's greatest and most secret power is its ability to make that abstract idea something sensual and shareable.

// // // // //

NOT EVERYONE WILL AGREE WITH this understanding of history . . . and especially not opera lovers.

The art we experience and the narratives we share ultimately cultivate opposing views on the past: as either open and changeable, or as closed and observable. Zooming out, we could apply the same characterizations to conservative worldviews—which idolize origins as perfect and consider change a degradation; or to progressive ones—which emphasize mutability, becoming, and the possibility of a better future by actively transforming the past. In one case, paradise is irrevocably lost; in the other, paradise is yet to come.

Opera companies are inclined to consider the works on display as representatives of a stable view of history. So many self-described opera lovers tend toward an obsession with bygone composers whose genius has not been rivaled; the towering singers of some long-ago "golden age" who (alas!) possessed a greatness we will never again witness; the glory of a civilization reflected in the harmoniously ordered gatherings inside a glittering hall, come to appreciate an unsustainable high point of human achievement.

The progressive view implies that there has never yet been a perfect opera, nor will there ever be a definitive realization of any single work. We interpret a work, whether it's one year or two hundred years old, and as we respond with our imaginations, we are all the while modeling what change and revision look like in action. Far from repudiating the past, we actively tangle with it in the act of inquiring who we are and where we've come from. If we engage with it in this way, opera can offer immediate proof of how deeply we need a sense of a past. If opera truly disappeared for good, we would lose not only cultural memory but an ideal mechanism (along with live theater) for its constant reinvestigation. Our ability to consider the past as representation, as a costume that we can don and remove, allows us to view history from a new perspective.

Today opera is primarily an act of *re-creation* rather than creation. Theater has its Shakespeares and ballet its *Swan Lake*s, but perhaps no other art form presents so many works distanced from its audience by well over a century. And every time we re-create, we make a choice. Those choices can either obliterate considerations of potential; or, with imagination, they can remind us of memory's essential malleability. Just as ideas passed down from previous generations never stop transforming as society, technology, and values change, the ideas within an opera never stop changing.

John Adams and Alice Goodman's *Nixon in China* offers a perfect model. What might have been a closed-door view of history in a ripped-from-the-headlines reenactment instead becomes something living and ever-changing—and, through the driving repetitions of the score or the just-irrational-enough imagery in the language, history becomes a field of parallel paths. (Nixon's unforgettable opening aria states it plainly: "News has a kind of mystery.") Our attitudes toward its central characters continue to evolve, and because the authors chose a decidedly poetic and *nonnaturalistic* approach to these real personalities, we experience the shifting relationships to our own history whenever a new baritone and soprano represent Richard and Pat Nixon. The same can be said of other historical characters as they are depicted in great operas— Queen Elizabeth, Malcolm X, Saint Francis of Assisi, Nero, or Federico García Lorca.

The living art of opera, as long as it's constantly reinvented, never stays still. We need to start considering the art form less as a bulwark and more as a blueprint, suggestions for a realization based on the inspiration of the interpreters and the exegesis of the moment. That means it is an entirely open form—open to the flux of time. And therefore opera, when it reimagines the past, reveals the past's reality as incomplete and evolving. Every opera production should strive toward being this incomplete, this temporary, this provisional.

There is urgency underlying the restaging of classic works: to keep an opera fixed in time is to confine it within the narrow cell of what we already know. We must follow the imperative to truly interpret these works from our contemporary perspective or risk the cultural stagnation that accompanies an iceberg view of the past. Historical accuracy has its place in academia and conservatories, but it should only function as research for contemporary operatic practice. Getting the past right is not what matters when we stage an opera; getting our present moment right as we replay and reinterpret works is of critical importance. We may be without Athenas and other descending gods, but art can be the force that makes it possible to imagine breaking the chain.

"There is only one way to dominate the past, the realm of things that have perished," according to the Spanish philosopher José Ortega y Gasset: "to open our veins and inject some of our blood into the empty veins of the dead. This is what the reactionary cannot do: treat the past as a form of life."

// // // // //

OPERA IS STILL AN UNEASY fit in America. Like the Pilgrims, opera started here as a European import imposed upon the land. Centuries later, it remains a repository for the feelings of inferiority the upstart colonies needed to jettison like so much English tea. I still smell a whiff of desperation when I see a regional company perform an Italian "masterwork" and strain for a sense of authenticity. There is always a sense of checking one's reflection in the storefront window: "Am I doing this well? Do I look the part? Am I emulating the ethos of this piece convincingly?" Opera became a holdover of nostalgia for the Old World, and even today, as new art forms emerge bearing the imprint of our own country's ethos, new operas are usually charged with looking and sounding like old ones.

The story of opera in America is far from over, but its future depends on an evolutionary attitude toward both the art form and the country's colonialist origins.

America was founded on genocide and slavery, and ingeniously indoctrinated generations to believe the country was conceived on the moral high ground of democracy and human equality. When we read about Abraham Lincoln signing the Emancipation Proclamation, a profound moment in the country's ability to self-govern, who doesn't want to shout: "Yes, but how could enslaving another human on these shores have been accepted *for so long*?" And as much as history would like to make that proclamation a marker of America's ultimate moral victory over racial inequality, we know from the subsequent 160 years that the victory was anything but decisive. That the proclamation preceded by a mere five days Lincoln's authorization of the largest mass execution in U.S. history, of thirty-eight Sioux warriors, betrays this country's cruel hypocrisy. Throughout our history, examples of an evolved nature run neck and neck with continued acts of aggression and delusions of grandeur, the ever-renewed manifestations of foundational sins. All Americans are born with blood in our bathwater.

But as pernicious as our past is, does that mean our future has no chance? Does humanity really have no hope of changing? As in the *Oresteia*, we could keep going further and further back, before national borders existed, to realize there's always another "original sin" that we can point to—primal acts of violence, aggression, and dominance—demanding restitution. There is power in the metaphor of America as a house built on a rotten foundation, therefore doomed to collapse. But there's a rigidity in that line of thinking that's a perfect mirror of the rigidity more conservative thinkers bring to their concept of the past. On both sides of the spectrum, the past is unchanging—and an unchanging, dead past that our present moment can't shape implies no possibility for movement or improvement.

The year 2020 was one of painful and intense reckoning with how our past makes present-day living impossible. Confederate statues began to fall in an effort to open the eyes of every citizen to the insidious mythologies attempting to control the American narrative. We heard calls for "W.A.T." (White American Theater) to listen up; demands that museums, publishers, and film executives drastically change their attitude toward inclusion and representation; and a small but growing resistance to how opportunities are apportioned in the classical live arts. Some companies opted for a tough-sounding slogan: "There is no room for racism in opera." But the hard truth is: There is so much room for racism in opera! Not to mention the casual misogyny and cultural xenophobia at the heart of so many of its plots. By presenting those plots uncritically, without questioning, addressing, and then revising how complex elements function within the universe of the work, opera companies have—wittingly or no—perpetuated a sense that the art form speaks for and represents an elite class of Americans, the very same people who have benefited from the cruelty of colonialism, capitalism, and patriarchy. Here, opera faces exactly the same dilemma as our country: until that unjust past is truly confronted, and its insidious tentacles into our present are amputated, we can't look forward to a more hopeful future.

But this is where opera has an advantage over something like a statue. A monument is a cold artifact, embodying the desire of a particular class to lionize an image of the past. This is what makes the public markers of Confederate soldiers so disturbing and why they should be relegated at least to a museum providing context—if not to a junk heap or, as in Moscow's Art Park, strewn in a disturbing and disorganized field of Soviet flotsam. A statue can't change, and even the addition of a bronze plaque at the base is a wimpy apologia for the trauma awoken by the spectral sight, unmistakable even at a distance, of a person responsible for the death of your kin.

Operas are not statues, and we must treat them as malleable. Let's consider Monostatos's Act II aria from Wolfgang Amadeus Mozart's *The Magic Flute* (1791). Monostatos, an enslaved Moorish man, lusts after the sleeping princess Pamina and bemoans the fact that love will always be denied him "because black is so ugly." In contrast, Pamina's whiteness makes her a paragon of beauty, which drives him delirious to the point of nearly raping her. Yikes! Don't touch this toxic opera with a ten-foot pole! Except that *Magic Flute* remains one of the most popular operas of all time. If the other racist and misogynist slurs in its text can be minimized, this aria's offensiveness is impossible to ignore. A contemporary producer might simply excise it (Mozart is no longer around to complain!). But if the aria is retained—for fidelity to the original or any such reason—with nothing done to express a critical viewpoint, its presence will end up saying much more about the company, the director, the conductor, and the singer than it does about Mozart.

Integrating a critical standpoint into a production while maintaining the ambiguous contours of a work of art is an extraordinary challenge. It takes imagination, insight, and empathy into how a contemporary audience might grapple with the constellation of words, music, and image placed before them. Yet nothing less than that is opera's charge now. When it is met with enough imagination, opera can be the most exciting art form in the world; maybe even the best art form for exploring ideas of our shared humanity.

Here we can identify another of opera's paradoxes. Because so many of the "standard repertoire" works are rooted in the past, they could easily shed more light on our contemporary circumstances than brand-new works. But only if they are given the chance to do so through stagings that actively interrogate in both directions, into the past and toward the future. Otherwise, every time *La traviata* is presented uncritically, a misogynist gets his wings. Every time Monostatos sings his aria in a production that presents it with a kind of historicist shrug, a white supremacist in the audience feels seen. It's shocking how recently it was still deemed acceptable to perform Verdi's *Otello* or *Aida* in blackface in this country—and productions of Puccini's *Madama Butterfly* still traffic in yellowface and other stereotypes of Japanese culture that would not be tolerated in any other art form. Opera has tried to rationalize these gaffes with calls for understanding the operatic context—and then usually proceeding with an uninvestigated and out-of-touch production, setting the case for opera back a century or more in the imagination of that community.

People suspicious of what I'm saying may think I'm advocating for revisionist history in the form of radical stagings of classic operas. Indeed, I do reject "originalism" as it relates both to our national politics and to the interpretation of classic works, as this may be the only way to salvage questionable documents (in the case of the U.S. Constitution) or to make sure the humanist impulse at the heart of many great operas finds its voice for contemporary society.

Mine is not an outlier position in other cultural fields. In her new translation of Ovid's *Metamorphoses,* Stephanie McCarter advocates for rethinking the mythic tales in light of contemporary concerns:

> If we do not rethink these texts through the lens of the present, they will cease to have meaning for the present. The inclusion of so many stories of rape in the epic suggests, in fact, that Ovid felt such violence was worthy of critical interrogation, just as he shines a light on the negative repercussions of masculine heroics or divine power precisely in order to question, not celebrate, them. Not to focus our reading on the theme of sexual violence, or to quickly explain it away, is in many ways to miss the point. It is also to miss the opportunity to trace the legacies of such abusive power in our own world so as to understand and combat them. To read Ovid with an eye toward his full complexity—his beauty *and* his brutality—allows us to scrutinize our own thorny relationship with the past and with the ambivalent inheritance we have received from it. To wrestle with the unsavory aspects of ancient literature is to do the hard work of self-examination. It is simply easier to talk about love rather than rape or to focus on ennobling values rather than try to grasp our own human failings. Yet it is precisely this hard work that Ovid invites us to do.

The journey of self-examination that McCarter proposes is perhaps even more accessible to opera than it is to classical literature. McCarter's translation will sit on a shelf, exactly as it is, next to many other translations. Her ideas and choices may ultimately be superseded by the imperatives of new translators. But in book format, her work will live on as a reference for as long as books are read, a product of its time as earlier translations are of theirs. In contrast, although video documentation is beginning to change the dynamic around live performance, performances of an opera are still ultimately ephemeral articulations of a work at a particular cultural moment. They are not meant to last eternally on a library shelf—and that, I believe, gives them even more license to be bold. Just as translators make choices based on their contemporary standpoint as a way to ensure a connection to the present, every new production automatically "translates" past ideas for modern times. In McCarter's case, her unromanticized view of the many sexual assaults in Ovid's stories is essential to forging a link between our current climate and the inherited psyche of the past.

Imagine if we thought of *La traviata* that way. We might discover the aspects of Verdi's work that were quite the opposite of misogynist. The opera is ultimately vicious in its attack of bourgeois hypocrisy and remains as close as Verdi ever came to wearing the badge of feminism. Great "translations" of these operas prove this to be true, while unimaginative productions reinforce a patriarchy that Verdi himself despised.

// // // // //

WE COME BACK AGAIN TO imagination and what is lost when we undervalue its function in contemporary opera practice. Without imagination, the past is a cold landscape of toppled dominoes, and operas become frozen in time. Rather than enacting a dialogue with the past, opera becomes a rehashed repetition of what was rather than what could be, and implicates its audience in an embalming ritual.

"Past history is fluid, labile, suspended, its sense yet to be fully determined," the philosopher Terry Eagleton writes in his book *Hope Without Optimism*. "It is we who can endow it retrospectively with a definitive form, not simply by choosing to read it in a certain way but by virtue of our actions. . . . We must strive, then, to keep the past unfinished, refusing to accept its appearance of closure as the final word, springing it open once again by rewriting its apparent fatality under the sign of freedom."

It takes imagination to do what Eagleton suggests: to envision the past as an open field, and to consider its reenactment onstage as one of the most powerful exercises of that form of creativity. A transfigured view of our own past: that is the promise and possibility contained in any single performance of an opera.

3

"THE POWER PLANT OF FEELINGS"

SINGING ACTORS AND THEIR EMOTIONS

ONE OF THE BEST OPERA SIGHTINGS ON THE BIG SCREEN must be the climactic ending of Francis Ford Coppola's 1990 film *The Godfather Part III*. The ruthless Corleone family gathers in Sicily to attend a performance of Pietro Mascagni's opera *Cavalleria rusticana* (1890). Mafia godfather Michael Corleone, having first spurned his son Anthony's desire to devote his life to music, now revels in his performance of the opera's main role, Turiddu. The performance turns out to be a decisive and definitive finale for an entire saga.

Coppola's choice of opera couldn't be more fitting: Mascagni's work began a school of thought known as *verismo,* which strove to capture reality in the larger-than-life dramas played out in small villages among everyday people. Likewise, Coppola uses the staged performance within the film to hold up an operatic mirror to the lush, bucolic Sicilian landscape he's shown us earlier in the film. The sets onstage may be more two-dimensional, but the audience revels in an authentic-looking reenactment of their social lives just outside the theater.

Throughout the opera's performance, Michael is stalked by an assassin in the lobby. A dramatic polyphony emerges, connecting *Cavalleria rusticana,* the assassin's plot against Michael, and another assassination attempt by his sister Connie against a traitorous old family friend sitting in another box (via poisonous cannoli, no less!). The tension mounts between those narrative strands, and Mascagni's music provides the soundtrack.

In the opera, Turiddu is killed offstage in a duel, and his murder is announced by peasant women screaming—not singing—the blood-curdling line *"Hanno ammazzato compare Turiddu!"* ("They have killed our neighbor Turiddu!"). For Mascagni's first audience, a spoken-screamed line at the climax was a shock, and it still is: it contributes to the dramatic effectiveness of the moment and creates a sense of verisimilitude (SEE PLAYLIST). Coppola cuts between these lines in the opera and scenes of the family's ruthless assassinations beyond the opera house. All remaining traitors to the family are cut down one by one in scenes that constitute an important contrapuntal line in Coppola's final fugue. Ordering killings from afar keeps Michael's hands clean of blood—just as the offstage death of Turiddu spares him the agonizing sight of watching an enactment of his son's death.

After the opera finishes, as the family is leaving the theater, the poised assassin finally opens fire. But instead of hitting Michael, his bullet strikes Michael's beloved daughter Maria. Spared witnessing one child's make-believe death onstage, Michael is now confronted with another child's real death on the steps outside the opera house. The scene's parallels to the opera border on the farcical: as Maria lies dying, we hear someone scream off in the distance, *"Hanno ammazzato Signora Maria!"* And Connie covers her head in a black veil, the exact same gesture the soprano made on the operatic stage on hearing of Turiddu's death. Underpinning the scene, the sweeping, cinematic music of Mascagni's "Intermezzo" pulls at our heartstrings.

What is Coppola trying to say at the end of his masterful family

saga by drawing these parallels with *Cavalleria rusticana*? Is the operatic scale of Corleone family life a cause for critique? Or is the final
scene a gesture toward myth? Could a proper epic sweep of the Italian
American experience really be complete *without* opera? Could Coppola be highlighting the artifice of his own film? (In addition to the
operatic parallel, a massacre staged on theater steps offers a clear nod
to the "Odessa Steps" sequence in Sergei Eisenstein's 1925 film *Battle-
ship Potemkin*—a scene referenced even more obviously in the climactic
scene of *The Godfather Part I*.)

Yet the crucial moment is yet to come.

One by one, with the suspense mounting, the various characters
look toward Michael, expectant and astonished at his reaction. When
Coppola finally turns the camera to him, we see Michael Corleone as
we have never seen him before: mouth gaping open, in a complete state
of shock. Al Pacino's performance at this moment provides an iconic
expression of unbearable agony. At first there's no sound other than
Mascagni's music—until finally, without his face or mouth changing at
all, a scream emerges. A primal vocal wail, singular in the entire trilogy,
that rightly deserves to be called operatic. The film ends minutes later,
with a silent, broken Michael dying alone, his only companion a small,
confused dog.

The ending can feel unsatisfying and abrupt. How can Coppola end
his family saga here, with so many narrative strands left unresolved? Yet
even if the rest of *Part III* is less consistently spectacular than the first
two parts, ending the trilogy with Michael's heartrending cry was an
ingenious, devastating choice. Throughout the films, we've watched a
character unable to express emotions other than violent anger—he frequently and literally shuts doors on all his feelings. Now, facing the devastating loss of his daughter, he opens his heart for a true howl to pour
out. It's not only shattering, it's definitive. His cry releases everything
that has been pent up since the first film. The totality is overwhelming
and transcends the moment: he bewails the devastating consequences of
all his life's actions. What could Coppola show after that? There's truly
nothing more we need to know.

Naturally, it's possible that watching an opera moments before his emotional outburst is exactly what put Michael in touch with his feelings—his scream replicating the more musical final cry of the soprano at the end of *Cavalleria*. That possibility likely smacks of the kind of elite self-importance that turns so many people off about opera (the subject of Chapter Seven). Opera doesn't have a monopoly on the passions, and yet there's something true about the juxtaposition of these two fictional circumstances. Emotions are confusing, and language's ability to communicate them is notoriously incomplete. Still: the biggest emotions call us to share them despite that disadvantage. If spoken language alone can't convey what we're feeling, maybe opera's mix of languages—musical, textual, visual—can give a more multidimensional picture of our interior lives.

The German philosopher Alexander Kluge famously called opera "the power plant of feelings," and perhaps no other art form offers the same opportunity of releasing and sharing emotions—complex, powerful, and elemental ones. Certainly no other art form allows them to appear as confusing as they are.

But talking about emotions in opera is tricky. There's the danger of explaining away the experience that every operagoer longs for: the moment a performance grips you, overwhelming you with an emotional connection. Words will never be able to capture that magical moment.

We also know how easily emotions can be manipulated by other media. A less inspired director than Coppola will use music to tell the audience what to feel. And outside the cinema, there's hardly a moment in our day when some commercial or political force isn't trying to grab our attention and trigger feelings, through social network posts, news outlets, or advertisements—which are impossible without music. Controlling our emotions becomes the easiest way to start controlling our minds and, invariably, nudging us to open our wallets. Surrounded by ceaseless attempts at emotional exploitation, opera can exist in our contemporary media landscape as *resistance* to all of that. Although the stereotypical depiction of opera revels in one-note, over-the-top emotions, the best operas honor and hone our emotional intelligence. We come back to them again and again for the subtle and complex expressions that change and evolve as *we ourselves* change and evolve.

But the main reason it's difficult to talk about how emotions work in opera is because, contrary to popular opinion, the emotions don't actually live in the music. Although this may sound surprising, think about it: the music is ultimately only notes on a page, a set of guidelines whose *only* validity is in performance. The score is a suggestion—and the genius of great composers is not their ability to "capture emotions" or "convey deep ideas." Instead, musical geniuses astonish us through their prowess at setting up the (sometimes unexpected) rules for performers to bring emotions and ideas to life.

Music only exists when it is performed and activated—and so the emotional life of an opera only lives through its interpreters, first and foremost the singers. There are obviously more interpreters involved—instrumentalists, dancers, conductors, and of course directors. But it's ultimately up to the singers to realize the promise of words and music on paper. And when an emotional connection is forged, it's carried and realized by the singing human onstage.

// // // // //

"THERE IS SOMETHING VERY FREEING about hearing a song sung in a language that you don't understand," Bob Dylan observes in his book *The Philosophy of Modern Song*. "Go and see an opera and the drama leaps off the stage even if you don't understand a word." When the language is obscure, feeling becomes the mode of connection: "Sometimes you can hear a song so full of emotion that you feel your heart ready to burst and when you ask someone to translate it the lyrics are as mundane as 'I cannot find my hat.'"

When I first read this, I instantly thought of Mozart's *The Marriage of Figaro* (1786), whose final act begins with a minor character singing about a lost pin. On the page, the text by Lorenzo Da Ponte looks innocuous and forgettable: "I have lost it, unhappy me! / Who knows where it can be? / I cannot find it, I have lost it! / And my cousin, and my Lord . . . / What will he say?" Judging purely from the libretto, you might expect music that comedically mimics the character's hectic search for the lost item. But what Mozart wrote to these words is a heartbreaking and mournful melody, the saddest music in an otherwise sunny opera (SEE PLAYLIST). If you heard the aria out of context (without knowing the words), you might think it was from Mozart's *Requiem* rather than from his most famous comedy. The music's deep feeling catches an audience by surprise every time the opera is performed.

An excess of feeling beyond the libretto is something that happens over and over in *Marriage of Figaro*. In a duet from Act III, for example, two sopranos are composing a letter: one is the wife of a cheating count, and the other a young servant girl, Susanna, who is the object of the count's affection. Their joint letter is a plot, part of an elaborate scheme to ensnare the count and expose his unseemly behavior. Like the text of the song to the lost pin, the words here are simple, even perfunctory: "'A gentle breeze will blow through the pines this evening'—he'll understand what this means!" Mozart could have set them in a way that underlined the comedy, exaggerating the phony seduction and playing for laughs. He could also have chosen to simply dispatch these lines in dry recitative. Or he might have highlighted the difference between the noble countess and the lower-class Susanna, setting their voices apart with an unmistakable dividing line. Instead, Mozart wrote a cascading melody that sounds deeply heartfelt (SEE PLAYLIST). The two vocal lines circle around each other, creating an enduring image of friendship and equality between two women of different social experience. It's the music that transforms this simple moment into something complex and magical, much larger than the words or the dramatic situation they imply.

This duet has its own cinematic cameo, in a famous scene from the 1994 film *The Shawshank Redemption*. An inmate in a soul-crushing prison broadcasts a recording of the duet, which makes every prisoner stop and take notice. Then a voice-over takes a page straight out of Bob Dylan: "I have no idea to this day what those two Italian ladies were singing about. Truth is, I don't want to know. Some things are best left unsaid. I'd like to think they were singing about something so beautiful it can't be expressed in words and makes your heart ache because of it." (I'm glad I'm not the guy trying to explain to these inmates what they are actually singing about!)

But in some urban settings, broadcasting opera has had a very different effect. At 7-Eleven convenience stores around the country, opera blares loudly through speakers to keep unhoused people from loitering outside. The owner of a 7-Eleven in Austin, Texas, told a local television reporter that he'd selected the music because "studies have shown that opera is annoying." The reporter also got a reaction from an unhoused woman, who called the music "absolutely obnoxious" and "a total nightmare."

These two examples offer us a mechanism for distinguishing two visions of opera's emotional impact: either expressing a feeling that can stop hardened prisoners in their tracks, beyond any literal comprehension; or making sounds that can be weaponized for maximum irritation.

I stumbled on a 7-Eleven in downtown Chicago deploying operatic selections in this antagonistic way—and it should come as no surprise that Mozart's sweet-sounding duet was not one of them. Instead, the "repertoire" featured arias depicting rage, despair, agony, or death, all sung at maximum volume by big-voiced tenors. Even I was repelled by the excess noise, since the music represented opera's most simplistic displays of emotions. I couldn't recognize which pieces were being played, but I certainly recognized the type: athletic showcases of a singer's power and volume, portraying a basic, primary color of emotional life. Excessive scale superseded any subtlety or complexity. No wonder there was no one loitering around the store—I couldn't wait to get away myself.

This, too, is opera: the over-the-top emotions and one-dimensional characters with a paint-by-numbers approach to inner life. It's a commonplace cliché that is sadly corroborated by plenty of examples in the operatic literature.

It may seem strange to blame music for anything, but with the advent of arias, opera took a turn toward a codification of emotions. In his essay *Metaphysical Song*, musicologist Gary Tomlinson argues that the aria—as an emotive moment that halts the drama—encouraged audiences to narrow their focus down to a single emotion at a time. Before then, in the early operas of Monteverdi's time, the less melodically fixed style of recitative contained a spectrum of emotions within a few lines. But as arias developed as an operatic convention in the late seventeenth and early eighteenth centuries, they created what Tomlinson calls "a lexicon of stable patterns" that mirrored the broader philosophical trends of the time. "Such codes answered the need, in the new representative order, for predictable patterns of signification. They are a musico-dramatic exercise in Cartesian habituation."

This development followed the Baroque-era aesthetic theory known as the "doctrine of passions," which maintained that an artwork's emotional composition could be coded in visual and aural signs. In his 1649 treatise *The Passions of the Soul*, the philosopher René Descartes categorized the six basic "passions" as wonder, love, hatred, desire, joy, and sorrow—offering opera composers a kind of checklist for what a well-rounded work must include. Even before the first words of an aria were sung, an orchestral introduction signaled to the audience which passion was in the spotlight. For a while, the unruly art form of opera became much easier to decipher and categorize, with set-piece arias conforming to recognizable tropes.

Take the example of the "rage aria": a furious orchestral introduction at a fast clip was often the only sign the audience would need to expect a character to unleash a torrent of wrath. Listen to the Act I aria "Non tremar, vassallo indegno" from Venetian composer Antonio Caldara's last opera, *Temistocle* (1736) (SEE PLAYLIST). Although little known today, Caldara was fiendishly prolific in his lifetime, with an astonishing eighty-five stage works to his credit and a rich catalogue of cantatas and sacred music. Some claim that his death at age sixty-six was due in part to sheer exhaustion: in the last twenty years of his life, he served as Vice-Kapellmeister to the Imperial Court in Vienna, a demanding position that required the constant creation of new compositions for the music-hungry emperor Charles VI. The operas written in that period betray a composer working under a serious time crunch; the more intricate musical textures of his early works started thinning out, as inspiration gave way to a craftsmanship that favored just getting it done. To churn out so many new works quickly, Caldara let a cookie-cutter approach to emotional development suffice.

The rage aria from *Temistocle,* sung by the Persian king Xerxes as he admonishes a disloyal confidant, offers a perfect example. With ample opportunities for dazzling vocal fireworks, a riveting performance (like the one in this recording by countertenor Philippe Jaroussky and conductor Emmanuelle Haim) can make Caldara's well-crafted music an exciting listen. But it's hard to imagine the aria doing much more than checking the "rage" box in the opera recipe. The scene may work well on a recording, but as part of a drama, isn't the reduction to a single color bound to make this character feel stagnant onstage? What is there for a singer to portray beyond the roulades of straight-up anger?

Compare Caldara's with the most famous rage aria of all time: the Queen of the Night's Act II showstopper from *The Magic Flute*, known as "Der Hölle Rache" (SEE PLAYLIST). In its first section, the aria, which depicts a hell-raising mother trying to convince her abducted daughter to murder her captor, seems as emotionally straightforward as Caldara's. Its perilous, almost freakish vocal acrobatics require machine-like precision, and it never fails to make an audience hold their collective breath. But the queen continues in unexpected ways. From four furious high F's, her next lines drop to a middle register, and leaving behind the wild leaps of the opening, she steadily sings about what will happen if her daughter fails to listen: "You'll be forever disowned and abandoned, and all the bonds of nature will be destroyed if the villain does not perish by your hand." The music briefly becomes more predictable, with the same vocal pattern repeating in ways that convey a character in absolute control. This cool-headed development can seem inconsistent with the nightmarish vision that arrested our attention just seconds earlier—but that's precisely why the audience continues to listen with fascination. Where a lesser composer would have stayed in the heat of the moment, Mozart shifts to complicate the emotional temperature.

But the aria isn't done shifting, and my favorite part comes next: the queen repeats the phrase "all the bonds of nature" in a covered, mysterious voice, once again sliding up and down her vocal range to trace an elliptical shape. Something has changed for her at the start of this run, but Mozart doesn't explicitly state what that is. Is she trying a new tactic with her daughter—say, maybe, hypnosis? Is she perhaps experiencing a brief moment of remorse? Or is she trying to scare her daughter with the vivid portrayal of a future vision, one haunted by her desolation and dejection? Whatever is happening in this section, the queen is clearly undergoing a change. She repeats her earlier "freakish" line but in a darker, more measured way, several steps lower and in a much quieter tone. She closes the aria with a final gaze to the heavens: "Hear me, hear me, hear me, you gods of vengeance! Hear this mother's oath!" Even here, in what could have been a straightforward conclusion, Mozart throws in a surprise. The three calls of "hear me" trick the listener into anticipating a stepwise ratcheting up of her intensity, but the last iteration jumps unexpectedly into a kind of hyper-drive. In his book *Opera and the Enlightenment,* musicologist Thomas Bauman describes this moment as Mozart's "masterstroke of transformation," since the listener "is led by musical logic to expect, after D and F, A. But the Queen sings a terrifying B♭ instead." What some might have considered a mistake against the mathematical conventions of composition becomes an unforgettable expression of a character's emotional truth.

Within three minutes and without ever straying from the recognizable contours of the rage aria, Mozart offers the singer depicting the Queen of the Night at least four major color shifts to explore. And the most gifted singers can bring out even more (on my playlist, the excellent singing actor Diana Damrau shapes each line with a fresh idea). While Caldara contented himself with the depiction of one stable emotion in his rage aria, Mozart demonstrates the real emotional potential of opera as something unpredictable, messy, and complex. Above all, Mozart shows his characters *changing.*

Opera does poorly when it presents the world as unambiguous and explicit—especially in the turbulent world of "the passions." The art form at its best constantly reveals human nature to be what it is: complicated, sometimes contradictory, and anything but straightforward. That's why "primary color" arias blaring through 7-Eleven speakers seem so absurd (and, for the uninitiated, "a total nightmare"). They paint our feelings as easy and one-dimensional, when any human knows first-hand that the opposite is true. Our emotions are never as clear-cut as Caldara; they're always as mercurial as Mozart.

// // // // //

WHATEVER INTERIORITY THE COMPOSER or librettist or director may have imagined for a particular moment, if the singers can't adequately communicate the idea, it will be as if the score itself doesn't work. Composers, librettists, directors, and conductors can only ever point at the truth of a moment; the singers put themselves out there to channel and embody that truth.

Consider the farewell soliloquy for the character Ottavia in Monteverdi's *The Coronation of Poppea* (1643), a brief monologue that begins, "Addio Roma" (SEE PLAYLIST). Queen Ottavia is married to the cruel and unfaithful emperor Nero, who openly flaunts his love of Poppea and wishes to make her his new queen. Over the course of the opera, Ottavia attempts to outwit her husband, his lover, and a whole court of "yes men" who uphold the status quo. She even goes so far as to order a hit on Poppea's life. When that plot fails, Nero gets the "out" from his marriage that he's been looking for; he now has recourse for banishing Ottavia and marrying his true love.

As the heartbroken queen prepares to leave her beloved homeland, she sings, "Farewell, Rome . . . farewell, country. . . . My friends . . . my friends, farewell!" The opening of this aria is unforgettable, as Ottavia struggles to articulate her first word. "Addio" begins to fragment, as the first syllable repeats: "A . . . A . . . A . . ." Language is opened up and almost abandoned as pure sound is mined for its expressive possibility. But nothing in the score indicates how this moment should be played. Rather than informing us what the character is thinking, the orchestra simply plays in unison with Ottavia's singing, creating a disturbed silence before and after each fragment of sound. If you compare recordings, you'll notice that some singers stretch these "A"s out almost like groans, while others perform it staccato in a series of sharp, painful jabs. Whether her stuttering represents Ottavia's last burst of futile rage, or the shock of realizing that she is leaving her home forever, or the mournful pangs of a heart already feeling nostalgia, the singer brings the true emotional character to this scene—and Monteverdi wrote a score that allows the music to bend in response to the choices she makes.

Such humility on Monteverdi's part indicates an unusual recognition that his music is primarily there to be interpreted. If you judged the role of Ottavia based purely on the written score, she may not seem a particularly exciting character to sing: the vocal range is limited, and the music seems closer to the dialogue of a play rather than the big melodies that show off what a voice can do. But Monteverdi wrote the role for the soprano Anna Renzi, arguably the most famous operatic performer of her time and renowned for her acting ability. The minimal intrusiveness of the score must have emerged from the trust Monteverdi placed in Renzi; spareness of instruction, ornamentation, and orchestral flourishes indicate how well he knew that his music would benefit from giving her license. When a performer recognizes the dramatic potential of this role and realizes how much interpretive responsibility she carries, she will quickly discover a liberating sense of possibility. She can make Ottavia her own in a way that's not afforded to other operatic characters, where the composer's score dictates every nuance.

Ottavia's aria features another ingenious meta-insight into the emotional potential of opera. As her farewell continues, she concedes, "Ah, blasphemous sorrow: you forbid my tears as I leave my country! I must not shed a tear while bidding kin and city farewell." The queen can't cry. And neither can the singer, mostly because she is required to keep singing. Unlike Al Pacino as Michael Corleone wailing at the loss of his daughter, opera singers can't abandon themselves to their emotions; they must transmute their emotions into the music. Even with the maximally flexible emotional life Monteverdi allows Ottavia, she must sing on— and so the performer must strike a seemingly impossible balance between restraint and freedom to bring a character convincingly to life.

Another scene of exiled farewell illustrates this point perfectly. In Verdi's *Aida* (1871), the title character is an enslaved princess from Ethiopia who, despite herself, is in love with her Egyptian captor. In Act III, she sits by the Nile River and imagines drowning herself, even if suicide means the death of her dream of returning home. Like Ottavia, Aida repeats a phrase obsessively throughout the aria: *"Mai più,"* or "never again"—as in "Oh, my country, I will never see you again" (SEE PLAY-LIST). In an opera otherwise characterized by bombast and excess, the subtlety of this aria is affecting; it's often the first moment in an *Aida* performance of authentic emotion.

You could hardly imagine a performance that captures this moment more profoundly than the American soprano Leontyne Price's final Aida at the Metropolitan Opera in 1985. One of the greatest Verdian sopranos of her time, Price considered Aida her operatic legacy; she brought soulfulness and interiority to a character often portrayed with the two-dimensionality of an Egyptian hieroglyph. "My skin was my costume," she avowed in an interview she gave in 2008 on receiving the National Endowment for the Arts' Opera Honor for lifetime achievement. "I was allowed freedoms with her, because she was—and still is very much—*me*." Price found deep satisfaction in "finally being able to express—not just vocally—that she is a princess, never a slave." A video capturing her farewell performance is most affecting during Aida's Act III aria. After singing with exquisite beauty, she finishes the final phrase and looks up to the rafters. The audience showers her with adulation while she stands stoically—everyone present, including the singer, knows they will never experience a moment like this again.

The applause, naturally, goes on for quite a while, and the camera lingers on an intense, almost intrusive close-up of Price's face. The expectation of an emotional dam bursting and overcoming her is palpable. Yet her stare is resolute; she will not break character or cave to the pressure of acknowledging the thunderous applause. She remains committed to her role. She must also be thinking about how much more singing lies ahead: before she leaves the stage, she still has two demanding duets to perform. She can't abandon herself to what she is feeling without sacrificing her best possible performance. But as the applause shows no sign of letting up, her face begins to quiver as she fights to stay in control, and it's hard not to think of this moment as a real-life version of Ottavia's "A . . . A . . . A . . . Addio"; she must not cry. Ultimately, Price prevails over her emotions.

Try watching this excerpt, available on YouTube; if the performance itself doesn't bring you to tears, witnessing a master's self-command pushed to the limit surely will. No wonder the Metropolitan Opera considers it, according to their website, "one of the most emotional evenings in the Met's history."

Describing Leontyne Price's voice as beautiful is easy. But what makes her voice beautiful for me is that it carries the imprint of her inner world. She trained her instrument to speak to a vast range of human experience. When she is portraying a character, Price uses every note and every word to deliver an intense *interiority*. Only when a singer shows that level of dedication to her own inner life—and the inner life of the music and her character—can a voice be considered beautiful. That beauty is where the emotional life of a character, a music score, or an opera ultimately resides.

It's a very special type of performer who can first master the techniques of classical singing and then successfully communicate the inner life of a theatrical character. On one hand, musical interpreters must "stick to the script," adhering to instructions with an exactitude that always threatens to turn music-making into a tyrannical experience; and on the other hand, their expression must never feel rehearsed, flowing as naturally and as truthfully to them as possible. But only after becoming adept at musical execution can a personal, subjective honesty in singers or instrumentalists emerge. Too much subjectivity and the performance devolves into vanity; but too much obedience and all you get is lifelessness. The excitement in theater comes from the paradoxical tension between discipline and individuality that gives a performance its soul.

That's why calling these extraordinary beings merely *singers* can't convey the full breadth required of them. The designation prioritizes the initial and ongoing process of musical training over all the other interpretive techniques they will also have to master to be successful. It's like continuing to call a scientist a researcher after they've won the Nobel Prize. If you are performing in an opera, it's a given that you are a well-trained singer; it's that next level of artistry, including but transcending the singing, that makes a great performer. For those who want to remain singers but consider acting, dancing, literary analysis, and a collaborative process with other artists somehow secondary, there are more than enough opportunities in concert halls.

If *singer* feels too narrowly focused, *artist* surely isn't specific enough, since the art form involves numerous different types of artists.

I like the designation *singing actor*. It may be the best way to understand the singular talent required to truly make an opera work. And it also recognizes acting as a fundamental aspect of the performer's responsibility, not always a given in the field of opera. A 2015 post on the blog *TalkClassical.com* poses the question "Should we expect opera singers to act?" One commentator drew virtual cheers from readers for responding, "Put on a costume, sing your heart out. That's my ideal opera performance."

For many people, acting implies the same naturalism we find in most plays and films. Performances influenced by the teachings of Konstantin Stanislavski and Lee Strasberg aim to reflect a reality the spectator can recognize. This is becoming an expectation of opera singers as well. But operas create their own universes with unique, not necessarily recognizable logic for sound, space, and time. Opera is *unnatural* but, paradoxically, emotionally authentic. Performers are called to discover a singular way to convey something essential and true in an environment that's essentially untrue. And since the singing actor moves in a transfigured space, where everything is magnified to an awe-inspiring scale, acting means something quite different for them than it does for Al Pacino playing Michael Corleone.

When audiences complain about "bad acting" in an opera, they will often cite the cliché of the singing actor's gestures. But no gesture in opera is inherently outdated. The issue is not the way a performer manipulates his hands in a gesture that has been disparagingly called the "baritone claw" (a wrathful, demonic, Shakespearean cupping of his hand), but rather the fact that the baritone may be leaning on a well-established gesture as a shortcut to his own authentic internalization. The same gesture, when emerging from a grounded performer, can be a riveting expression of his inner experience. The clichéd gesture is not the problem; it's the all-too-often occurrence of that externalization standing in for "acting" that makes for an unsatisfying performance. Whether in gesture, presence, or facial expression, the acting part of the singing actor's craft is fundamentally about internalization. Everything else is contingent on the universe the opera is trying to conjure.

We can find a powerful analogue in a non-Western performance style: the ritualistic theater from Japan known as Noh. Invented more than 200 years before Monteverdi's *L'Orfeo*, Noh began from an entertainment known as *sarugaku*, a form of musical performance involving dancing, acrobatics, and other tricks. Troupes adept at *sarugaku* began to integrate narrative elements into their performances, and a new kind of musical theater emerged as its own genre. Zeami Motokiyo, the playwright and actor who's considered the "father" of Noh theater, defined an actor as a performer who could *show* internalization. Zeami considered this ability both a spiritual and natural process, akin to a flower budding, blossoming, and then withering. In his treatise "Mirror Held to the Flower," he gives actors a famous instruction: "When you feel ten in your heart, express seven in your movements." It's quite a different approach from naturalism, which demands that ten in your heart finds an expression of ten in your movements. But for Zeami, "A truly great artist has for many years succeeded in training both his body and his spirit; he can hold back much of his potential in reserve and perform in an easy fashion, so that only seven-tenths of his art is visible."

Zeami's approach to acting is perfect for opera, as Leontyne Price proves in her final *Aida*: it's undeniable that her heart is swelling at the maximum level (ten), but her ability to hold back not only allowed her to perform with total control; it also allowed us, the spectators, to perceive the character Aida and reflect on a deeper meaning. The same phenomenon makes someone holding back tears much more emotional than if they were actually crying. As a well-known acting adage has it, "If the actor cries, the audience won't."

The "singing actor" label also conveys an ethos of collaboration. Singers may stand alone on a concert stage, with a piano or accompanying instrument, and call all the shots. But the singing actor never stands alone, and even in a solo aria they never perform in isolation. The cliché of singers as divas who demand that everything adapt to them has become an outdated phenomenon. Singing actors, like every other artist involved in opera, must navigate a space between what they offer as individuals and what the work as a whole needs. (I'll talk more about opera's ludicrous-seeming spirit of collaboration in the final chapter.) Every aspect of their performance must harmonize with the work of their fellow singing actors and the two primary leaders of the performance, the director and the conductor. This situation must sometimes feel like Odysseus navigating Charybdis and Scylla, trying to locate an impossible middle passage between a whirlpool and a monster. Surely the different imperatives of the director and the conductor can make for a very narrow needle's eye for a singer to thread, as the leaders' instructions may sometimes conflict. When directors and conductors fail to model a mutual respect for each other's ideas, the singing actors are the ones caught in the crossfire. It is they, after all, who must appear onstage to carry the interpretations of both alongside their own.

An essential part of a singing actor's training is the practice of accessing and expressing their emotions. Most singers just starting out play the emotion ("I'm sad"), which will almost certainly result in a purely external performance. Although some remarkable performers can pull this off, especially when coupled with an amazing voice, the result is unlikely to transcend the superficial. Directors can help these young novices by asking them to play an activity rather than an emotion. Singers engaged in an activity ("I'm digging my beloved's grave") will have something to do, which can often keep them from focusing on the emotion; and even if this may bring the danger of "telegraphing" an emotion rather than properly communicating it, such a focus can help guide them to what's really demanded of them.

The most skilled singing actors do not play the emotion and do not need activity, because they can find action in every moment. Action may or may not have an activity related to it ("I'm seeing before my eyes the memory of my lost love"), but it will trigger a communicability that keeps the relevant idea alive. Within one aria, the more that internal action changes, the more alive the performance will be. The most effective singing actors have long left behind emotions in favor of action-oriented interiority.

Expert singing actors also know how to harness the excitement of emotional contrast, even contradiction. A novice singing actor will no doubt want to begin with the straightforward emotional idea of an aria: in Mozart's *Don Giovanni,* Masetto and Zerlina are joyous when they sing their first duet, and Donna Elvira is indignant when she warns Zerlina of Don Giovanni's roving eye. Sticking with the one idea of joy or indignation takes us back to the paint-by-numbers approach of *Temistocle,* where the human psyche is portrayed simplistically.

Musicologists have dubbed such direct illustration of music "Mickey Mousing," a perfect pejorative for the unambiguous merging of sight and sound. When singing actors embrace in a passionate kiss exactly at the moment of a huge orchestral climax, the result is almost laughably one-dimensional. Although avoiding Mickey Mousing is a large part of a director's responsibility, the task also falls to the individual singing actor. The great ones understand how to add complexity to even the most straightforward musical moments, injecting dramatic heft into a scene. In his joy at being with Zerlina, an excellent Masetto can also find moments in his first duet with her to portray the jealousy and hot-headedness that characterize him throughout the opera. And even as she is indignant, a great Donna Elvira will know exactly where she can struggle with her ongoing love for Don Giovanni.

(We can look once again to the Noh theater of Zeami, who wrote in his acting treatise "Style and the Flower": "When an actor plans to express the emotion of anger, he must not fail to retain a tender heart. On the other hand, in a performance requiring Grace, an actor must not forget to remain strong.")

The real beauty of opera is that there can be no single correct interpretation; there should be as many different characterizations of Donna Elvira as there are humans alive to sing them. The emotional life of the music will only speak when the singing actor finds their unique internalized expression. I hesitated to discuss Leontyne Price in this chapter because I didn't want to fuel the familiar wail of opera fans who love to lament the loss of an imagined golden age of singing: "No one sings like that anymore!" Not only is that kind of moaning tedious, it's also unhelpful in forging a path toward a more vibrant future for opera. I don't want performers in Price's wake singing like her; they should sing and perform only as themselves. The greatest performers today will continually open up the field of the possible rather than aspire to past standards. And while some claim that an increased attention to theatrical aspects minimizes the primacy of the singing voice, I see instead a wealth of new expressive possibilities as we set new benchmarks for today's and tomorrow's singing actors.

// // // // //

ONE OF THE MOST IMPORTANT roles I play as a director is as an inspiration and support for the singing actor on their process of self-discovery. I would therefore feel remiss in only talking *about* singers without creating space for them to speak for themselves.

Of the many amazing artists I've been lucky enough to work with, I've selected three who embody what it means to be a singing actor. I asked them about their process, how they handle the big emotions of their characters, and how they were able to unlock their unique voice. Each one has carved or is carving out a singular path that matches her particular qualities (you will never see these three women competing for the same role!). Opera is no doubt richer for being able to sustain individuals with such distinct forms of artistry.

Paula Murrihy is a mezzo-soprano with whom I worked at the Santa Fe Opera for my 2023 production of Monteverdi's *L'Orfeo*. Paula played the Messenger, who brings Orpheus the news that Eurydice has died. In what is certainly the emotional high point of the opera, the Messenger sets the scene in loving detail, in a way that shows how much the death of her friend affects her.

"Words are always so central to me—sometimes to my vocal detriment," Murrihy humbly admitted to me during a rehearsal break. I had to ask why she thought that way, since I'd never seen her musical skill suffer from the intense emotional life she brought to the Messenger's heartbreaking words. "Sometimes I feel in bigger, grander opera, or on a larger scale, I'm thinking too much about the clarity of the word. But actually, I don't regret it—because the power of the word brings you to the heart of the matter. I always start with the text—sitting down, writing out the text, and working with a language coach before I go to the music. I put words ahead of the tone, so the thought goes first. The thought, of course, is also the emotion. So from the words, I can start

Radical empathy: Paula Murrihy as La Messaggera in *L'Orfeo*
at Santa Fe Opera (2023).

to consider: What causes the character to say this? Where is she right now? Where are the color changes? Before the collaborative aspects start shaping my view, I get to form my own *scena* in my head—developing the background, with lots of images, engaging my own imagination. I start by becoming a director in my own head."

Paula's care for the words explains why she creates such an indelible presence in the work of Monteverdi, where the flow of the music closely follows the natural cadences of the Italian poetry. "I like to think of the orchestra as the river of my thoughts," she said, "and I look to articulate that ebb and flow."

I wondered whether the music might demand a specific kind of acting style, perhaps different from other operas, where the big sweeping melody takes precedence over the language. Paula didn't think so, although she acknowledged that "if you are inherently open to how a musical style is realized, your body, your gesture, your gaze all react in a different way." She lets the director in her head take a backseat as the style develops collaboratively with the director and her fellow artists onstage. "In a very strange way, I don't enjoy being a soloist; I love the team element and how many people it takes to make an opera happen. From the porter who greets you on your way in to the building to the gentleman at the cafeteria, who has likely forgotten more opera than I'll ever learn. We singers do not exist in a vacuum; we are informed by the team around us.

"I feel fortunate when I think about how I came into acting in the first place: I started in folk theater as a member of the National Folk Theatre of Ireland from the age of eight. Looking back now, I think that folk theater at its heart is about telling the story of people and re-creating the story of our heritage—and I think that little seed has somehow informed me throughout. Especially when I consider the link between folk music and Baroque music: there is a directness, a vulnerability, and a truth when you are telling these stories.

"Finding the balance between the structure of the music and the directness of the emotions is always a journey," she said. "But I think you have to be honest above everything. My teacher Patricia Mislan always talked about the search for truth in the music. Patricia was about 'the inner rhythm'—not an accurate rhythm but a vitality, the life of the note, the life of the word, the life of the music. I think that aspect is too crucial. Whether they know it or not, people react to honesty; they sense when someone is in the moment, giving something that is *them* . . . in all their imperfection."

The second singer I want to introduce is the soprano Whitney Morrison. I had the chance to work with Whitney at the Lyric Opera of Chicago on an unusual project called *Proximity,* a trio of new American operas that premiered in 2023. One of the three works dealt with gun violence on Chicago streets, with music by the eclectic and energetic Daniel Bernard Roumain and words by the renowned actor and playwright Anna Deavere Smith. In her iconic style, Smith created a libretto from interviews with real Chicagoans, forming a mosaic of perspectives that provokes the audience to an empathetic investigation of her subject. Roumain responded with inimitable music, weaving Bach chorales, R&B, hip-hop, and trap music together to form a nervy and galvanizing sound world for a city on edge.

Whitney closed the evening with a heart-wrenching final scene taken from the words of a young woman named Yasmine Miller.

Miller lost her six-month-old son Sincere on her way to the laundromat, when an unknown assailant shot up her car—a shocking crime that remains unsolved. The scene is daunting, beginning with Yasmine's joy in becoming a mother and leading to a report on the shooting. In her interview, Yasmine simply said, "He didn't make it," with a crushing lucidity. Roumain made this one of the most emotionally charged moments in the score, as the orchestra quiets down to a solo synthesizer, which supports her as she comes around to uttering the full sentence: "He didn't...he didn't...he didn't make—he didn't...make—he didn't...make—he didn't...he didn't. He didn't make it. He didn't make it. He didn't make it."

As the scene goes on, Miller's journey is an emotional rollercoaster: we hear about her depression and sleepless nights; her outrage at the police's complete lack of action and urgency; the pain of knowing her son is never coming back; and finally the bittersweet joy of announcing the arrival of a second child. "Her name is going to be Serenity," she tells us. Roumain sets her final line with another stutter, a hesitation to reach the final word: "It won't fully mend a broken heart, but it will be some kind of... It won't fully mend a broken heart, but it will be some kind of... It won't fully mend a broken heart, but it will be some kind of... *peace*." Whether or not Roumain was consciously invoking the emotional power of Ottavia's broken singing in *Poppea*, he created a similarly unforgettable effect and gave the singer an enormous interpretive opportunity to bring herself to this role.

The emotional maturity and range required by this aria makes it a formidable assignment for a singer of any age. That Morrison could bring so much honesty and natural poise to the scene was nothing short of astonishing. She never held back in a single rehearsal and used every repetition as a chance to try something new or go deeper. She was always remarkably present—what actors call "in the moment"—in a way that never betrayed self-awareness; and she was always able to channel Miller's emotions rather than choke up on her own. All of that—while also singing with rich beauty and freshness.

"I've been trying to think if I had to dissociate to perform this role,"

Bearing witness: Whitney Morrison as Yasmine Miller in *Proximity* (2023) at Lyric Opera of Chicago.

Whitney told me six months after the performances of *Proximity*. "And I don't think I did. But my passion was in my resolve to tell the truth. Whereas other people may have needed truth to show up with tears, the intensity of my presence and my resolve was more important than needing to be a first-hand experiencer of Yasmine's pain. There's no way I can do that—I don't have children, you know; I can only imagine, really, so my entire performance is a function of imagination anyway. But the resolve to see and use my social skills to say, 'Okay, how do I empathize and show sympathy for this person?' And if I can use my imagination to feel her sadness, I can use my imagination to tell the truth.

"I err on the side of service and truth-telling," she continued. "And when it comes to emotions, my approach is very integrated. I don't think about emotion as separate from truth-telling and *is*-ness—meaning to embody something as fully as I can." Whitney frequently calls upon her spiritual background and her upbringing in church, and for her the fear of "bearing false witness" urges her to dig as deep as she can into the language and the history of a character. She's not bothered by showing up truthfully in the highly artificial world of opera: "Acting is a series of tools for you to use so you can let go of your inhibitions and find the truth."

When it comes to Yasmine, Whitney claims that a sense of responsibility helped her grapple with the emotional demands of the role. "Growing up in the south suburbs of Chicago, one generation out of the projects on both sides, I've been navigating a complex social landscape for a long time. And when I see people from other areas of Chicago who have a very different experience from mine, I have a lot of sympathy. I know their story could have been mine. So especially as a Chicagoan, who has the most contact and context for Yasmine Miller, I felt a responsibility that was singular. When it was hard, I kept thinking, 'That woman lost her baby, and she's going to be in that opera house, and I want to tell the truth.' Nothing else was more important.

"I don't think we have vastly different experiences," she said. "If I dig all the way to the bedrock of humanity, socially and emotionally, I can find common ground with anyone—with people from all sides of the city, or with Mimì from *La bohème*."

I have only rarely witnessed a performance like Whitney's—and rarely witnessed a singer with a process so deeply rooted. Yasmine Miller was present on opening night, a fact that would have thrown a less anchored singing actor into an unnatural self-consciousness. Not Whitney: her musical, psychological, and spiritual preparation all paid off. The truth of the character's emotions communicated at the overwhelming scale that is, ultimately, opera at its best.

The final singing actor I spoke with was the great German soprano Waltraud Meier. Her career is full of legendary performances of searing intensity, especially the demanding roles in Wagner's operas—Isolde, Kundry, Sieglinde, Waltraute, and Ortrud—that have become her signature. Before I worked with her, as Ortrud in *Lohengrin* at Bayreuth in 2018, I considered her such an astonishing performer that I would go out of my way to see her onstage. After working with her, my esteem of her enormous gifts only increased.

Among the many unforgettable performances in Waltraud's legacy, one of them stands out for me as an exemplar of her extraordinary gifts.

Complete mastery: Waltraud Meier as Ortrud, with Georg Zeppenfeld as
König Heinrich and Tomasz Konieczny as Telramund, in *Lohengrin*
at the Bayreuther Festspiele (2018).

In Berlin in 2002, she jumped in at the last minute for a sick colleague
to perform Fricka in Wagner's *Die Walküre*, a role she had not sung in
years. The problem was, she was already singing the much larger and
more demanding role of Sieglinde in the same production. Waltraud, at
a moment's notice, simply performed both, and ended up delivering two
completely different vocal and dramatic characterizations in the same
show. Although Fricka and Sieglinde never appear together onstage,
Waltraud's astonishing feat that night would have had anyone believe
that she was capable of somehow splitting herself in two.

Our conversation took place as she was preparing her own farewell
to the stage, in a final performance of the haunted mother Klytämnestra
in Richard Strauss's *Elektra* (1909) at the Staatsoper Berlin.

YUVAL: If anyone can consider herself a singing actor, I think it's you.

WALTRAUD: I do consider myself a singing actor. When I was inducted as a member of the Bayerische Akademie der Schönen Künste [Bavarian Academy of Fine Arts], I was not categorized in their music department. Instead, I am a member of their Darstellende Kunst [Performing Arts] department, alongside directors, playwrights, designers, and theater actors. And that's a bigger honor for me than if I was considered just a singer.

Y: When you begin approaching a role, how is your work on the text different from your work on the music? Do you have a preferred way "in" to a role—through text or through music?

W: The music and text are two different things, but they belong together; the composer thought of them as a combined thing. So to analyze it, I have first to . . . start with one and then with the other, before considering them together. When I started looking at the role of Klytämnestra in *Elektra,* I didn't know the opera very well. So I started by listening to it once, only to get an impression of the sound of it—the general impact. And then I read the text, and I read it out loud. That is important: to hear the sound of the words. As we know, words are already music. The vowels, whether they are light vowels or dark vowels, are very important. Or the consonants: there are singing consonants, sounding consonants like V, like L, or rhyming consonants. That's why I read the text out loud; I get the sound into my ear.

Then I read it as a story. For that, it's important not to read it from the score. Because as a singer, you can't help but also read the music; you can't help but see there's a quarter note, or a pause, and so on. It's important to read it as a story and to read it in your own words. That way, it creates a movie in my mind. I start seeing pictures—and I keep these pictures for later on when I go to the stage.

Finally, of course, I bring that together with the music. But very often, even in between productions, I'll go back and I will read the pure text again. I remember after years and years of singing the role, I sang Kundry in *Parsifal* at the Paris Opera in 2010. I sat in my dressing room during an intermission and I read the text again. Despite all my work on the role, I still came to new understandings. "Ah, I've never thought about that word—what does *that* mean?" Or "Oh, he's saying this line to *them* and not to me." And it's always very important not to read only my lines; I read the whole thing, everybody else's lines as well.

Y: I remember that so well from *Lohengrin*. You knew everyone else's lines by memory.

W: I think you need that kind of knowledge. Otherwise you cannot react; you don't know what's really going on.

Y: Isn't that a lot to keep in your head? Don't you have enough to keep track of just for your own role?

W: Not at all—it actually helps me remember what I have to say, how I have to react, or what I should play. It always helps, and I cannot understand why the others don't do it.

Y: It's true that you can sometimes find yourself with singers who behave like members of an orchestra. In a way, the act of learning a piece musically rather than dramatically habituates that mentality.

W: True, but for me, staying in the energy of a performance is so much easier. It's much more difficult stepping in and out of a role. When I go onstage, I'm *in*—all the way until I exit. And then it's a flow.

Y: You've already said a few things about text and where you look for insight into the character from the sound of the words...

W: Yes—that's the technical point of view. But now we are getting to the emotional and the incarnation of it. For this, I have to recall something very important I learned from the director Klaus-Michael Grüber. He told me, "Never take what you say as a comment; never take it ironically or sarcastically. You have to identify with what you are saying, without commentary." A comment would be something like "I'm the happy one now!" Or "I'm the bad one now! I'll show you how bad I am." Or "I'll show you how intriguing I am." Then you are distanced. That doesn't mean it should be about your own private emotion; you have to enter into the emotions of the person that you are showing onstage. Take it seriously; don't mock them. That's why, when I'm playing Ortrud, I must feel like I'm completely right in what I'm doing. I must leave it up to the audience to judge. It's up to the audience to cry, to be furious, to love, whatever. Instead of judging, when you are onstage, you have to enter into your character's skin with all that you have.

Y: But how do you go from that technical analysis—of the language, the music, and the space where they come together—into the incarnation?

W: Klaus-Michael also told me, "Onstage, you must be as honest as you can. If you want to communicate something, imagine you are telling it to an eleven-year-old child." I was surprised and asked him, "Why an eleven-year-old?" And he said, "Eleven is an age where a human being already knows about love, hatred, betrayal—all those big emotions. But in that age, you don't have cynicism, sarcasm, or irony. You must never do these three things onstage." And when I see singers today performing ironically or cynically, all I can see is their pretending. There's nothing honest.

Y: But opera is such an artificial medium—how do you find that honesty in it?

W: Yes, opera has many artificial layers, but at its core, it's all about love, hatred, betrayal—all those things that will always be with us. We can wear lots of costumes, but the essence of it surpasses all time. Generations after us will experience the same problems we do. And if you concentrate on that essence, then you have something to say. You're onstage, looking out to see Mrs. Smith in Row 15, and you tell her how you were betrayed by your lover; you tell her how it hurts. And then you have truth!

Y: So, for you, the artifice is more of a costume—the rules of the game—that enables something true?

W: Depending on the possibilities that a director gives me, with costumes and lighting and everything else. It's true that I sometimes walk onto a set quite different from what I'm imagining, and then I have to wonder, "How can I play in this situation?" And then I play with it. All the many elements that make up opera are so important for the performer; costumes, for instance, are terribly important for me, because they funnel how I feel and how I move. I love costume designers who are at the rehearsals from the very beginning; they watch what we have to do and how we move as a person. Because everybody has their own unique body language. I think the director and the costume designer must support that.

Y: It's true—and it gets to the heart of what the rehearsal process is about. Rehearsals are not the place to simply enact what you've already discovered but rather the place to undergo a discovery process. Which means staying open for things to adapt to the specific performers. Are there other rehearsal methods you use to develop an internalized response to a character?

W: Yes, although the director Patrice Chéreau always laughed at me when I did this. After every rehearsal, when everybody goes away, I stay back and I walk it through on my own.

Y: Yes, I've seen you do this in Bayreuth!

W: And I use my own words—not the character's lines. I'm walking the character of Ortrud but with Waltraud's words. That way I can discover the emotions as they live within me—not the poetry but more direct, personal language. That awakens my imagination for the scene, and for the emotions I need. With my own words, I can be furious, or mean, or jealous, or anything.

Y: And beyond your words—what aspect of yourself appears in your characterizations?

W: I'd say *every* aspect! I'm convinced that the more you live normally (not as a star or a diva) and you live everything in life—mourning, joy, surprise, all the emotions—then you know how things feel, and you remember how you reacted. And you know how your body reacted. Those are tools that you must remember when you are portraying a character.

Y: It makes me think of the Japanese Noh theater, where some troupes insisted that to play a teenage character, the actor must be at least fifty years old. Because you can't possibly understand what it means to be an eighteen-year-old in love until you're past that. It's a bit extreme and very different from the expectation that a singer should look the part. But as a fifty- or sixty-year-old actor, you can reflect on what it means to be young and can *show* it better, rather than simply living it.

W: Except by then, the bones don't work anymore!

Y: Isn't that what costumes and lighting are for?

W: It's awful walking onstage and thinking, "Oh shit—don't build any more stairs!" Or, "Don't make me kneel down!"

Y: But it doesn't matter about the creaky knees and the inflexible hips when the spirit is right. That's what I think the Noh masters were getting at: your ability to communicate a spirit *increases* with age. The bones may not work the way they used to, but the experience and the memory inside those bones can radiate.

W: But that's why it's also important that performers practice exercises in awareness. What can your body do, and what does it express? What is your *hand*, just your hand, able to do? It can be a fist; it can hold; it can be cramped; it can invite; feel; caress. Just one hand can do a thousand things. And then the head, just the way you hold your head: when it's straight, you appear strict; if it's tilted to one side, you seem doubtful; and when tilted to the other side, it makes you look flirtatious. Just your head can show so many things. So I spend a lot of time in front of the mirror just watching and discovering what my body is communicating even without saying a word. You are never just standing and singing. Everything you do is already telling a story. That's why I always say that as soon as you go out onstage, you are telling something. And it's up to you if what you are telling is the story you're actually trying to tell!

Y: It always amazes me how performers are so completely transparent when they are onstage. I'm not sure all singers are aware of how much an audience sees inside them.

W: Yes. You can read everything.

Y: *Everything.* There's actually no place to hide, no matter how many layers of makeup or costumes or wigs . . .

W: Performing in opera takes a great deal of awareness.

Y: Absolutely. Although that's really hard to come by when there's so much external stuff surrounding the conventional operatic performer.

W: Yes, of course.

Y: Whether it's the constant insecurity around your voice, which you can never adequately hear because you are literally *inside it*; or the fear of the wrath of an autocratic director or conductor, which may cost you future jobs; or the feeling that you need to be a brand and constantly promote yourself on social media—our field makes it very hard to tune all that out and focus on craftsmanship.

W: Yes, it's difficult. One way to escape that while you are onstage is to stay communicating—and ideally to someone else onstage. It helps you connect to emotions when you have somebody you send the emotions to. You must have a recipient for what you say.

Y: Absolutely.

W: In Paris, I worked with Patrice Chéreau on a play at the Louvre Museum. I sang Wagner's song cycle *Wesendonck Lieder,* and with each song, I took the audience from room to room. There were only about 250 audience members, and they didn't have seats. Instead, I would sing *among* them and I would approach them very closely—sometimes only one meter away. The reactions were fascinating; some people were totally shocked at how close I was, while others were crying. The emotions were suddenly so direct.

Y: Yes, the intimacy must have been overwhelming. I always wish audiences could experience what I get to experience in the rehearsal room, when I'm so close to you and other singers. I'm sure that if more people experienced opera like that, *everyone* would be fighting to get tickets. The humanity of what we do would just be immediate, instead of the huge distances of traditional opera houses.

W: Distance never makes emotions. Total distance in opera is not possible, because the music overwhelms you. Instead, I always look to express things as strongly and directly as I can.

// // // // //

KLUGE'S CONCEPT OF OPERA AS "a power plant of feelings"—an image I initially considered generative—now strikes me differently after working with singing actors like Paula Murrihy, Whitney Morrison, and Waltraud Meier. For these artists, the purpose of their craft is not self-indulgence or an emotional manipulation of the audience—both of which can easily arise when we focus on "feeling." Instead, the best singing actors provoke their audience to connect with their own interiority—or, as Waltraud put it, to make up their own minds. And as different as these three performers are, each emphasizes imagination as one of her most important tools. Whether it's Paula becoming a director in her head, or Whitney respecting her position as witness, or Waltraud using her own words to inhabit a scene, the creative act of imagination is an essential animator of her musical skill. And for all three, the result is something they call truthfulness and emotional honesty.

There's much more to performing, then, than simply "feeling." Singing actors must forge a bridge connecting the music to what's inside them and to the audience. The potential for a direct empathic connection between humans from different times and circumstances—at the heart of Whitney's imaginative characterization—is one of the most profound reasons for pursuing opera in the first place. The igniting of that empathy at operatic scale has the power to overwhelm our hearts, to open our minds, and to manufacture a sense of astonishment.

So if we are to talk about opera in industrial terms, let's consider another metaphor: opera as an engine of empathy and awe. Because every production and every artist within that production has the potential to engender both. And the conduit for that electricity is the singing actor.

4

A STRANGE FORM
OF STORYTELLING

NARRATIVE, AMBIGUITY, AND DIRECTORIAL AUTHORSHIP

THE COMEDIAN ADAM SANDLER ENTERED THE ANNALS OF opera history in 1992 when he introduced the character of "Opera Man" on the TV show *Saturday Night Live*. Donning a tuxedo and cape, Opera Man became a regular guest correspondent on the show's satirical news segment "Weekend Update." He relayed the week's news in song, waving a white handkerchief as if conducting an invisible orchestra. Delivering brief digests of the latest headlines in a half-English, half-Italian mash-up, Opera Man deployed a virtuosic parade of operatic clichés while parodying current events. Lamenting the Buffalo Bills' Super Bowl loss in 1993, for example, he sang: "Buffalo destroyedo / el choko third year-o / Opera Man devastateo / Lose-oh mucho dinero! / Ah ah ah ah ah!"

A year after he was introduced, Opera Man left the news desk to open an episode of *Saturday Night Live* as the star of his own tragedy: "Opera Man Comes Within One Number of Winning the New Hampshire Lucky Five Scratch-Off Lottery." A tuxedoed Phil Hartman sets the scene: Opera Man, having just filled up his car at a gas station, purchases a lottery ticket. Each number he scratches off brings him closer to the million-dollar prize, and even though the title of the "opera" gives away the ending, Sandler plays the suspense so brilliantly that the audience can't help rooting for him to win anyway. But once he scratches off the final box and realizes he didn't win the jackpot, the music becomes tragic. "No millionaro, / back to jobo, / securito guardo / Montgomery Ward-o!!!"

The absurdity of Opera Man—the incongruity between his text and his grandiose delivery—relies on the absurdity of opera itself and its strange way of telling stories. By lavishing a full-throated delivery better suited for eternal tragedy on trivial, forgettable events, the excesses of operatic delivery come across as preposterous (and hilarious).

Unlike its sister arts, opera can only tell stories in an arcane manner—often in foreign languages, with curious dramatic pacing out of step with modern storytelling techniques and surrounded by alienating conventions. Comprehension is anything but a given, even when the story being told is as well known as *Romeo and Juliet*. While most other narrative art forms can usually satisfy an audience's longing for recognizable elements to connect with, opera as a genre is always on the verge of incomprehensibility.

Take, for example, the fact that when listening to an opera sung in Italian or German or even English, an audience is not expected to understand the lines directly from the mouths of the singers; even Opera Man's language relied on subtitles for comprehension. Operatic language is primarily understood through *reading* rather than listening, originally by way of printed libretti but now mostly through titles projected over the stage (or in some cases on the seat in front of you). I'm grateful for supertitles, remembering the off-putting experience of seeing my first opera without them. Still, they have obscured the fact that comprehension in opera is only achieved through distance. You start to understand the difference between a Broadway audience, hanging on every word emanating from the live performers, and the detachment of an opera audience, relying on the mediation of a projected translation to follow along. Titles at a commercial musical would likely signal a failure on the performers' parts, as if they couldn't deliver their lines with clear enough diction to be understood.

Then consider how opera doesn't seem to value a sense of suspense as to what will happen next. Other storytelling media, like episodic television, hold an audience by keeping them guessing how the story will unfold. Opera, on the other hand, shows no need for spoiler alerts: the entire story is given to you in advance in the printed synopses of your program book. Most companies encourage audiences to get to know the story before you arrive. I couldn't fathom this practice as a teenager: if I already know how the opera ends, why should I sit through the whole thing?

I've come to realize that opera's strange way of storytelling is not a design flaw. Yes, the interplay of word, music, and production rarely results in the kind of unambiguous clarity we have come to expect from other narrative arts. But as popular culture and mass media maintain a staunch resistance to ambiguity, opera's inherent complexity and layers of signification give the art form a singular and vital fascination: as a space for a multiplicity of meaning, for indeterminacy and ultimately enchantment. The creation of that space, and the director's role in holding that space, is the focus of this chapter.

READING OPERA POETICALLY

Ambiguity, appropriately enough, has many definitions and might best be thought of as an image. Let's use a telescope as an analogy. Its multiple lenses need to be calibrated just right to create a sharp image. When the image is perfectly clear, there's no ambiguity about what you are seeing. The shape is crisp, and the object gives the illusion of nearness. But shift the focus and the lines become blurred. Now the eyes must interpret what they are seeing. Rather than one identity or one conclusion emerging, multiple possibilities encircle your vision. The image becomes mysterious.

Ambiguity in opera implies this kind of blurred view, a resistance to complete legibility. It's a telescope kindred to a kaleidoscope, created not for the purpose of seeing clearly but for seeing *differently*. I like to think of ambiguity as referring to a work's *purposeful inconclusiveness*, always resisting a perfect focus. An ambiguous work involves a complex of possible meanings rather than the resolute pursuit of just one.

Popular culture remains averse to ambiguity in all its forms: enigma, paradox, and indeterminate meaning. The clear-eyed telescope, with its singularity of meaning, is prized higher than the kaleidoscope, with its shifting, unstable signification. This must surely be due to a desire for legibility and understandability—the antitheses of ambiguity—among the general public, and even among many art lovers. An audience's satisfaction with legibility is a constant struggle for artists who gravitate toward the unknown. Pablo Picasso, for example, famously lamented the fact that "everyone wants to understand art. Why not try to understand the songs of a bird? Why does one love the night, flowers, everything around one, without trying to understand them? But in the case of a painting, people have to *understand*." In the intervening century, and unquestionably in part because of the pioneering work of artists like Picasso, painting and sculpture have largely overcome expectations for comprehensibility. Mood, color, and composition are prized higher than legibility, and ambiguity has become a treasured quality of paintings. Great works of the past in pursuit of enigmatic realities, like Diego Velázquez's *Las Meninas* (1656), emerged from a long period of neglect to become exemplars of art's powerful mystery.

In his novel *Starbook,* the Nigerian writer Ben Okri best articulates the shortsightedness of a spectator's wish for comprehension. In depicting a mythic community of master artists, Okri characterizes their appreciation of art as auspicious:

> The masters knew that works of art could not be understood. And that the desire to understand was not only a fatal presumption, and an arrogance, but that it also got in the way of

seeing or hearing or being inspired by the work of art at all. For (so they believed) once a work is thought to be understood, its magic is dimmed, not in the work, but in the person seeking to understand. And so such people become closed to its light, its power for continual inspiration and regeneration. The world is thus diminished; for a light, a source of light, has then been hidden by false understanding.

As hard as it may be to deny Okri's praise of art that passes all understanding, his perspective remains in the minority. (And we'll come back to the "arrogance" of false understanding that Okri describes here in a later chapter.)

Ambiguity as an agent of indeterminacy has a long history of offering both frustration and fascination. In a 1962 article for the *Journal of Personality*, Dr. Stanley Budner created a scale to gauge an individual's threshold for uncertainty, a measure he called "ambiguity tolerance," or AT. After responding to sixteen different confusing situations, participants in Budner's experiment either scored as intolerant, tending to interpret "ambiguous situations as sources of threat," or registered enough tolerance or pleasure in uncertain situations to consider them "desirable." Budner was building off the work of Else Frenkel-Brunswik, an Austrian psychologist who first introduced the concept of ambiguity intolerance while exploring the qualities of the authoritarian personality just after World War II. Her findings are not surprising: the more individuals reacted negatively to ambiguity, the more they responded to the pleasing order of totalitarian leadership. Developing a tolerance for ambiguity offered a potent tactic in the effort to rewire a population brainwashed by the era's fascist governments. Psychologists began turning to art as a therapeutic medium for building AT in patients, under the assumption that art has an inherently ambiguous character.

But that assumption is becoming increasingly difficult to sustain, as all aspects of life are moving toward more uniformity at the expense of complexity, variety, and multiplicity. The German professor Thomas Bauer, best known for his descriptions of Islamic cultures as innately tolerant of ambiguity, views AT in Western culture at an all-time low.

Bauer connects this occurrence to both a rising tide of religious fundamentalism (which insists on a singular, black-and-white approach to truth) and the triumph of capitalism (the populist demands of the marketplace defining tastes and trends): all are succumbing to the same social impulses. The move away from ambiguity in art, for Bauer, is what accounts for the inundation of realism and reality-based entertainment in a culture that prizes understandability. And in his essay "The Disambiguation of the World," Bauer uses the history of opera to illustrate his point, contrasting extravagant Baroque superficiality with the popular naturalism of later *verismo* operas. "Melodies became gradually more 'realistic,'" he writes, "with coloratura accused of unnaturalness. The sung line got closer and closer to speech, as can be found in Puccini and operettas."

To understand what Bauer means, let's compare two scenes depicting the same dramatic situation: defiant men on the brink of their execution. In George Frideric Handel's Baroque opera *Arminio* (1737), the title character is the chieftain of a Germanic tribe defending his country against a Roman invasion. Arminio is captured, sentenced to death, and at the beginning of Act III brought to the scaffold before a crowd gathered to watch him die. Unflinching in the face of this dreadful scene, Arminio bravely prepares to meet his death . . . when a sudden attack on the Romans forces the execution to be postponed. As the chieftain is rushed back to his prison cell, he sings a proud aria: "I return to my chains, but what is it you want from me, oh my Fate? This strange alternation between prison and death only strengthens my faith" (SEE PLAYLIST).

His music is a straightforward example of a *da capo* aria, the format Handel loved best. An initial musical theme, sometimes known as the A section, is introduced with the first line of the text—in this case, "Ritorno alle ritorte" (I return to my chains). The music then develops and morphs in the B section, before the A section is repeated (*da capo* means "from the top"). The return of music and text the audience has already heard allows the singer an opportunity to riff freely. Part of what makes moments like this feel "artificial" in Baroque opera is the pausing of dramatic time, even when the stakes are high (the Romans may be under attack and Arminio hurried off, but how much urgency can there be if he has enough time to repeat himself with flourishes and embellishments?). Unnatural, too, is the elongation of words: the image of "ritorte" (chains) is constantly opened up with each pass, giving the singer ample opportunity to both express a defiance of his imprisonment and show off his coloratura skills.

"Ritorno alla ritorte" is not one of Handel's most original arias, but it makes a useful comparison with a different pre-execution meditation— the haunting Act III aria for Puccini's rebellious tenor Cavaradossi in *Tosca* (1900) (SEE PLAYLIST). The politically radical painter has run afoul of the lecherous police chief Baron Scarpia and faces a shooting squad at Rome's Castel Sant'Angelo at dawn. In the last hour of his life, he tries to write a letter to his lover Tosca but finds himself choked up:

And the stars were shining... and the soil smelled fragrant... when I heard the creak of the garden gate and a furtive footstep. I recognized her by her scent as she fell into my arms. What sweet kisses and caresses we shared! I found myself trembling as I undressed her. But that dream of love is now vanished forever: the moment is gone, and I die in despair! And never have I loved life so much!

This charged scene is famous for an emotional verisimilitude and directness that could easily make Handel's scene feel arcane and distanced. Puccini, taking a cue from his idol Verdi, gives the melody to the orchestra while the singer declaims his first words in a monotonous and haunted half-voice. The sobering effect is of emotional shock, a numbness that gradually gives way as the erotic charge of his memory ignites a new lust for life. Cavaradossi's melodic line strictly follows the syllabic contour of the words—no elongations or mutations like Handel's—and only the last two lines are half-repeated, either for emphasis or to hammer home the impression of a man wailing against his destiny. Without losing musical expression, the moment feels more like a confession than an aria.

Before we arrive at this showstopping moment, Puccini sets the scene with a picturesque tone poem evoking the quiet Roman streets at dawn: a shepherd boy sings in the distance (offstage) in a Romanesque dialect, while church bells toll indeterminately. According to legend, Puccini was so dedicated to an accurate depiction of his setting that he notated the exact pitches and rhythms of the bells surrounding the fortress. Everything points to a you-are-there naturalism, the ultimate dream of Puccini and his *verismo* colleagues (like Mascagni, composer of *Cavalleria rusticana*). Opera's artifice and ambiguous reality are vehemently denied in the pursuit of an authentic reenactment of a recognizable real world.

In the recording on my playlist, the extraordinary tenor Giuseppe di Stefano adds an emotive cry to his delivery of the final lines, *"mai tanto la vita!"* This naturalistic touch is something you could never get away with in the formal constraints of a Handel aria, where all the emotions must be expressed purely within the words and the melody. Puccini's more realistic musical setting lends itself to this kind of emotional outburst, part of why the aria ranks among the most beloved moments in all of opera. While di Stefano always managed to convincingly sell such emotive gestures, lesser artists have used the trick so often as a shortcut to an audience's emotional engagement that it has devolved into an example of opera's over-the-top artificiality. (And frequently deployed by Adam Sandler's Opera Man.)

For Bauer, Puccini's obsessive pursuit of realism poses "an existential threat to opera, because opera is in its nature a highly artificial art form and can never truly become realistic." The situation is actually more nuanced, especially when one considers the alternatives to realism that composers explored throughout the twentieth century. American composer Robert Ashley achieves a bewildering effect from the everyday language and familiar situations of American society. His most famous opera, *Perfect Lives* (1983), premiered on television rather than in a conventional theater; the story, according to Ashley, includes such commonplace Americana as "bank robbery, cocktail lounges, geriatric love, adolescent elopement, et al., in the American Midwest." The natural ebb and flow of spoken American English makes up the majority of the score's music, which eschews conventional operatic singing entirely.

And yet the effect is anything but naturalistic. The ultimate strangeness of *Perfect Lives* and the rest of Ashley's body of work has nothing in common with what Bauer describes as opera's tendency toward a reflection of reality. The *Los Angeles Times* called his operas "so unconventional that they tend to be received as either profoundly revolutionary or incomprehensibly peculiar."

Bauer is surely not considering Ashley or other prominent experimentalists when talking about opera with a capital "O." Even the most perspicacious critics and musicologists today turn a blind eye to the essential work of composers actively expanding the definition of opera. How much more vibrant and provocative would opera be if we considered Puccini and Robert Ashley as equally important contributors to its development? As Ashley told the *New York Times* in 1983: "The actual word ["opera"] means far more than our narrow usage of it." Still, Bauer is absolutely right that a cultural predilection for realism is life-threatening for opera—but only so long as we succumb to that pressure to disambiguate, to present the world in sharp focus in operas that behave like reality television and are devoid of Ashley's strangeness. If we wanted to cultivate the *opposite* of realism instead—an ambiguous view of reality—opera would be a natural place to start.

To a modern spectator, opera's inherent ambiguity is a confrontation. Do we listen as we would at a concert? Do we gaze as though at a painting or sculpture? Are we following a drama, as we would at the theater? With its numerous overlapping voices, opera is a chaos of interpretive modes presented in a dizzying simultaneity. All the various layers that make up a work unfold at the same time, like a clown car stuffed full of arts. Opera's proliferation of meaning can seem like a heap of confusion.

In the face of so much ambiguity, a clear narrative might seem able to come to the rescue, offering the audience something to hold on to against the competing elements and alien rituals unfolding—the way a dreamer may try to decode the chaotic images that confronted her at night by consulting a "dream dictionary." But I'm struck by another paradox that opera faces, as an art form buttressed by two complementary ideas of narrative: the rising-falling action in the dramatic structure of the "well-made play," which audiences have come to expect; and the abstract dimension of music. Music is easily cheapened when made subservient to narrative. But much musical education in this country still insists that audiences listen to symphonies as "dramas," with the principal theme as a kind of protagonist struggling toward resolution. It's easy to give in to the mind's insatiable urge to create a narrative. All the same, music's dramatic logic doesn't easily fuse with narrative logic; in opera, musical form must come to grips with the messy imperatives of storytelling, like dramatic pacing and character development.

Maybe there's something about opera taking place in a theater, with its clear separation of artist and audience, that implies a kind of spectatorship more connected to plays. As if the architecture tells us what to anticipate when the curtain goes up: the expectation of a dramatic representation we can recognize from traditional theater.

Theater, after all, originated from a culture's urge to examine itself through the telling of stories. In ancient Greece, the entire populace would attend a representative narrative, which offered each spectator an opportunity to reflect simultaneously on the microcosm of themselves as individuals (by identifying with the characters onstage) and on the macrocosm of a community made up of many individuals (the chorus). Theater unified the personal and the political in the imagination of the spectator and posited a vision for the continuity of their worldview. Holding it all together was the story. Opera originated as a resurrection of that antiquity, employing the same mythological narratives (Orpheus, Daphne, and the like) that populated the ancient amphitheaters.

As opera developed, the story started becoming a flimsy pretext for impressive displays of a singer's virtuosity. Centuries later, narrative deficiency remains one of the most common critiques of opera—as embodied in Opera Man's overly dramatic reaction to losing the lottery or Bob Dylan's remark that the text of highly emotional music in another language may mean something as simple as "I've lost my hat." Even an acknowledged masterpiece like *The Magic Flute* frequently elicits the judgment that "the music is sublime, but the story is stupid." In an article for *Slate,* Jan Swafford describes his experience of learning to love the opera despite initially assessing "the story of Prince Tamino and his journey to love and wisdom" as "unmitigated flapdoodle." And "even if you love it," Swafford argues, it's hard to deny that the piece has "a creaking assemblage of a plot."

A prime example of an opera with a story so stupid that even Verdi's great music can't save it is *Il trovatore* (1853). The librettist Salvadore Cammarano took a convoluted play by the Spanish playwright Antonio García Gutiérrez and somehow made it even more difficult to follow. The opera begins with a lengthy recap of what happened to the Count of Luna. When his brother fell ill, their father blamed it on an innocent Romani woman. As she is burned at the stake, she commands her daughter, Azucena, to avenge her. Azucena grabs the count's sick brother and throws him on the same stake as her mother. The father dies of a broken heart, and the count is charged to seek revenge. A complicated love triangle ensues between the count, a lady-in-waiting named Leonora, and Azucena's "son" Manrico—whom we later discover is actually the count's brother (it turns out that Azucena had accidentally thrown her own child in the fire). The count eventually executes Manrico, and the opera ends with Azucena exclaiming, "He was your brother! Mother, you are avenged!" The audience is somehow supposed to take all this seriously. You can almost hear Verdi and Cammarano shrugging through the piece, as if to say, "I don't really understand it either, so let's try and dispatch all this nonsense as quickly as possible and get to some ravishing music."

Trovatore remains one of Verdi's most frequently performed operas, but even Adam Sandler couldn't sell the plot. Watching a performance, you can't help but wonder: can it be that opera's storytelling, far from making the genre more engaging, is actually one of the reasons it feels so arcane today?

If that's the case, then contemporary opera is in trouble. For the most part, new operas try carving out a place for themselves in an oversaturated media environment by *leading* with story. What an opera is about is now more important than what it actually is. This can sometimes yield provocative and remarkable results, as when the life of Malcolm X or Nixon's landmark visit to China serves as the narrative. But in other cases, the composer and the poet become secondary attractions to easily understood or relatable subject matter. This is also why much contemporary opera looks to plays, novels, or films for their stories— the art form is demystified in exactly the way Bauer lamented. Before we know it, the expectation that opera will tell stories in an equivalent manner to theater and film begins to rob it of its unique power.

With the narrative now the main organ for making meaning, the magic space created by music, text, and visual is minimized or eliminated. The effect is only to reinforce opera's alien relationship to contemporary culture. Rather than bridging the divide between the art form and our time, an operatic version of a great film usually pales in comparison. It's not fair to compare Wagner's *Ring* cycle with J. R. R. Tolkien's *Lord of the Rings* (in either its novelistic or cinematic form), because literature and film tell those stories with a swiftness and fullness that opera can't manage. Narrative-driven operas usually reveal the genre to be the most unwieldy and indirect way for a story to be told. And if the public is being told that story is what matters most, why should they continue to engage with "irrelevant" works from the past, with their "stupid stories"?

We then need to ask: if opera has such a difficult time with narratives, why haven't we eliminated them altogether? Perhaps that's a more viable approach to opera's magic ambiguity, as Philip Glass and Robert Wilson suggested with their landmark *Einstein on the Beach* (1976). In this singular work, image replaces narrative and non sequitur stands in for drama for four uninterrupted hours. Language becomes a texture rather than a mechanism for storytelling—even if, in the opera's final scene, a hymnlike description of two lovers at a park bench feeds our need for a "soothing story" at bedtime (SEE PLAYLIST). The theorist Hans-Thies Lehmann called this kind of piece *post-dramatic theater*—that is, theater in which atmosphere and composition replace the structure of a narrative, giving shape and meaning to a new kind of theatrical experience.

But much as I find the boldness of a non-narrative work like *Einstein on the Beach* thrilling and inspiring, I must admit that I'm not ready to give up on story. Narratives that take full advantage of opera's idiosyncrasies still have much to offer artists and audiences. Sometimes I like to think of a story as a rope hanging from the top of a well, giving audiences something to hold on to as they climb down into a murky obscurity. With a story, the insatiable need to understand has an outlet, and even the most casual observer has something they can grasp. And, as Ashley's *Perfect Lives* illustrates, the inclusion of a narrative can still leave ample room for ambiguity. A story can give artists the license to tackle what they *really* want to explore: the network of themes that invisibly influence that same story, while always pointing beyond it. (Ashley ultimately called *Perfect Lives* "an opera of ideas.") We need to divert the audience away from confusing the red herring of narrative for the main event. *The opera is not in the story; the story is in the opera.*

When the narrative is the main event, and everything else follows from it, the mechanics of the art form appear clunky and old-fashioned. But when the story is in the opera—or when it becomes one element among others that make up a less predictable composite—opera escapes the structure of conventional theater and becomes its own magic space. Scenes that a dramatist might dispatch quickly could, in opera, become epic explorations of ideas that go far deeper than the words alone would imply. One spoken line when sung can open up worlds of emotions when stretched, repeated, chopped up, or otherwise transformed (as Monteverdi's exiled queen from *Coronation of Poppea* proves).

The "stupid story" in Mozart's *Magic Flute* follows a young prince searching for his beloved, and having to undergo extraordinary trials to unite with her. But can anyone say that this is what *The Magic Flute* is actually about? Beyond the plot mechanics, the work is much more interesting and complicated. Perhaps on the surface a story of dragons, magical instruments, and mysterious trials seems nonsensical—if we expect the narrative to be the driving factor. But read symbolically, the piece reveals an enormous capacity for wisdom and interpretation (see Chapter 5).

Opera-in-the-story asks us to consider a narrative concretely; story-in-the-opera teaches us to read a story in symbols. Throughout his career, the Swiss psychiatrist Carl Jung advocated for a symbolic reading of religious texts as a mechanism for understanding who we are. In his late essay "The Undiscovered Self," he looked for the generative possibilities in religious myths that don't hold up to factual analysis. A story like the resurrection of Jesus is an example of "impressive mythological symbolism which, if taken literally, comes into insufferable conflict with knowledge." For Jung, a congregation understanding a story's truth as merely symbolic is less likely to lose faith than a congregation asked to consider a story too literally. "Is it not time that the Christian mythology, instead of being wiped out, was understood symbolically for once?" Joseph Campbell elaborated on Jung's concept in his own lectures (which can be heard on the excellent podcast *Pathways*). Campbell proposed that the resurrection of Jesus is not a factual, material reanimation, nor does the story of Exodus retrace the geographic steps of the Jews fleeing Egypt. Both stories for Campbell become symbols of a refusal of the status quo in favor of a future possibility still to be realized. (Maybe religion is one of the only mechanisms remaining to us beyond fiction for developing our ability to read the world symbolically.)

Opera resembles religious parables in their elasticity; they also present dramatic circumstances that signify much more than what we see. While Puccini's exacting description of a Roman dawn in *Tosca* may make anything other than a literal reading of the scene difficult, other operas take on increased power the more we approach them on symbolic terms. Take Leoš Janáček's *The Cunning Little Vixen* (1923). Its surface story, based on a Czech comic strip, follows a sly female fox constantly outwitting the myopic humans around her. If we perceive the work as a narrative suited for illustrated squares in a newspaper, we might quickly dismiss it as breezy entertainment. And many productions stop at that surface story, with singers dressed as animals jumping around the stage and trying to imitate animal behavior.

But a naturalistic production of this opera is a huge mistake—not only because most singers trying to mimic animal movement usually end up looking embarrassing. The opera is reduced to *only* its surface level—which is ultimately the least interesting layer. Listen to the luxurious music that Janáček pours into this seemingly simple tale, with heartfelt depictions of the changing seasons, extraordinary orchestral waves that bring the inner world of the animals to life, and a profound sunset at the Finale, as the human character reflects on love's mysterious effect on the cycle of life. (No wonder the composer asked for this moving soliloquy to be played at his own funeral; SEE PLAYLIST.) The score keeps reminding its audience that the work is much more than the story; it's a deep meditation on nature and humanity's complicated distance from it.

A symbol is only as strong as its multivalency—that is, its ability to be constantly recontextualized and reinterpreted according to the standpoint of the reader. Symbolic readings demand ambiguity because they die once they start dictating; a symbol is no longer a symbol the moment it becomes easily understood. If the painter René Magritte's pipe in *The Treachery of Images* can only be understood as a stand-in for a phallus, there's not much true symbolism left. But anyone with an intolerant attitude to ambiguity will seek out that single meaning, and explanatory texts on the wall next to a painting satisfy those viewers at the expense of the artwork. Discovering the best way to invite an audience away from the urge to decipher—away from the dominance of narrative—and toward the symbolic should be the primary mission of all opera-makers.

And yet, the mission poses a challenge: opera needs to somehow play out in the material world, that nuts-and-bolts world of concrete things. Understanding the story of Exodus or the resurrection in symbolic terms is relatively easy when they are words on a page. But as soon as those stories are embodied and presented, open-ended symbolic readings become more difficult. In any production of *Cunning Little Vixen,* the singers must still somehow represent foxes, chickens, mosquitoes, badgers, and more if the piece is going to have any relation to its original material. I dread to imagine how she would feel if I asked the soprano to play "the symbolic manifestation of nature" instead of the darting consciousness of a fox.

The humanity of opera is ultimately the most difficult thing to render in symbolic terms. Actors, singers, and dancers can be understood as symbols only when presented in clear-cut allegory—like the figure of Music in Monteverdi's *L'Orfeo.* As captivating as the opening scene may be, the abstract representation of music rarely moves us very much, even as she speaks of music's ability to console the heartbroken. But when the grieving Messenger sadly recounts Eurydice's death, she ends up making a stronger claim for the consolations of music than La musica herself. As long as operas are performed by flesh-and-blood humans, readings that are purely symbolic will result in disembodied allegory.

As an alternative to the realistic and the symbolic, I propose *poetic* readings as the most rewarding path—especially for an art form like opera. Unlike most narrative fiction, poetry possesses a natural aptitude for ambiguity; it's looser, more associative, and more interested in potential meanings that arise from familiar words being used in unfamiliar ways. Aristotle contrasted poetry—how things might have happened—with "chronicle," or history, an account of how things actually happened. Narrative fiction is inclined to adhere closer to the experience of a chronicle, and opera, in the era of cinema and realistic theater, now tends to that experience as well. But opera, born of actual poetry (the libretto), truly achieves its power when considered poetically.

In a poetic reading of *Cunning Little Vixen,* the singers can be both the animal and not the animal at various moments. In a poetic reading of *Trovatore*, perhaps some resonance can be drawn from all those babies being thrown into fires (although I must confess to not being able to find one myself). We can inflect the story without being subject to it—as when reading a great poem we can be taken on an allusive journey to meanings much deeper than anything literal. The audience makes the meaning for themselves.

The French philosopher Jacques Rancière suggests a useful way to understand the potential of a poetic reading over a literal or realistic one. At a lecture he gave in Los Angeles, he spoke of fiction not as a world but as a *framework* of objects that instigate a dialogue with the reader's subjective experience. If we think of a performance in those terms, we begin to resist the idea of a coherent and closed universe onstage in favor of the variety of possibilities that might emerge from our active engagement with what we are experiencing. In his book *The Emancipated Spectator,* Rancière writes:

> The spectator also acts, like the pupil or scholar. She observes, selects, compares, interprets. She links what she sees to a host of other things that she has seen on other stages, in other kinds

of places. She composes her own poem with the elements of the poem before her. She participates in the performance by refashioning it in her own way—by drawing back, for example, from the vital energy that it is supposed to transmit in order to make it a pure image and associate this image with a story which she has read or dreamt, experienced or invented.

In the freedom enjoyed by every audience member, Rancière imagines the mechanism for an almost utopian social equality:

> In a theatre, in front of a performance, just as in a museum, school, or street, there are only ever individuals plotting their own paths in the forest of things, acts and signs that confront or surround them. The collective power shared by spectators does not stem from the fact that they are members of a collective body or from some specific form of interactivity. It is the power each of them has to translate what she perceives in her own way, to link it to the unique intellectual adventure that makes her similar to all the rest in as much as this adventure is not like any other. . . . What our performances—be they teaching or playing, speaking, writing, making art or looking at it—verify is not our participation in a power embodied in the community. It is the capacity of anonymous people, the capacity that makes everyone equal to everyone else.

What Rancière describes as an ideal, liberated state of spectatorship is only possible with productions that leave space for poetic flight. He builds off an idea developed by Roland Barthes in his book *Image— Music—Text*: "the death of the author is the birth of the reader." In other words, the power of a work of art is centered not with the artist but with the receiver and interpreter of that work. This is still a radical idea when applied to opera, with its cult of authorship surrounding the familiar works of the canon. The reverence for past masters—Mozart, Rossini, Verdi, Puccini, and so on—places power squarely in their cold, dead hands. It is not *our* agency as the living spectator that is actively cultivated and addressed. The works become a closed entity, a locked-up world we can only ritualistically reenact. Poetry, on the other hand, points beyond itself to create what I described in Chapter Two as an open form—or what the Italian semiotician and novelist Umberto Eco considered an "open work." For Eco, an open work is a celebratory title for ambiguous and inconclusive art:

> The poetics of the open work posits the work of art stripped of necessary and foreseeable conclusions. Every performance explains the composition but does not exhaust it.... Every performance offers us a complete and satisfying version of the work, but at the same time makes it incomplete for us, because it cannot simultaneously give all the other artistic solutions which the work may admit.

Some of the most fascinating operas are literally "incomplete": Arnold Schoenberg's *Moses und Aron,* Alban Berg's *Lulu,* Puccini's *Turandot.* But what would happen if we considered all operas incomplete? Meaning, as the artist Marcel Duchamp put it, that the audience completes the work. Then every opera would become a work of poetry, an open work, trying to break free of the confines of the surface story.

Which brings us back to narrative: in the "open work" approach to opera, story can serve different purposes—as a hook for the audience, a springboard for the artist, a spine for the event—but the opera itself becomes much more than just story. Narrative may ground the audience in an argument or situation, but it always leaves space for a poetic engagement that goes far beyond the literal.

So instead of emphasizing narrative and topicality as a way to disambiguate, and instead of jettisoning narrative altogether to preserve its function in poetic readings, a middle path seems to offer the best solution: let's simply *decentralize* the role of narrative in opera. Let's use the narrative as needed and cast it off as quickly as possible to explore complexities and paradoxes as only opera can. Then the narrow narrative may no longer obstruct an audience's meaningful encounter, and an openness to the genre's multiplicity is much easier to accept.

Operas with decentralized narratives abound in the twentieth and twenty-first centuries, offering exciting examples of what "narrative-in-the-opera" can achieve. When the Hungarian avant-garde composer Péter Eötvös announced that his first large-scale opera would be based on Anton Chekhov's *Three Sisters*, his contemporaries were surprised that such an experimental artist would choose such a traditionally constructed drama, which depicts the slow burn of family strife in a Russian dacha. But rather than following Chekhov's narrative arc, Eötvös ingeniously transformed the four-act play into three sequences that present the action from three different characters' points of view. Musical gestures and dramatic moments reappear in different form across all three sequences, always revealing a different perspective. Two separate orchestras—a chamber orchestra in the pit and a larger one far upstage and unseen—create an acoustic illusion of music drifting through indistinct spaces, as if from the past. Fittingly, the opera begins at the end: the three sisters' famous speeches that close Chekhov's play are placed at the beginning in a spellbinding trio (SEE PLAYLIST). Chronological time gives way to the haunting, cyclical experience of memory; Chekhov's original play becomes merely a reference point in a musical-dramatic work that stands entirely on its own.

After a fascinating, ambiguous treatment of Nixon's visit to China, composer John Adams and director Peter Sellars turned their attention to Robert Oppenheimer for their opera *Doctor Atomic* (2005). The first act begins with action-movie energy, depicting the race to prepare for the first-ever test of an atomic bomb on July 16, 1945. But the musical and the theatrical languages change drastically in the second act: although superficially dealing with the hours before the test's successful execution, all sense of narrative arc is suspended. Instead, a tapestry of perspectives disrupt the first act's linearity, and the audience is drawn in to the interwoven psyches of people on the brink of the "brave new world" the bomb will introduce. Poetry, prophesies, dreams, and nightmares take center stage, as markers in narrative time occasionally reappear to give the audience a faint grasp on the chronological story. Adams's music holds this all together with a cohesive, symphonic unfolding that allows each audience member the space for reflection and contemplation. The piece doesn't end with an illustrative depiction of the bomb's blast—what orchestral or theatrical effect could ever hope to match that horrific act? Instead, a distorted, scarred electronic soundscape absorbs past, present, and future the same way the explosion's fireball transformed the white sand of Alamogordo into green glass.

Just as Adams and Sellars resist the "biopic" treatment of Oppenheimer and Nixon, the French composer Olivier Messiaen shows little interest in a step-by-step biography of Saint Francis, the central character in his towering epic *Saint François d'Assise* (1983). Despite its five-hour duration, the opera lacks any conventional dramatic development: there is no antagonist and ultimately only one scene of conflict. Instead, Messiaen depicts stations in the life journey of Saint Francis as he teaches young apprentices, preaches to birds, and performs or experiences miracles. The libretto, written by Messiaen himself, presents each figure in archetypal terms. And the language, rather than introducing us to recognizable situations and relationships, always veers toward the poetic. We see a Saint Francis prone to cosmic visions, declaimed in a poetry that's almost Dadaistic. He interrupts sensible dialogue with his disciples to offer ecstatic prayers in enigmatic images. In Act II, a young monk remarks that it's springtime, which elicits this response from Saint Francis: "A celebration! An exclamation point! An island like an exclamation point! An island of the ocean and beyond the ocean! Where the leaves are red, the pigeons are green, the trees are white, where the sea changes green to blue and from purple to green like the reflection of an opal!" The monk, standing in for the audience, can only respond in bafflement: "What are you saying?"

With story and text so elliptical, it's up to the music to create a cohesive journey. And an ingenious musical mind like Messiaen's is more than capable of fulfilling that charge. His eccentric and ecstatic style makes the sound world of this opera unlike any other piece written for the stage. One moment evokes Japanese kabuki theater, the next harks back to science fiction B movies from the 1950s. Five hours of musical fascination alternate between the beguiling, the terrifying, the honeysweet, and the psychedelic. And despite its potentially off-putting elements (duration, lack of narrative, unabashed religious sentiment), a

performance of *Saint François* invariably sells out and ends with rap-
turous applause—in large part because of the music's undeniable pull.

But Messiaen outdoes himself in the opera's central scene, nearly
fifty minutes long, centered around a sermon Saint Francis preached to
a flock of birds. This symphonic scene becomes the massive culmination
of Messiaen's lifelong love of birdsong, an essential feature of his music.
Decades of research, studying bird melodies around the world, went
into creating an overwhelming musical tableau in which "nothing seems
to happen" except an elderly man singing hymns to his aviary compan-
ions (SEE PLAYLIST). Despite the scene's centrality to the opera, even
Messiaen's most zealous supporters admit that it can try your patience.

Imagine the poor director charged with staging this scene! How are
they to keep an audience engaged and tuned in to the expansive arc of
the music, when so little seems to happen in the story? Are they really
supposed to somehow depict birds flying around the singers' heads for
fifty minutes while the music creates an image so much larger than any
stage can hold?

In fact, the work of the director is crucial for a work like *Saint
François,* in the bird sermon scene above all. To understand how, we
first need to separate out the strands of an opera—music, text, and
production—and examine how directors weave them together.

OPERA UNBOUND

I recently took a friend to a very poor production of an opera, set in
a vaguely modern period and staged in an aimless way. My friend is a
smart film and event producer who had seen "twenty or so" operas but
had never developed a love for the art form. At intermission, she was
cagey, not wanting to risk seeming ignorant or rude in front of her opera
director friend. But once I expressed how awful I thought the performance was, the conversation got interesting. As we dissected individual
elements or moments, her own perspective started to develop. We pulled
up pictures of other productions of the same opera, so she could see the
range of possible iterations the piece might inspire, and compared the

implications for what we were watching. Swiping through different sets, she stopped at one of an abstract space and remarked, "I don't know how that one makes sense with the story, but it certainly looks like how the music sounds."

When a performance is not going well, it can be difficult to pinpoint precisely where the problem lies. Is it a director's bad idea? Are the singers not strong enough actors? Maybe the orchestra hates the conductor and is purposefully playing badly in revolt? (Yes, this does happen!) Or is the opera itself just not very good? Even for professionals and music critics, parsing out why a performance doesn't gel is a challenge that can spark heated debate.

In her difficulty to distinguish where the music starts and the scenery ends, my friend unwittingly revealed how opera suffers from what neuroscientists call "the binding problem": the fact that simultaneous stimuli appear to us as a singular experience, even as they activate different modalities in the brain. When we see a red ball bouncing, for example, the color, the shape, and the movement are all processed by different parts of our brain. How, scientists and philosophers of the mind want to know, does consciousness synthesize such varied information into one unified experience? A paper on the subject for the National Institutes of Health suggests that we can learn how by focusing on a single element at a time. Likewise, in an art form that seems like one enormous "binding problem," separating out the various elements can give audiences a greater command over their own perception.

The binding problem for opera is not a conflict between just two principal components, as summed up by the title of an opera written in 1786 by Antonio Salieri: *Prima la musica e poi le parole*, "First the music and then the words." Since the music is almost never actually written before the words, Salieri's motto advocates rather for music's primacy in a two-headed race for opera's dominant voice. If only opera were that simple! But this art form is never just words or music; those two elements are forever triangulated by an intervening element. It's tempting to call the intersecting third party *the visual*—namely, the staging and designs. A better name might be *the production* (closer to the French term *mise en scène* or the German *Inszenierung*).

The production is the animation of the words, the music, and the conditions surrounding their materialization in time and space, born in the imaginations of the director and their designer colleagues. No mere referee in a ping-pong game between words and music, the production creates a distinct and *dynamic* third avenue of meaning. It's like an electrified third rail running alongside the musical and textual tracks.

I think of the three planes less as a binding and more of a braiding, the ensuing pattern becoming an unpredictable weave. Since two stable, document-based entities (a music score and a libretto) require this anarchic, transient third element (a production) for life, the three tracks should receive equal weight. It's not just a question of *prima la musica* when it comes to opera, especially when Salieri's catchphrase leaves out everything theatrical.

(Then again, even thinking in terms of "three tracks" is reductive. Music, for example, shouldn't be limited to simply what's heard. Our nervous systems as well as our ears are processing the waves of sound emanating from an orchestra pit, revealing many forks in the road to our understanding of a piece as it unfolds. The myriad possibilities at any one moment of a performance are exponential—but we'll never get anywhere if we keep atomizing all the things opera binds together. So let's consider the three primary tracks as a starting point.)

Disentangling these constituent elements is an essential exercise during the performance of an opera. The German playwright Bertolt Brecht argued this point in the first half of the twentieth century. Brecht hated the Wagnerian model of merging the arts in opera, calling it a "witches' brew" that cast a narcotic spell over its audience. The effect was a sleepwalking public, robbed of all critical faculties and surrounded by an undifferentiated fog. In the ultimate elaboration of his theatrical theories, called *A Short Organum for the Theater,* Brecht set out a solution for separating the various artistic strands that make up a performance. He also considered story a red herring, unifying the experience just enough to allow each artistic voice some autonomy. Coordinated action will still be the hallmark of a theatrical evening, but the blurring of artistic lines should be avoided: "Let us invite all the sister arts of the drama, not in order to create an 'integrated work of art' in which they all offer themselves up and are lost, but so that together with the drama they may further the common task in their different ways."

The purpose of Brecht's unbinding—similar to Adorno's dream of radio broadcasting rehearsals—is to produce inquisitive and awakened spectators. An audience that doesn't just go with the flow but questions, dissects, and reflects would realize the potential for change in our societies and ourselves: "Humanity does not have to stay the way it is now," Brecht urged, "nor does it have to be seen only as it is now, but also as it might become."

Thanks to Brecht, European theater has had a century of practice in unbinding its constituent elements. Audiences have been trained to appreciate the difference between the production and the text, making it easier to understand the creative interpolation of the director when *Hamlet*, for example, is set in modern-day dress. But American opera-goers have mostly been spared the hermeneutical challenge Brecht set in motion. In keeping with a general intolerance for ambiguity, performances in our country mostly minimize the production element by syncing it up cozily with instructions in the libretto. The linguistic and production tracks are thus fused together, clearing the way for the first track—music—to dominate (*prima la musica*).

This is why *Carmen* tends to look the same no matter where you see it in the United States. The title character will likely wear a frisky red dress, her matador lover will carry a red cape, and the incongruity of French music within an "authentic" Spanish setting will be shrugged off as a given. All because we have come to assume that this is what *Carmen* originally looked like—and therefore, like the music and text, must remain unchanged. Production in this way becomes reduced to *image*, most often the original image connected to the first performances. It's an unimaginative attempt to simplify matters, usually defended as fidelity to authorial intention (what the Germans call *Werktreue,* or "loyalty to the work"). That attitude assumes, of course, that Bizet actually liked the original sets and costumes. Perhaps, like composers today, he never had a say in how his work was visualized. All the more tragic, then, to think that *Carmen* is now bound in an endless, unthinking repetition of those original choices.

There's something inherently American about "Mickey Mousing": aspiring for a complete reinforcement of sight and sound. In this case, binding is not a problem but a goal. The fathers of the American musical, Richard Rodgers and Oscar Hammerstein, pursued a unified aesthetic that they called "integrated"—so that, as Rodgers put it in his autobiography, "the orchestrations sounded the way the costumes looked." Entering a theater in this country has begun to take on the assumption of a pact between artists and audience: what shall be put before us is a closed system that will be entertainingly explicable; every sensation shall correspond perfectly to every other; and any mysteries will be resolved by evening's end. What is heard shall reinforce what is seen as frequently as possible, if not exclusively.

When music never veers away from a one-to-one relationship with the words, it quickly becomes dull and predictable. And when the production underlines that same idea *again*, there's hardly any interest left to find. To return to the telescope analogy: when the lenses are perfectly calibrated to create an unambiguously sharp image, there's not much compelling you to look for long.

The notion that the music, text, and production tracks benefit from some independence from one another is not widely accepted by opera audiences, no matter how sophisticated. The distance can be unsettling, especially in relation to the music and the production. Many an audience member who saw *La bohème* set on the moon, as the director Claus Guth has done in Paris, found the dissonance between what they saw and what they heard intolerable. Likewise, an audience that came to my reverse-order *Bohème* in Detroit may not have suspected that the work's authors didn't originally intend to begin with Mimì's death and work backward. Opera's version of the binding problem is the expectation that all elements in a performance have only one way of belonging together.

Film and television have only further entrenched an audience's expectation of sight and sound in sync. The cliché of sappily swelling strings to signal a film's emotional climax has come to epitomize a demand for lock-step coordination between what we hear and what we see. I recall as a teenager visiting Universal Studios in Florida, where a special exhibit for the children's television network Nickelodeon particularly captured my imagination. In a replica of a sound stage, a spooky campfire scene from the show *Hey Dude* played on a monitor with its original score; brooding sound effects and long-held bass notes prompted a foreboding sense of danger as the characters told a ghost story. The scene was then shown a second time, with the visual edit exactly the same and the actors delivering the same lines, but the music changed to a bouncy, lighthearted score with whistles and kazoos. The exhibit might sound like a manifestation of Adorno's or Brecht's dream of making an audience aware of the constituent parts of an artwork. Instead, we had been given evidence that the ominous soundtrack was "correct," while the silly soundtrack was out of step with the storytelling. It was a perfect illustration of Hollywood's factory precision in calibrating sight and sound in a way that has cultivated our eyes and ears to respond identically. Audiences have carried this kind of expectation with them into the opera house, even if, as the German director Walter Felsenstein put it, opera is a unique place where "the ear sees and the eye hears."

The pleasure we feel in an art form with multiple tracks of meaning derives from its possibility of divergence, even contradiction. In their *A History of Opera,* Carolyn Abbate and Roger Parker use the character of Wolfram in Wagner's *Tannhäuser* (1845) to illustrate the richness that arises when music and text do different things. Judged merely by what he says, Wolfram comes across as square and pious; but he is given sensual and searching music that reveals another perspective. Abbate and Parker distinguish such complexity as the "plot-character," rooted in the music, and the "voice-character" as we hear it in Wolfram's words. It's a useful way to parse out the joys of opera—to which I would add the third voice of interpretation. The singer's individual vocal color, physical demeanor, and expressivity can't help but alter our view of the character. And the way Wolfram is costumed—as schoolboy? punk rocker? medieval minstrel?—reveals another layer. In addition to plot-character and voice-character, we must consider the contingency of "production-character."

To unbind opera, imagine the three principal tracks as having three distinct authors:

The musical track has the composer;
    The literary track has the librettist;
        The production track has the director.

If the first two authors are living, all three tracks have equal weight and intersect with each other. If they are deceased—as is the case with the majority of operas produced today—then the director assumes a different responsibility: to prove why we should still be performing the work even after the first two authors have died.

The director has the license to take whatever means necessary to make the piece come to life—including cutting, rearranging, and editing. While directors must be well versed in the original intentions of the composer and librettist, they understand that a production is only interesting if it intersects the other two elements in an *unstable* relationship. Otherwise, the Mickey Mousing predictability will make the experience tedious. Then again, if the production is *always* countering the words and the music, it becomes predictable in another, more cynical way. The responsiveness demanded of the director to lead the audience on the opera's journey is its own unique form of authorship.

As Brecht put it, narrative becomes the place where the three authors meet. The story may begin with the librettist, who puts character, environment, and situation into words; but in creating music from those words, the composer also takes on a storyteller's responsibility. A director then considers how the narrative unfolds on both of those tracks to decide how the production will relay drama to the audience: what may be elaborated, alluded to, or contradicted in the language and the music to offer continuous fascination. All three are master storytellers: the narrative is everyone's responsibility and belongs to no one. And like the lenses of a telescope, the more they shift in and out of focus, the more enthralling the overall storytelling becomes. What then opens up is a field of potential meanings beyond the narrative. The music and text can be understood as engines of nonliteral significance; and the production becomes the temporary articulation of a *limited range* of what's possible.

The questions posed and contradictions offered by the third track can help an audience find their way to a poetic reading of the work. A spectator's attention zooms in and out of what's happening onstage, sometimes taking in the sensory overload of the experience, other times honing in on what's occurring on each individual level: What is the music doing? What is the poetry doing? What is the production doing in relation to those two tracks? And then come the deeper, more profound questions of interpretation and subjective meaning. If the language of a love duet is curiously scored for four saxophones: *why*? If the production seems to be playing against the music: *why*? If the director has changed the ending: *what does that illuminate*?

There are micro and macro ways a director helps a spectator understand their interpretation. The macro level is more obvious: the entire apparatus of set, costume, lighting, and video choices ranging from the time period the piece is set in to the color of the stage furniture. But a powerful interpretation really lives on the micro level—the articulation of individual moments. Choices made around any one individual line can illuminate an entire interpretation.

The totality of a director's perspective on Debussy's opera *Pelléas et Mélisande* (1902) can be read from how the soprano delivers her first line as Mélisande, the beautiful young woman encountered by the hunter Golaud in a mythical forest. Having lost his way during a hunt, Golaud discovers her crying by a well. When he approaches her, Mélisande rapidly but quietly sings, "Don't touch me, don't touch me, or I'll throw myself in the water!" It's a memorable first line for a character who will remain an indecipherable mystery for the entire (rather indecipherable) opera.

The soprano, working with the director and the conductor, may choose to present the line as a feral act of self-defense or with a dreamy, detached half-smile. She may be staged threatening the hunter with a knife, or she might be tied to a tree, indicating a traumatic backstory. Does she come across as damaged and deranged, or is she calm and in control of the mysterious world around her? In less than ten seconds, this single line will inflect the character and the drama as a whole, setting the rules of engagement for the audience with her and the production. It tells you how the interpreters view Mélisande—and, by extension, what they think about a wide range of broader ideas, like the roles of women in society. If the line carries no particular insight and simply plays out "as written"—if the interpreters defer interpretation—that, too, tells you the production track is deferring to the first two tracks and isn't likely to offer a strong perspective.

The production interprets and comments as much as it articulates, and with every choice at the smallest and largest scale, it can reveal the inexhaustible flexibility of an opera that is falsely viewed as eternal and unchanging. By adding a living and conditional voice to the authorial constellation, the production makes the entire work open and alive. This is particularly important for operas with deficient narratives like *Il trovatore*; the production can de-center the narrative from our experience of the work and perhaps lead us to a poetic reading. A hyperactive, steampunk-styled 2013 staging of *Trovatore* at the Bavarian State Opera in Munich by the director Olivier Py was described by Mike Silverman of the Associated Press as "a crazy-quilt approach that is bound to horrify traditionalists." But singing in that production led tenor Jonas Kaufmann to consider the deeper resonance of the story. He described "the overall theme of the production" as the impossibility of escaping your family history: "Everything they say, they do and they feel is a result of those awful things which happened in the past; therefore they don't have a chance to live their own lives." This is what happens when the story is in the opera, rather than the opera in the story: the plot's absurdity becomes secondary to a poetic reading that brings life to an otherwise deeply problematic work.

In the case of operas that already feature a de-centered narrative, the production can supply a cohesiveness that may otherwise seem elusive. To return to the long bird sermon scene in Messiaen's *Saint François*: since the sermon consists of so little action and so much music, the director needs to devise a theatrical mechanism to shape the time as if the scene depicted a dramatic situation. This is not to impose conventional modes of drama on an unconventional work; instead, it's about finding a corresponding mechanism for *visual evolution*, to keep the scene stageworthy rather than suited for the concert hall. The traditional recourse of conflict between a hero and villain isn't necessary—especially in an opera that Messiaen himself proudly explained features very little conflict to keep the focus on joy, bliss, and transcendence. Tensions, processes, and explorations can all shape a scene wherever narrative takes a backseat.

Even if a director's idea for the bird sermon is jaw-dropping and brilliantly executed, any isolation it betrays from the remaining three-plus hours of opera will render the scene a gimmick, spectacle for spectacle's sake. In a poetic reading, the images, ideas, and actions need to resound from the beginning of the performance until the end. A director engages with the music, the text, and the broader context to draw out ideas beyond the narrative. What is the opera ultimately exploring, and how can those themes be transformed into a theatrical process? The bird sermon scene will only be effective if it's also placed in a resonant relationship with all the other production decisions. Any theatrical mechanism devised for the scene doesn't need to follow the narrative, but it must resonate with the larger ideas of the work.

The examples of *Pelléas, Trovatore,* and *Saint François* illustrate how critical it is for a director to take a stand on the narrative. There are endless choices directors make with their teams to articulate a vision, including the level of reality or artificiality to strive for and which meaning—of a work's many possible meanings—will become the focus. No single production can exhaust the possibilities of the music and text. This is a cause for celebration and wonder: through the production track, old texts can reveal themselves to us in ever-new ways. So we must approach each and every production as a *perspective*, a reading specific to the worldview of the author of that perspective.

The director Peter Brook, in his seminal book on theater *The Empty Space,* observes that "theater is always a self-destructive art, and it is always written on the wind." Any production has only about five years' validity for Brook because "all the different elements of staging . . . are fluctuating on an invisible stock exchange all the time. Life is moving, influences are playing on actor and audience, and other plays, other arts, the cinema, television, current events, join in the constant rewriting of history and the amending of the daily truth." In short, "the theater is relativity."

The joy of directing lies in being a *relational* artist—not a stand-alone artist like a novelist or painter. Everything we do is in relationship to the work and to the other artists co-creating with us. And each project offers an opportunity to explore a new facet of the world. I take that to be my constant challenge: not to rest on the discoveries I've already made but to engage the music, the text, and my collaborators in a dialogue that will push us all into ever new ideas, new language, and new experiences.

THE *TURN OF THE SCREW* PROBLEM

In developing a strong, thematically resonant reading, a complicated danger lies in wait for directors: the seduction of oversimplifying, of limiting the work to a single reading. Is it possible to make decisions about the work's material articulation that will maintain ambiguity rather than reducing it?

Thomas Bauer, in his essay "The Disambiguation of the World," takes aim at the opinion that "everything must be explained; everything must be understood; and when it's not understood, it won't matter. In theater—in its essence a refuge for ambiguity—this task is taken up by the director, who must lead the audience (not always successfully) through the meaning of the play or opera, according to their opinion: why it is relevant to our times and what message it has to offer those of us living today. This experience is now obligatory in art, as it allows . . . multiple meanings to take the form of a singular meaning."

Bauer is a bit harsh to us poor directors here. After all, it *is* our responsibility to lead an interpretation of the work. Yet the kind of production he criticizes is easy to recognize: one that falls into the common trap of placing an opera in a decipherable (usually contemporary) setting and forcing every action to correspond perfectly to this cogent universe. Let's say that instead of nineteenth-century Seville, a director places *Carmen* in a modern Seville shopping mall. On the surface, there's no reason to believe this idea shouldn't work—in fact, it seems to take advantage of the freedom that staging brings. But such productions often fail to rise above the clever. They quickly become straightforward guessing games for the audience, predicting how the director and designers will transport key elements into their alternate universe. (Carmen's deranged lover will likely be the mall's security officer, while the cigarette women vape safely indoors.) The idea can boast the patina of boldness—as a clear divergence from Mickey Mousing—but drawing clear correspondences between the opera's original world and our own results in a circle as closed as traditional productions. Lacking in anything but a superficial divergence, such productions ultimately disambiguate. The telescope is once again perfectly focused: the forms are crisp, the colors vivid, and the desire to continue watching usually short-lived.

This type of production is particularly popular in Germany, which offers the most opera performances per capita of any country in the world. As Alex Ross reported in a 2022 article for *The New Yorker,* Germany's eighty state-supported opera companies have created a "quasi-utopia for the art form." The repertoire is varied; the audiences are democratic; and "with so many productions, directors feel free to try out new ideas, some outlandish and some revelatory." We thus credit (or blame) Germany for the notion of *Regietheater*—a German portmanteau defining the type of production driven by a strong directorial hand. (Less generous spectators prefer the term "Eurotrash.") A multiplicity of meaning is not demanded from any one production; rather, multiplicity emerges from comparisons between several concurrent productions of the same work. Concepts are therefore free, and often encouraged, to be completely single-minded. In some circumstances, this approach can indeed be revelatory, but too often an audience can smell a director's desperation to make their own brilliant contribution outshine the brilliance of any other contributor.

Each time I work in Germany, I sense the expectation to devise productions as though I were a scientist presenting a study: start from a point of hypothetical meaning and rationally move through the work to prove my point. A successful experiment maintains a sharp focus of the telescope and dispels any entropic pull toward ambiguity. Such productions are highly analytical, intellect-based, and accompanied by lengthy program notes. A frequent gauge of success for a German production—if you ask critics and dramaturges—is called *Konsequenz*, meaning "consistent" and "consequential." A *konsequent* production achieves the coherence of a formal argument, where any idea introduced by the director threads the production thoroughly. Inconsistencies—even intentional ones in the name of paradox, disruption, or openness—mark a faulty argument/reading/interpretation and brand the production an *inkonsequent* failure.

This situation is surely what irritates Bauer: the directors forcing us all to see the opera through their funneled perspective, with everything considered only in relation to one idea. But as a response to Bauer's critique, we must concede that the production track, as a material realization, will always struggle to maintain ambiguity. We might call this "the *Turn of the Screw* problem."

Henry James's novella famously lives in an unresolved space around a central dilemma: a governess charged with taking care of two young children believes ghosts are terrorizing them. The nature of these ghosts—a figment of the governess's hysterical over-imagination?—remains open to the reader's interpretation. But in Benjamin Britten's 1954 setting of the story, the reality/fantasy ambiguity is difficult to maintain when the ghosts require a flesh-and-blood tenor and soprano onstage: the ghosts are unmistakably *there*. Their real presence in the house is even more clearly proved by the beginning of Britten's second act, depicting a private scene between the ghosts with no human perspective (SEE PLAYLIST).

In *Metaphysical Song*, Tomlinson argues that the opera's lack of ambiguity is "in part a simple by-product of dramatic representation. The way [Britten] chose to present the ghosts, with direct interactions between them, and between them and the children, threatened already to render them too solid." When Tomlinson considers how a production might grapple with the challenge of the ghosts' physicality, he shares Bauer's contempt for the disambiguating presence of the director: "One could imagine, for instance—if without much enthusiasm—an ambiguity preserving operatic *Turn of the Screw* presented as the governess's internal monologue, in the fashion of Schoenberg's *Erwartung*." His lack of enthusiasm for a production that comes down so hard on one interpretation arises from the story's central indeterminate tenet having been explained away.

A frequent response to the *Turn of the Screw* problem is to "let things remain ambiguous"—to try and make *no* choices, ostensibly to allow the audience complete interpretive control. This may sound refreshing, but the results are almost invariably indistinct. Music and text ultimately come across as fuzzy and formless, as the simple playing out of a piece without perspective. Without the clarity of strong choices, a production can hope for none of the precision and luminescence that can bring it to life. Through a telescope, it would be *so* out of focus that the image you see has no definition whatsoever. (Or, put another way, "It's all a blur.")

American audiences should have no difficulty recognizing this sort of experience; the third track pretends it isn't there and tries to draw no undue attention to itself. The focus is placed solely on the music and the text (an experience that can just as easily be replicated in a concert presentation or at home with a recording). The design, by default, falls back into the recognizability of past productions and "staying true to the author's original intention." I've heard conservative operagoers argue that no interpretation at all is preferrable to a self-involved and "outlandish" one. It can be hard to convince someone who thinks this way that protecting a work from a confrontation with reality robs it of any opportunity to reveal fresh insight and new resonances.

The Overworld and Underworld in Monteverdi's *L'Orfeo* at Santa Fe Opera (2023). Set design by Alex Schweder and Matthew Johnson; costume design by Carlos Soto; lighting design by Yuki Link. (RICHARD BARNES)

A fairy tale that becomes a nightmare: Wagner's *Lohengrin* at the Bayreuther Festspiele (2018). Sets and costumes by Neo Rauch and Rosa Loy; lighting design by Reinhard Traub. (© BAYREUTHER FESTSPIELE / ENRICO NAWRATH)

Exploring unknown territory: Meredith Monk's *ATLAS* at the Los Angeles Philharmonic (2019). Set design by Es Devlin; costume design by Emma Kingsbury; lighting design by John Torres; video design by Luke Halls. (CRAIG T. MATHEW / MATHEWIMAGING / LAPHIL)

Tamino at the tree of knowledge, Papageno at his suicide tree:
Mozart's *Magic Flute* at the Staatsoper Berlin (2019). Set design
by Mimi Lien; costume design by Walter van Beirendonck;
lighting design by Reinhard Traub. (MONIKA RITTERSHAUS)

Childhood as the ultimate divinity: the Three Boys come to Pamina
and Papageno's rescue; in the Finale, we discover that children
have been pulling the strings all along. (MONIKA RITTERSHAUS)

Two scenes from The Industry's *Hopscotch* in Los Angeles (2015) that blur the boundary between inside and outside a car. (above: CASEY KRINGLEN; below: DANA ROSS)

The Central Hub, a bespoke pavilion created to experience the simultaneous performances of *Hopscotch*. Designed by Constance Vale and Emmett Zeifman. (JOSH LIPTON)

Christopher Cerrone's *Invisible Cities* with The Industry
and L.A. Dance Project (2013). (NIM SHARON)

Christine Goerke in *Twilight: Gods* in Detroit (2020). (MITTY CARTER)

Let's also imagine singers trying to find their own way in one of these uninflected productions: resisting any interpretation, the director can only offer them unhelpful vagueness. When a soprano playing Britten's governess needs to decide whether to play a certain monologue as bewitched or clear-headed, her director can't give her guidance that might fire up her imagination. She can make up her own mind—but so can the tenor and soprano playing the ghost characters of Peter Quint and Miss Jessel, who might decide something completely different. In the resulting production, a familiar sight on operatic stages, the singers all seem to be in different worlds: a director hasn't unified them around a common vision or at least created a consensus for what's happening in any given scene. Avoiding making a choice is itself a choice—and quite possibly the only one that will always be wrong.

In these circumstances, you can understand how directors might end up taking the scientific, or *konsequent*, approach. The *Turn of the Screw* problem makes clear that production choices lessen opera's ambiguity. And if that's the case, why not go all the way with a bold, unambiguous direction?

How each artist grapples with this problem defines their contribution to an operatic experience. In my case, I have evolved a perspective distinct from the German *Regietheater*. I've always been drawn to *Inkonsequenz* because of opera's proximity to poetry, with its irrationality, flights into the unknown, and expansion of language and therefore of our perceptions. I want to encourage poetic readings of a work rather than follow a fixed goal, through productions that *oscillate* between specific meanings.

In 2014, when I staged Adams's *Doctor Atomic* in Karlsruhe, Germany, I wanted to visualize and thematize the opera's narrative shift between the more expository first act and the expansive second. Leaning on expectations posed by the title for superhero rhetoric, I turned Act I into a comic book: behind a projection scrim of hand-drawn animations, the singers appeared in boxes revealed by sliding doors. The years of World War II, the opera's setting, were in fact the "golden age of comic books" with the debuts of Superman in 1938, Batman in 1939, and Doctor Fate in 1940, among many others. A comic-book approach also conjured America's sense of moral clarity then, as if the line between good and evil were black and white, and action unfolded in a causal and linear manner. An apparent conviction of moral mission, in the face of suspicions that the Germans were creating their own weapon of mass destruction, motivated Oppenheimer to begin working on the atomic bomb. But moral clarity quickly darkens, both historically—with the criminal deployment of the new technology on Japanese civilians—and in the context of the opera, which asks us to reconsider the mythic narrative Americans still use to talk about this era. The comic-book aesthetic of my production, then, started to unravel as the first act continued.

A *konsequent* production would carry the comic-book aesthetic from beginning to end. But just as the opera makes a leap from narrative to a post-dramatic landscape, the projection-heavy first act of my production gave way to the many performers inhabiting one enormous, curved piece of graph paper. The more choreographic language of Act II was resonant with the work's themes: the blank page at the discovery of a primal creative/destructive force and the onset of a new "nuclear" era; the illusion of any division between the opera's characters; the ingenuity and horror of the human mind. Naïve faith in a clear story as promised by Act I's comic storytelling was exposed as a tragic fallacy.

Although the production earned me the Götz Friedrich Prize that year, the expectation for *Konsequenz* has become so deeply ingrained in German culture that some audiences had a difficult time making the leap with me from Act I to Act II. At the award ceremony, I used my acceptance speech to justify a choice that some claimed was illogical: changing the language in a production to keep it open and encourage poetic rather than linear readings. My conceptual process didn't begin with a preconceived meaning, which I then used to rationally "explain" the opera from beginning to end. Instead, I engaged the imagination of my entire team to search for what felt true moment by moment through the piece. The meaning isn't formulated before work begins, but emerges only once the production is complete. That's the poetic and nonscientific approach that I think makes for the most exciting opera.

In my own productions, I aim for a high specificity on every detail—each word, each note, and each movement—but I don't believe in forging the composite into a closed circle. The more that individual choices keep opening up the opera to continuous *reconsideration*, the more I can preserve ambiguity and grant agency to the spectator, as Rancière, Barthes, and Eco would have it. I want a production to contain as much of the original work's multitudinousness as possible, without vanishing into vagueness. A director must seize the spectators' attention with the specificity of a strong interpretation, and at the same time leave space for their own interpretations.

I don't know that I have a solution to the *Turn of the Screw* problem, but if I were ever to direct Britten's opera, I would look for a way to constantly evade closure. Instead of deciding whether the entire opera is in the governess's imagination or the ghosts are real, I would look to create *a constantly fluctuating stage reality, specific in each moment but not reaching any final conclusion.* One scene might articulate a particular reading (the governess hears the voices of the ghosts but doesn't see them); the next might support a contradictory reading (the ghosts inhabit the physical world of the manor, moving the furniture and starting a fire); and perhaps the next would suggest a completely unexpected reading (the wealthy landowner who engaged the governess has actually paid off his kids and hired actors to play the ghosts in a twisted social experiment). Maintaining concurrent possible readings from scene to scene, and always with a committed specificity, can allow an ambiguity of multiple perspectives to flourish.

Not every director (or every audience member!) will find this kind of storytelling satisfying. The key point is that any interesting idea must evolve and become more complicated as a performance continues. Just as music develops and never stays stationary, the time-based nature of a performance demands unceasing change. A concept that is introduced and does not evolve will remain inert. The opera, in the flow of time, will pass it by. But when a production concept accompanies the audience in that process of duration—shifting, progressing, morphing, falling apart, transforming—then the work has been brought to life.

The telescope a director invites an audience to look through should therefore always be shifting in and out of focus, never staying at one calibration for long. The degree of blur should entice us to look deeper, to search for clarity, even while realizing that any lucidity will be short-lived. The result can be an invigorating openness, with ambiguity maintained (paradoxically) by precision. It's a precarious but pleasurable balancing act that defines, for me, my role as director: preserving possibilities beyond my own interpretation.

THE ENCHANTED SPACE

Let me sum this chapter up not as a conclusion, but as a starting point for further exploration.

Rather than considering opera imprisoned by outdated modes of storytelling, we should think of it as occupying an excitingly indeterminate space beyond narrative. Opera is fundamentally a musical art form, and yet it's so much more than music; it's inherently theatrical, and yet it's so much more than a play; it demands a proper spatial relationship, and yet it transcends architecture; the visual aspects dominate, and yet it is not to be confused with the visual arts. Its interstitiality is what makes opera so bewildering and difficult to decipher—but it's also what brings the art form close to contemporary life.

Audiences must be able to tolerate a large amount of ambiguity if they are to find pleasure in an experience created by multiple authors. The director takes them on a journey away from the safe and recognizable haven of narrative into an uncharted and barely explicable meeting place of music, text, and production. With three primary tracks running as a performance unfolds, opera simultaneously offers different meanings that sometimes converge and sometimes clash. The effect is kaleidoscopic and contrapuntal; opera's potential for the layered meaning we find in poetry is the reason it remains the only narrative art form whose masterpieces include "stupid stories."

I would love for opera audiences to stop worrying and learn to love ambiguity. Maybe one way to achieve that is a bait and switch: what if we called it something else? Say we started calling ambiguity "enchantment"—since in any case I believe theater's true capacity for magic consists in its ability to hold multiple realities at once, to make a paradox visible. Let's consider opera's nonreality not as a deficit but as a power—to create an enchanted space, with many meanings and possibilities somehow coalescing. Opera would become not a punishing exercise in developing a "tolerance" for ambiguity, but an experience that makes ambiguity and complexity so pleasurable that we long for *more* in our daily lives.

When an art form offers so much potential, any single interpretation is bound to feel partial and incomplete. Surrounding every choice is a maze of forking paths, pointing in all directions to every choice passed up. We can confidently believe in a future for opera only if we can preserve that multidimensionality. The opera house is not a place where various media come together to be reduced to a single meaning or even a single story. Instead, different voices offer as many diverting stories as possible without losing a certain amount of coherence. True opera is a state of tension on the precipice of the possible, always threatening to collapse but somehow, miraculously, sustaining. Even sometimes triumphing.

5

CASE STUDY:

THE MAGIC FLUTE IN BERLIN

GETTING BOOED IS STRANGE.

Not the booing of a lone dissenter or a handful of disgruntled patrons, like the two grumpy critics on *The Muppet Show*. That isolated expression of displeasure pops up occasionally in American theaters but often seems out of place. (The current default reaction at the end of any live performance in this country, the standing ovation, used to signal great enthusiasm but has since become as customary as a 20 percent tip.) I mean the type of booing where an entire audience seems out for blood—the kind you read about happening at the Paris premiere of Stravinsky's *The Rite of Spring* (1913) or at the opening of Patrice Chereau's centenary production of Wagner's *Ring* in Bayreuth (1976).

The practice is alive and well in Europe, and especially Germany. Booing the singers or conductor happens occasionally, but at most opening nights of an opera, a "booing chorus" greeting the director and design team at the curtain call has become as commonplace as our standing ovation. (I've recently seen a marketing campaign for an opera company that read, "Come for the music, stay for the Standing O." In Germany, you could update that: "Come for the music, stay to boo the director!")

I've been on the receiving end of this kind of reaction only once, at the 2019 premiere of my production of Mozart's *Magic Flute* at the Berlin Staatsoper Unter den Linden. I knew our "booing chorus" would be extreme, since the audience had already begun to boo at the end of Act I. And sure enough, the wall of sound that greeted our bows was unlike anything I'd faced before.

What, you might ask, could I possibly have done to receive this kind of public shaming?

I wish I could claim "ambiguity intolerance" as the reason. Instead, I must admit that the performance just didn't gel. The rehearsal process was one of the most turbulent I've ever experienced, and although we were supported by the theater's intendant, Matthias Schulz, the general hostility toward me and my team was perhaps best encapsulated by a technician I spotted in the wings during the curtain call with his camera out, ready to film us being trashed. Even after a rocky process, every imaginable obstacle on opening night—sicknesses, cancellations, technical malfunctions, even bad weather—seemed to conspire against us. Watching the opening performance was like observing a working rehearsal for a show that needed a lot of work.

Still, when we took our bows, I felt surprisingly calm as the avalanche of boos socked us. (And perhaps also relieved that no one threw anything!) The first performance may have been flawed, but my team's colorful, loud, fantastical, complicated production had crystallized my perspective on this opera. There was no question that I could stand behind our work.

More surreal than the actual booing was Matthias's genuinely enthusiastic reaction after the curtain fell. If this had been America, the theater's management would surely have proffered at least superficial consolation: "Don't listen to them," or "Their reactions are all politics," or "It has nothing to do with you and your great work." Instead, Matthias seemed elated despite the negative response. He acknowledged that the production was not going to be to everyone's taste, but he was sure it would make an impact after this tumultuous premiere and achieve what he called "cult status."

Directors usually stay with a production only through opening night—a dispiriting tradition, implying either that a production has become complete, closed, and immutable after the first performance, or that our meddling is no longer welcome. We therefore miss out on the continuation of the process the conductor and the singers undergo as a show finds its momentum. (I always tell people to attend the last performance of an opera rather than the first, because it's invariably a stronger and more confident show.) And we also miss out on that untranslatable sensation of what transpires in an audience as they experience the work. As word of mouth travels and audiences begin to arrive with expectations, a palpable shift can be felt in the auditorium. At the premiere, the ideas are new for everybody equally; that level playing field is exciting but much harder to read. For example, I later learned that our opening night audience had included its share of enthusiastic supporters. Afterward, I had to make do with reports that Matthias's vision of cult status was starting to materialize: performances were well sold, and the audiences were younger and genuinely fascinated by the production. Reviews of the opening were scathing, but critics who attended subsequent performances began to rave. And the set designer Mimi Lien and costume designer Walter van Beirendonck won that year's Beazley Award from the London Design Museum—a satisfying rejoinder to initial criticisms of the show as garish and "*bunt*" (meaning "colorful," with not entirely positive connotations).

Could it be, after our public drubbing, that my team actually came out on top?

// // // // //

IT HAD BEEN A GREAT honor for me to be invited to direct at Berlin's Staatsoper, not only one of the oldest opera theaters in Europe but a stage that carries enormous personal significance. When fresh out of college, I spent a bohemian year in Berlin, learning to speak German and absorbing all the theater, opera, and dance I could. With three opera houses, a dozen orchestras, and countless theaters, the breadth and depth of live arts in the city made my time there a kind of self-directed second education. As I was still learning about opera, frequent (and dirt cheap) visits to the Staatsoper shaped much of my understanding of what the art form could be. Every experience there was exciting, regardless of what was playing. I got to know the building inside and out, including the best ways to sneak in to a show (the paltry sums I earned teaching English were stretched awfully thin that year). I'm still in touch with members of a social circle of other people my age who went out after every show to argue over what we'd seen. Twenty years later, the invitation to direct my own production at this theater felt like a circle closing.

And not just any opera but *The Magic Flute,* probably the most beloved opera in Germany. For thirty years, the Staatsoper had performed the work in a reconstruction of Karl Friedrich Schinkel's original, iconic set designs—partly to honor Schinkel's role as architect of the building, and partly to have something "historical" to offer tourists. Mounting a new production of this tremendously important work—displacing a legendary museal staging—was not for the faint of heart.

Whenever I am asked to name my favorite opera, *The Magic Flute* usually springs to mind first. This often surprises opera fans, who expect me to name a more obscure or thorny contemporary piece—or at least one that's a bit more logical. "*Magic Flute*? Really? But it barely makes any sense." The Egyptologist Jan Assmann considers Mozart's opera alongside the pyramids as among "the greatest enigmas in human culture." Its resistance to the tidy rationality of more straightforward narratives makes it a piece people love to trash: the story is "stupid" or "meaningless" and defies reason; the music, although sublime, shifts registers so often that you have no idea where it belongs; and the reliance on "magic" and spectacle is childish, not dignified or deep enough for the operatic stage.

Such complaints echo the stubborn adults in Antoine de Saint-Exupéry's beloved book *The Little Prince*. At the beginning of the first chapter is a six-year-old's drawing. We are asked to identify the ambiguous shape: is it a boa constrictor that has swallowed an elephant? or simply a lumpy hat? The critical eye of the adult fails to see the more fantastical intention of the child, who is deemed an artistic failure. The child would be better off studying sensible topics like mathematics, history, and grammar. "Grown-ups never understand anything by themselves," the narrator learns, "and it is tiresome for children to be always and forever explaining things to them."

Like *The Little Prince*, *The Magic Flute* illustrates a conundrum of maturity: why do so many children intuitively understand the opera, while adults dwell on its irrational, inexplicable, and contradictory aspects? Grown-ups tangle themselves up in search of consistency and causation, disdaining the opera's lack of coherence and closing off its direct communication to their inner child. The opera may indeed be confounding in its shifting modes from kaleidoscopic to Shakespearean, from naïve to philosophical—but it's best appreciated when we can approach it with the eyes and ears of children.

Mozart, who wrote his first opera at age eleven, is sometimes called "the eternal child." To the serious classical music lover, the label may seem like an insult, but *Magic Flute* proves its validity: his penultimate work for the stage (written when he was only thirty-five) is a loving ode to a childhood he never quite left. The opera is a paean of hope that music can help us return to the uncorrupted nature of our younger selves, before mature self-consciousness made everything so complicated.

The ideal spectator of *Magic Flute* is the young girl in Ingmar Bergman's film version, who sits in the audience with wide eyes, delighting in what she sees. Bergman begins his adaptation as if it were a theatrical presentation that gradually becomes cinematic: two-dimensional sets grow more and more three-dimensional, and a presentational style gives way to close-up confessional delivery of the text and music. But the camera throughout constantly returns to the girl in the audience, a framing layer of reality that undermines the audience's tendency to believe in what is being depicted. The montage of images—the world of the opera cutting directly back to the face of this little girl—implies that the film's cinematic leaps are actually the result of her imagination. It is she, not Bergman, who is transforming the artificial presentation onstage into an authentic, immersive, and internal experience.

We do this instinctively when we visit the theater as children; we trust what we see, and the theatrical universe extends well beyond the wings. We watch a performer exiting the stage and assume that character is entering some other out-of-view space, just as our parents leave our room to go on existing someplace else. As adults, we might imagine that performer smoking a cigarette on their break, as Bergman's actors are seen doing. We adults have learned to read the clear delineation of fiction and reality, and we recognize the theater's proscenium arch as the frame dividing the two. But for the child, the boundary between worlds is porous, and the proscenium arch is invisible.

What prevents adults from recognizing the boa constrictor in Saint-Exupéry's drawing or following the lead of Bergman's young spectator is the loss of childlike wonder that so often accompanies growing up. Like Tamino, the prince at the center of the opera's story, each adult faces a rocky road of maturity marked by disillusion, temptation, tragic loss, and fear of death. Those challenges tend to alienate us from our childlike state; the world around us becomes disenchanted. *The Magic Flute* doesn't deny that life is full of suffering and despair—but the true trial is to never lose our youthful joy in the face of those hardships.

The opera makes childhood divine, as personified by the only faultless characters in the piece: the three "beautiful and wise" boys, who sing in perfectly spaced harmonies and always show up in the nick of time. They first appear as mute guides to Tamino and his mysterious, bird-catching companion, Papageno. Throughout, the young trio repeatedly intrude on the scene to save the adults from destroying their lives. They are this opera's equivalent to a *deus ex machina*—in place of Athena, Mozart gives us these charming little cherubs.

The Three Boys have one moment, at the beginning of the Act II Finale, where they address the audience directly:

> *Soon the dawn will come,*
> *And the sun will begin its golden path.*
> *Soon all delusion will vanish,*
> *And the wise will be victorious.*
> *Oh blessed peace! Descend again*

And return to the hearts of humans:
Then this earth will be a paradise
And all mortals equal to gods!

This is the kind of language we imagine issuing forth from Sarastro, the sagacious high priest who sings with a sonorous bass. Sarastro is a confusing character. Because of his stentorian voice and patriarchal authority, audiences are socially conditioned to consider him wise and truthful. He sings two arias, each resembling a lullaby—the slowest music in the opera. The chill that Sarastro brings to the party can either indicate that he has achieved a sublime level of tranquility, or that he is now far removed from what the philosopher Hannah Arendt would call the *vita activa*. While the Three Boys sing hopefully of a utopian future, where humanity can reach a divine status, Sarastro's most famous aria, "In diesen heil'gen Hallen" ("In these holy halls"), tries to portray the present state of his temple as perfect—a hard pill to swallow, since we have seen how the temple is run by enslaved "Moors" who are mercilessly whipped if they disobey. As the opera continues, Sarastro's own unchecked authority seems to be his only "virtue" and gaslighting his only remaining skill. On the other end of the spectrum, the Three Boys—always active, always a life force—are offered as our true guides. They carry with them the hope that we will find our way back to paradise, our natural state, back to the childhood we've lost. If Sarastro's music aims to put us to sleep, the Three Boys constantly try to wake up our dormant inner child, as if to say: When we keep the child in us alive, even in the face of death, we may realize the full potential of our lives.

Dismissing magic as a child's game is easy for the serious, adult spectator. But even the simplest forms of magic, like sleight-of-hand illusions, provoke a sense of wonder at the suspension of our perceived limitations. "Magic" has everything to do with reality: the opening up of possibilities we have long taken for granted as closed, or the return to an enchanted vision of the world. (Wonder was one of humanity's six essential passions for Descartes.) Theatrical magic is the same magic accepted by children, who believe that Tamino's journey continues when he leaves the stage. And a similar awe takes place when characters manifest seemingly unimaginable acts: grace instead of revenge, as in Mozart's operas *Idomeneo* and *La Clemenza di Tito*; forgiveness rather than refusal, as in *The Marriage of Figaro* and *Così fan tutte*; courage overcoming fear, as in *Magic Flute*. We may berate others for "magical thinking," for believing problems will magically solve themselves or that consequences can be outrun. But opera reminds us why we need to believe in magic—not in the sense of delusional living but in the spirit of seeking out what remains possible even when all the odds are against us.

In the first act Finale of *Magic Flute,* Papageno attempts to rescue the princess Pamina, daughter of the Queen of the Night (and, for me, the real hero of the opera), from Sarastro's temple. But they are trapped by Sarastro's enslaved henchman Monostatos. "Now it's all over for us," they sing in despair. Then, out of thin air, Papageno summons the will to fight for their lives: *"Wer viel wagt... wer viel wagt... wer viel wagt gewinnt auch viel!"* The sentiment is not particularly deep: "Whoever risks big... whoever risks big... whoever risks big can often win big!" But the music depicts Papageno rapidly ratcheting up his courage, repeating *"wer viel wagt"* higher and higher, before taking action. And his action is the kind of "sleight of hand" magic that might seem childish: he plays a music-box melody on his magic bells, instantly hypnotizing all the angry guards and rendering them harmless.

This swift little scene is one of the opera's most humorous moments, a comedic counterpart to the more serious bravery that Tamino and Pamina are called to generate. But even here, Mozart is showing us that magic begins with an act of will in our hearts. Papageno discovering his courage supplies the true sorcery of the scene; his magic bells and Tamino's magic flute are only effective tools for "stage magic" once the characters commit *internally* to seizing their destiny. This is the deep secret that the opera demonstrates each time it's performed: all external magic emerges from a more powerful, more beautiful inner alchemy.

// // // // //

NOTHING IN *THE MAGIC FLUTE* is what it seems. The story revolves around sudden shifts of perception, which constantly confound the prince Tamino. When he first hears the Queen of the Night's account of Pamina's violent abduction by Sarastro, Tamino takes her words at face value and vows revenge. But approaching Sarastro's temple, Tamino is surprised to see that the doors are inscribed with virtuous words, denoting a "Temple of Wisdom," a "Temple of Reason," and a "Temple of Nature." "Did I reach the seat of the gods?" he wonders. This is certainly not the nightmarish realm he was expecting. Instead, Tamino confronts a cryptic character known only as "The Speaker." What follows is one of the opera's weirdest and best scenes. The Speaker bars Tamino's entry to the temple and asks him to reconsider his assumptions. "Has what you've heard been proven?" The complete 180-degree turn leaves Tamino dizzy to the point of despair: "When will you dissipate, endless night? When will my eyes find the light?" An unnamed chorus replies: "Soon, soon . . . or never!" It's an inscrutable scene that would feel right at home in a Kafka novel. (Ingmar Bergman used the music of this scene powerfully in another, much darker film, *The Hour of the Wolf.*)

Aristotle's fantastic concept for what Tamino experiences was *peripeteia,* or the sudden turning point in a story as a character's fortune changes. But in most Greek tragedy where *peripeteia* played a crucial and recognizable role in the drama, the reversal of fortune occurred shortly before the play's final denouement. The change of perspective in *Magic Flute* appears quite a bit earlier—at the beginning of the Act I Finale, with much more opera still to come. Additional reversals will take place—most famously when the grieving, sympathetic Queen of the Night reveals another side of her personality in "Der Hölle Rache" (described in Chapter Three). Brilliantly and confoundingly, *Magic Flute* introduces one *peripeteia* after another—and because nearly every character undergoes at least one sudden shift of perception, the audience is not at all clear whom they should trust. In the course of a performance, you may find yourself wondering, like Tamino, "When will this eternal night be over?"

Peripeteia is probably my go-to narrative device when creating a production. Beyond their function in the narrative, such moments help keep the circuit of meaning open. They become the essential scenes in a production by overturning our assumptions of the stage reality, pointing to other possibilities and other interpretations. As mentioned earlier, I try to place spectators in an unstable relationship to the work, where surprising new perspectives or unexpected new ideas demand that they reconsider the terrain. To avoid the closure of an airtight argument (the German concept of *Konsequenz*), I want a production to constantly unsettle the audience and ask for continuous renegotiations of their experience. As I began work on *Magic Flute,* I knew that whatever mechanism I came up with had to keep pace with the frequent shifts and reversals of the piece itself.

I conceived the opera as a marionette theater, with the singing actors as life-size puppets. I imagined restricting all entrances and exits to the space above rather than stage left or stage right, to maintain the marionette illusion of appearing and disappearing from the sky. When it became clear that not every entrance could be vertical, we supplemented moments of actual flying with a system we called "fake flying": the singing actors kept their feet on the ground but stayed attached to the fly system above by three elastic yellow strings, so the audience never lost sight of the main characters' inherent artificiality as manipulated puppets. Other characters surrounded our protagonists as wind-up toys, jacks-in-the-box, or simply shadow puppets. In short, the opera's motley crew of characters all became figurines in a children's theater, blown up to human scale.

Mozart's music pairs nicely with the lightness and simplicity of a marionette. The score must always sound as effortless and natural as child's play (despite how challenging it may be to perform). But what really interested me was how easily the marionette as an image could evolve through the production, with moments of *peripeteia*. An operated toy is a perfect symbol of the quintessential human dilemma: do we act from our own free will, or is some invisible force pulling us to perform roles in a theater we mistake for reality? A poetic reading, maintaining the childlike wonder of the toy theater, also allows the opera to chart the evolution of

Marionettes reaching for divinity: Anna Prohaska as Pamina
and Florian Teichtmeister as Papageno.

individual consciousness. The marionette's wood giving way to humanity
mirrors the alchemical procedure of converting our inner metal into spiritual gold.

Early in the opera, Tamino receives a portrait of the queen's daughter Pamina and is seized by an unexplainable paroxysm of feeling. "This
portrait has an enchanting beauty...I feel something I've never felt
before. Could this be love?" In the way the melody unpredictably twists
and turns, Tamino's aria serves as a microcosm for this wily opera. His
strong emotion inspires a blissful state of confusion, catalyzing his transformation. However, since it's still early in his journey, he doesn't display
a hero's secure sense of self. The aria shows him questioning, doubting
himself, and unsure of what to do. In my production, Pamina's portrait
became a small marionette that the puppet Tamino could manipulate with his own (manipulated) hands. Like a series of nesting dolls,
a marionette holding a marionette was a powerful image for me of the
character at this stage: unaware and impossibly far from self-perception.
Pamina is not yet a subject for him but an object, a thing. And (as our
digital age still proves true) falling in love with an image is an egoistic

illusion. Nevertheless, his initiation has begun, and the humanizing process, quickened by music, becomes possible.

At the end of the production, Tamino and Pamina remove their strings and stand on their own feet. Our two marionettes face their greatest fears—gravity and abandonment—to become conscious of their strings and gain mastery over their condition. Through confusion and trials, they find a way together to become noble—to become fallible—to become human. Without ever losing a fairy-tale veneer, *Magic Flute* accompanies the audience through a reenactment of all the misperceptions and difficulties that keep us from our potential for such transformation. Faced with endless reversals, feints, and illusions, Tamino and Pamina nevertheless achieve a transcendence from the material world. Overcoming received prejudices and superstitions from the previous generation (Sarastro and the Queen of the Night) has enabled them to become enlightened humans beyond any doctrine.

How could anyone call the story of *The Magic Flute* stupid?

// // // // //

NOT LONG AFTER THE FIRST performances of this opera in 1791, the German playwright Heinrich von Kleist wrote a short but influential text (far too little known in the United States) called "On the Marionette Theater." The article appeared in three installments of the *Berliner Abendblätter*, the daily newspaper where Kleist was employed as a theater critic. His critical voice was harsh, befitting his status as a neglected genius (in his own time, only three of his plays were ever performed). But his relative obscurity also meant that the theater was still essentially a theoretical proposition for him, and the speculative tone of this essay carries an unmistakable air of philosophy.

The article relates a dialogue between an unnamed narrator and "Herr C.," the leading dancer at the opera. The narrator is surprised to have often noticed Herr C. on the street "among the rabble," enjoying performances by a marionette troupe. What could such an educated and accomplished artist find to amuse him among such a lowly form of entertainment?

(From the first paragraph, Kleist captures a central conflict between "high" and "low" art that remains an eternal conflict in opera, to which I will return in Chapter Seven. The conflict applies to *Magic Flute* as well, since the opera wasn't written for Vienna's dignified and grand court theater, but for one of the independent theaters on the outskirts of the city instead. Just as Kleist's narrator begins by believing that nothing worthy of the great artist's attention could be uncovered in a childish art form, *Magic Flute* is similarly and all too frequently dismissed as inherently juvenile.)

Yet Herr C. claims that human performers can learn much from their inanimate counterparts. The puppet, lacking in basic consciousness, doesn't suffer from the self-consciousness that Herr C. calls an "affectation" in his human counterparts. He reflects on the image of a boy removing a splinter from his foot, a "graceful" gesture because it's unperformed. The boy exhibits no self-consciousness in his action, which makes his posture arresting and beautiful. As we mature, Herr C. argues, such spontaneous acts of unaware poise become impossible; as adults, we are too locked in our own heads and too conditioned by society to act with this kind of simple, elemental grace.

Herr C. seamlessly shifts the argument onto the metaphysical plane when he suggests that watching the puppet move with a grace lost to adults is a reminder of our fallen condition, "unavoidable ever since we ate from the tree of knowledge. But paradise is barred up and the cherubs left behind. We have to journey around the world to see if maybe we can get in from the back." The puppet's defiance of gravity—the force human dancers fight the most—also becomes a metaphysical symbol: "the power from above that lifts us up is greater than what keeps us chained to the earth."

Herr C.'s ability to glean spiritual dimensions from a marionette leaves the narrator gobsmacked. The essay ends with a cryptic and penetrating return not just to the imagery of the Garden of Eden but to a surprising End of Days:

"Well now, my dear friend," Herr C. said, "you now have everything you need to understand where I'm coming from. In our material world, as intelligence dims and weakens, the grace within it emerges proportionately brighter and more powerful.

Just like ... an image appearing in a concave mirror, after disappearing into infinity, suddenly reappears complete before us; so too, after knowledge has passed through some infinity, grace comes back—most purely in the forms of the human body that have either zero or infinite consciousness. I mean, either the marionette or the god."

"Which means," I interjected despite my bewilderment, "we will have to eat from the Tree of Knowledge again to fall back into a state of innocence?"

"Without doubt," he answered. "That is the last chapter of the history of the world."

With Kleist's essay and Bergman's young spectator as my inspirations, the concept for the marionette theater production began to take shape. I gathered a fantastic group of collaborators—in addition to Mimi Lien and Walter van Beirendonck, the team included Hannah Wasileski on projections, Reinhard Traub on lights, and Krystian Lada as the dramaturge—to start to articulate how the ideas would become animated.

(As I will discuss in the final chapter, everything a director does demands so much cooperation and co-articulation that pinpointing the place where I start and the myriad other musical, visual, and technical artists end is a near impossibility. The collaborative reality in creating an opera means I can hardly call anything in this production solely "mine.")

We decided early on that our marionette theater would be anchored in the visual notion of collage—just as the musical world of the opera constantly shifts registers and genres. We looked to create composite identities for each character rather than straightforward reproductions of existing puppets and toys. So Tamino and Pamina seemed fashioned out of wood, but they wore bright red boots and gloves reminiscent of Osamu Tezuka's classic manga character Astro Boy. The slaves became sleek onyx robots infused with accoutrements from *Star Wars* and S&M clubs. The Three Ladies serving the Queen of the Night appeared as three neon-colored heads emerging from one voluptuous, Rubenesque naked body, a kind of grotesque excess of maternal presence that threatens to suffocate the budding prince.

The magic animals Tamino enchants with his magic flute became the frozen animals of a carousel, liberated from immobility and set free to dance into the wild. And the all-important Three Boys perched on a cloud wearing monkey masks, recalling the Japanese myth of Mizaru ("see no evil"), Kikazaru ("hear no evil"), and Iwazaru ("speak no evil"). Mimi's sets played with two-dimensionality and emphasized verticality—set pieces descending or ascending rather than the more conventional stage left and right—and always involved a sense of visual assemblage. The effect was a never-ending phantasmagoria, fitting with the opera's frequent *peripeteia,* and taking full advantage of the theater's elaborate stage machinery.

Krystian connected our ideas to the work's historical origins. Mozart's opera has much in common with what were known in seventeenth- and eighteenth-century Vienna as *Maschinenkomödien,* popular stage works driven by a fascination with the theater's mechanisms for creating illusion. Circus-like quick changes and special effects dictated the story and dramatic situation of these works, transporting audiences to exotic locales and astonishing them with moments of stage magic. Some argue that *Maschinenkomödien* conveyed a philosophical and religious perspective of the world as full of illusions, with humans as mere puppets in a larger machine. This popular form of entertainment helps explain why *Magic Flute* is structured the way it is; but the opera goes further by treating some of the characters as manic machines themselves. The frenetic, proto-electronic coloratura of the Queen of the Night's rage aria is an obvious example of an utterance from a woman who feels at least part cyborg. The obsessive, music-box mechanics of Monostatos's gruesome Act II aria are also clear evidence of the widespread craze in Mozart's time for automatons and early forerunners of artificial intelligence. Toys and marionettes feel completely at home in this opera.

Maschinenkomödien and their popular counterpart *Singspiele* are sometimes considered precursors to the American musical—and like musicals, *Magic Flute* alternates between music and spoken dialogue. For a director, the music is far less a challenge than those dialogues: once music has disappeared, life seems to have vanished from the stage, as if the floor has just dropped out or something has gone terribly wrong, forcing the show to grind to an unexpected halt. Singers who can project their arias unamplified to the back of a large auditorium rarely know how to use their speaking voice in this way, resorting to either booming, old-timey declamation or, to preserve intimacy and truthfulness, a cinematic low volume that the audience can barely hear. In either case, the production's energy is sapped. Even if a director manages to get the delivery right with one set of performers, once the cast changes, that specificity becomes very hard to maintain. I may have fond memories of frequenting the Staatsoper when I was younger, but the *Magic Flute* production I saw back then featured wonderful singers struggling mightily with the spoken sections. They delivered their dialogue in a clunky, sing-song way that indicated a lack of real understanding of the language. Music can disguise a singer's lack of comfort with a language, but spoken dialogue makes it painfully obvious. The alternation between brilliantly executed music and schlocky dialogue often makes a performance of the opera a highly uneven experience.

I've never enjoyed the dialogues of *Magic Flute* more than during a performance by the Salzburger Marionettentheater, where a recording reenacted the full opera on a miniature stage with classic marionettes. The performance captured the piece's essentialized mode of storytelling, far removed from any psychological realism, and watching the puppets during the spoken sections was an enchanting experience. Still, when it came to the musical moments, the marionettes were less compelling. The work's depth couldn't be conveyed without the human voice and a body responding in direct and subtle ways with the movement of the music.

I leaned on that experience in Salzburg to find a solution for the dialogues in Berlin. I decided to have the singers use their own voices to sing but mutely mime all action to a recording of their dialogues. We prerecorded them with child actors, which the singers pantomimed with a puppet-like physicality: stiff and inhuman, as though they were made of wood or metal. Their mouths did not move along with the dialogue but stayed frozen, even if their eyes remained alive. Amplifying the recordings helped keep the energy of the performance from sinking, with enough sound effects to maintain a sense of sonic structure (as opposed to a deafening silence around each spoken word). And then, each time the music began, as spoken voices of children gave way to the singers' own singing voices, music magically made their physicality fluid, graceful, and organic. Music became an animating force, awakening the puppets and giving them essential human emotions and a lightning-quick intelligence.

In preserving a separation of spoken voice and physical body—one of the hallmarks of puppet theater—we invited the audience to reenact the imaginative activity of Bergman's young spectator. Just as she gradually reads the artifice of the stage world with cinematic immediacy, a spectator of my production could come to believe that inanimate objects have taken on a soul. And each time the music began and the separation of body and voice was erased, the score transcended the stage illusion, reigniting the spark of life lying dormant in the toy.

The idea held promise—but to save the production from growing predictable and repetitive, I had to find ways to make the dialogues evolve and grow more complex as the performance went on. One way, I thought, might be to let Papageno speak with his natural voice as he interacted with the muted singers. He would identify completely with the puppet world—befitting a character who refutes any search for higher wisdom. Papageno as a sidekick offers comedic relief from the serious journey undertaken by Tamino and Pamina, and he invariably becomes the audience favorite.

Part of *Magic Flute*'s anarchic and anti-elite power lies in its treatment of Papageno as an equal hero to the questing Tamino. The opera refuses to claim one path to truth, as Sarastro or the Queen of the Night would have the young characters believe. The role was originally written for Emanuel Schikaneder—the librettist and also the impresario who ran the Theater auf der Wieden, where the opera debuted. No wonder Papageno is given the lion's share of stage time, even though Schikaneder apparently couldn't sing very well. Mozart responded ingeniously to his particular gifts by writing a role of folk-like simplicity with a limited range, driven more by comedic delivery than the kind of musical precision demanded of the other characters. Papageno in fact describes himself as a *Naturmensch,* the Enlightenment ideal of an innocent human in their natural state, uncorrupted by society. He doesn't seek transcendence or anything beyond worldly pleasures; he identifies fully with his artificial environment and is happy staying exactly who he is within it. Making Papageno the master of his dialogue—speaking with an ease in this artificial world that the other characters can't achieve—positions him comfortably in the illusory world of the puppets, as well as adding complexity and ambiguity to his dialogues.

An important evolution in the treatment of dialogues occurs after Pamina's devastating Act II aria "Ach, ich fühl's" ("Ah, I can feel it"). Fearing she has lost Tamino forever, her thoughts turn to suicide, and the marionette's greatest enemy—gravity—seems to win. She slowly sinks to the ground to sing her aria weighed down by grief. But her anguish has also given her a clearer, deeper look at her reality. In the subsequent dialogue, Tamino and Sarastro continue pantomiming their dialogue, but Pamina can suddenly hear her lines recited by some other voice. "Stop it!" the singer cries in her own speaking voice, for the first time. "Who is that speaking for me?" While Papageno relishes his puppet world, Pamina becomes aware of it as an oppressive system, one that silences her voice. Despair in the face of the machine's injustice may be the prerequisite dark night before the dawn of full realization—and indeed, Pamina emerges from her suicidal thoughts to face that dawn (thanks to the intervention of the Three Boys, naturally).

Allowing Pamina to recover her speaking voice on the way to becoming an equal hero to her male counterparts became a way of critiquing the work's misogynistic aspects—which also frequently undermine contemporary productions. Residents of Sarastro's temple hardly miss an opportunity to denigrate women: "Women blab and don't act," "Protect yourself from feminine treachery," and "A woman needs a man to lead her" are just a few of the smears parroted by the temple priests. Tamino himself, after having been called to act by the Queen of the Night, mimics the priests' perspective in the second act quintet, by disparaging women's "claptrap."

What, then, are we to make of Pamina's journey through the piece? While we first see Tamino terrified and fainting at the sight of a snake, one of Pamina's first lines reads, "I don't shy from death." And after her emotional devastation, she emerges to *lead* the male hero through a final ordeal, a direct confrontation with death known as the "Trial of Fire and Water." In the face of what Tamino describes as a "portal of terror," Pamina reacts with natural grace: "I myself will lead you, just as love guides me by scattering roses on our path—because roses grow where thorns are found." Pamina, then, rather than serving as Tamino's obedient handmaiden, sets the example of courage. If he had listened to the chauvinism parading as wisdom in Sarastro's temple, he would have never completed his spiritual journey.

It's impossible to imagine Mozart identifying with the misogynist trends of his time. Not only do the women in his operas possess an interiority that their male counterparts lack, they also find opportunities for agency within a system built on their subservience. The greatest example of this must be the end of *The Marriage of Figaro,* where the countess confers forgiveness and mercy on her cheating husband. She is elevated to a status equivalent to that of Emperor Titus in the composer's *La Clemenza di Tito*, embodying a grace the men in *Figaro* frequently fail to realize.

So if *Magic Flute* itself is *not* misogynist, how are we supposed to interpret the crudely sexist sentiments sometimes expressed? It can be hard to understand that the text given to a dramatic character is not necessarily a position endorsed by its authors. But if we practice separating music, text, and production, we find that opera offers myriad ways to create diverging points of view. Disentangling the tracks opens up a distance between a character's perspective and authorial intention, and what may seem like confirmation can quickly become critique. When you consider Pamina's role in the final scene, it becomes easy to see that *Magic Flute* actually exposes sexism as a shortsighted social weakness and foolish prejudice standing in the way of true wisdom. If a production fails to call out misogyny as it appears—either by letting it slide or by affirming it—an audience will not be able to make sense of what it means for Pamina to lead Tamino at the end. Such is the power of opera when we stop looking for a Mickey Mousing relationship between music, text, and production. Refutation and contradiction, derived from interrogation and exploration, become essential tools in drawing closer to what the piece is truly saying.

Sarastro's priests are not only notorious misogynists, they are racist as well: the Black, enslaved Monostatos is constantly flogged and denigrated by Sarastro, who ends up administering much more cruelty than wisdom. As discussed in Chapter 2, the one aria given to Monostatos is a a self-loathing screed, claiming "ugly" Black men can only win a "beautiful" white woman by force. As he does for the misogynistic duet of the priests ("Beware of women's wiles"), Mozart allots almost no time to this prejudiced view of humanity: Monostatos's aria rarely takes longer than a minute to perform. When Sarastro stops the attempted rape, he preaches one of his platitudinal cradle songs: "In these holy halls, we forgive our enemies, and whoever doesn't is not deserving to be human." How should an audience reconcile the character's sagacity with what they just witnessed—the fact that his sacred temple enslaves and punishes fellow humans and excludes women? I believe Mozart was exposing the duplicity and closed-mindedness of his "enlightened" eighteenth-century contemporaries. The libretto scoffs at superstition as the antithesis of wisdom, but Mozart ultimately ridicules the prejudices that render all forms of ideology regressive.

The marionette once again offered for me a perfect symbol of how racism, misogyny, and prejudices of all sorts turn each of us into puppets who unthinkingly accept the status quo. Tamino and Pamina can only evolve when they are liberated from any manipulation by the previous generation. One of the central mysteries of the production would then become: Who is pulling the strings? Who is controlling the events of the opera?

In a more conventional production, Sarastro, like Shakespeare's Prospero in *The Tempest*, would likely be revealed as the opera's grand puppet master. His "wise old prophet" vibe carries a superficial veneer of the divine, substitute father, and he gets the work's last triumphant solo. But that concept affirms a sense that his ideology is correct, prejudices and all. Some directors might present the Queen of the Night as puppet master: we certainly watch her manipulate Tamino, Pamina, Papageno,

the Three Ladies, and Monostatos. But we also recognize that her ideology is built on power and violence, a perfect mirror to Sarastro's ultimately egocentric worldview. Placing her in the Svengali position would
likewise affirm her position as correct.

For a while, I imagined a production with Sarastro and the Queen
of the Night as a warring couple—more like Shakespeare's Oberon and
Titania in *A Midsummer Night's Dream*—not agreeing on how their
play should proceed and which of them is really in control. They would
fight over the stringed characters, pushing and pulling until one of them
(most likely Sarastro) eventually won out. Instead, I decided that both
Sarastro and the Queen of Night should become marionettes. This act
undercut any sense of their power; rather than master manipulators,
they themselves were manipulated. The self-centered and partial views
of humanity they espoused no longer seemed eternal but provisional.

I could have opted for complete ambiguity and left the question
of puppet master unanswered—not unlike the silence surrounding
Tamino at the beginning when he ponders, "Has some higher power
saved me?" Tamino, more than any other character, is plagued by the
possibility that behind reality is a mere void, an "eternal night" without
light. Keeping that potential reading open as long as possible created a
tension and suspense in the production, but I ultimately needed to provide an answer—not least to ensure the production resisted a nihilism I
can't endorse myself.

So in the final scene, I revealed who was pulling the strings all
along. All set pieces and puppet characters vanished, and a smaller-scale
version of the theater appeared on the empty stage. Looming above that
stage-within-a-stage, were the puppeteers: six children, the singers who
played the Three Boys (now in contemporary clothes) and three young
girls. Sarastro sang his final triumphant lines offstage, lip-synched by
one of the boys, while all six lip-synched the offstage chorus. There were
no adults in sight, and the children jumped around and celebrated *their*
triumph as the curtain fell.

The prerecorded dialogues connected this idea to the rest of the production, as the characters were all voiced by the six children we would
meet at the end. As opening night unfolded, the overheard intermission

chatter indicated to me that this was a bewildering (and for some, deeply annoying) choice. I offered no clear indication why we were hearing children's voices; only at the very end would the audience understand that the recorded voices were the young puppeteers, animating the characters in their play.

We did, however, drop obvious hints throughout. In the first scene, the traditional sound effects of wind, thunder, and lightning crashes were supplanted with children's exclamations of "Pow!" and "Bang!" In the first major scene change, the children read the original stage directions, interrupting each other as they stumbled over the old-fashioned, ridiculous depiction of the slaves' quarters. "What weird language," one of them said, before the scene began. Most important, during Monostatos's self-hating aria in Act II, the children's voices supplied real-time critique. "This must be a *very* old text," commented one. "None of what he's saying is true—why should we see him as evil?" Other young voices tried drowning out his language with cries of "Stop! Stop!" Finally, unsure how to proceed with the drama, one child ambivalently suggested, "Maybe we should just let him sing."

The children, then, provided a contemporary rejection of the work's racism in real time. The temptation to merely excise the offensive aspects of *Magic Flute* by cutting this aria and dialogue is a difficult one for contemporary productions to resist—and surely cutting them is far better than simply taking no stance at all. Instead, in my production the warts-and-all text remained but was actively negated as it unfolded. The voices of the next generation modeled an act of refutation.

The ideas embedded in *Magic Flute* that I wanted to highlight were perhaps best captured by giving children this supernatural authority at the end. Children carry the ever-renewing hope of evolving human consciousness and repairing the world.

// // // //

IN THAT POWERFUL MOMENT WHERE Pamina begins to lead Tamino, the key transformation of my production occurs: she shows him how to remove their marionette strings. The two puppets have become humans and they embark on their final trial together, the Trial of Fire and Water (SEE PLAYLIST).

What's most curious about this climactic trial is how Mozart scores it. He passed up the chance to impress his audience with an imagistic soundscape, as he did to describe the turbulent surface of the ocean in his earlier *Idomeneo*. Instead, music for what's meant to be the most terrifying ordeal of the evening is written as sparely as anything else in the opera: just solo flute and quiet percussion. After a long evening of two-dimensional drops and (literal) flights of fancy, this scene demanded something different from our dramaturgy. I took the quietness of Mozart's music as the inspiration for a final trial that would also feel subdued, humble, and unexpectedly ordinary. So Tamino and Pamina removed their strings, found their "sea legs" as humans, and left the puppet theater. They entered a modest, unadorned but three-dimensional kitchen. Their quiet task: lighting the stove (fire), filling the pot from the sink (water), and cooking a meal they would quietly share.

This decision was the one that *truly* enraged the opening night audience; their boos drowned out Mozart's gentle march.

I've given much thought to why this everyday image provoked so much wrath, as I found its frailty quite touching—refreshingly honest after a great deal of artifice. A recognizable, contemporary kitchen pulls the rug out from under the audience's feet—perhaps, as Tamino discovers, everything we've been led to believe in this production was wrong? Such moments of overturned expectations are the ones I find the most exciting. For Germans, maybe less so: the sudden shift to the kitchen was read less as an illuminating *peripeteia* than as resolutely *inkonsequent*.

Since the production opened, I've been asked to "explain" the choice on several occasions. It's a depressing proposition, implying that you only meant one thing. ("If artists truly despise you," Joseph Campbell once said, "they'll tell you what they meant by their art.") When I offer an explanation, it's as if there was one magic solution all along that I've purposefully withheld from the audience. That would make directors more like teachers asking the class a question for which there's only one right answer. Instead, I am looking to create an open field of possible meanings to be considered and completed by the spectator.

"Death is a kitchen": Julian Prégardien as Tamino and Anna Prohaska
undergo the Trial of Fire and Water.

Even now, the move to the kitchen is one I resist explaining. I can discuss how the scene describes the most important trial for a mature couple: finding the magic in everyday life. Falling in love with an image of someone is easy, but it's much harder to keep love alive in the daily tribulations that truly make up a relationship. I could mention the other associations that make this decision feel right—but since there isn't only one key to the riddle, I am ultimately more interested in how others read production choices. I would even consider it among the primary reasons I direct: to perceive how a choice I make resonates with someone else. It's a way to broaden an appreciation of a work's mystery and, by extension, the mysteries of the world.

So when Krystian heard my idea for the kitchen, his mind immediately leapt to a beautiful image expressed by the Chilean poet Pablo Neruda: "After death, heaven will be an endless kitchen." We shared this association with the singers, who absorbed it to the benefit of the scene. Mimi's impulse was to design the kitchen as a kind of utilitarian, almost featureless container of space, offering maximum contrast to the colorful and mostly flat images that populated the rest of the production. Both artists took the initial idea and elaborated on it, enriched it, made it more multi-perspectival. They demonstrated how collaborative thinking and sharing a vision ultimately secures a sense of multiplicity.

// // // // //

THREE YEARS AFTER THE TUMULTUOUS opening night, Intendant Matthias Schulz invited me to return and make some adjustments to the production—an all-too rare opportunity in opera. Unlike commercial theater, where a lengthy preview process gives everyone involved a chance to revise their work, what you see on the opening night of an opera is basically what you will get for as long as the show exists. I wish that opera could find a way to introduce revisions to the production process more regularly, especially for world premiere operas (imagine the pressure on composers and librettists, who spend years writing a work that must emerge perfectly on opening night!). It would require a systemic shift away from product and toward process—and, considering the economic implications, seems difficult to imagine.

Under normal circumstances, I would not have been given the chance to revise my *Flute* production. But after Covid-19 arrived, the flying system the Staatsoper rented to create the marionette illusion was no longer available. The singers' more intricate flight paths would need to either undergo a simplification or be reassigned to the "fake flying" tracks. I was disappointed at first, since the technical wizardry of the flying anchored what I originally thought would make the production distinctive. If the singers flew less, the production might no longer capture the music's anti-gravitational fascination. But Matthias saw an opportunity here: if the production could be simplified, it could be performed more frequently throughout the season, rather than in discrete pockets around the flight system's availability. Much to his credit, when Matthias could have walked away from a controversial production, he chose to reengage and reinvest in it instead. With that commitment, I went back into the world of this production.

This rare opportunity proved a revelatory experience. Without changing any of the ideas or the basic design, the clarity and communicability of those ideas exponentially increased. It probably shouldn't have surprised me to discover that the production was much stronger with *less* real flying. The singing actors landed more frequently on solid ground, with the "fake flying" strings indicating their relationship to a mysterious higher power. Entrances and exits may have been more conventional—more horizontal, stage left or right—but none of that ended up speaking as strongly as what the performers themselves could do. Being grounded gave them the security to *play* the marionette rather than experiencing its hung-up reality. More important, the spirit of the production was reclaimed from the technical machinery and put back where it belonged: with the performers.

Other changes helped the overall production read better, such as the reintroduction of projections we originally cut because of a lack of proper tech time. But one decision in particular truly changed everything—and may seem completely contradictory to my praise of ambiguity in Chapter Four. I disambiguated the entire production by restaging the overture.

In the first version, the identity of the puppet masters was withheld until the very end. But as my friend and collaborator Du Yun so aptly put it after seeing the production, "Opera is bad at the reveal." It's true. Perhaps because opera already challenges an audience's capacity for comprehension, any additional mystery becomes much harder to communicate.

Only a handful of operas are built around a big last-minute reveal, in the spirit of the films *Sixth Sense* and *The Usual Suspects*. Leoš Janáček, the Czech composer of *Cunning Little Vixen,* created one prime example in one of the strangest operas of all time, *The Makropulos Case* (1925). The opera revolves around a beautiful, youthful woman who confesses in a stunning closing monologue that she is 337 years old. The opera gives absolutely no indication that this is where the whole piece is heading: the first act is almost relentlessly banal, set in a lawyer's office and centering on a complicated legal battle in rapid-fire Czech. Mundane twists and turns—set to music that is anything but mundane—finally give way to the exquisite final revelation, which, for those with a high level of ambiguity tolerance, is well worth the ninety-minute buildup.

The opera is a director's dream, because its fantastical aspects open up a broad field of visual possibilities. On the other hand, directors invariably spend a lot of time trying to disambiguate the work at the beginning so that the audience can have something to hook onto, some reason to stick with it through the legal debates and convoluted intrigues. The opera remains somewhat of an oddball rarity, produced on occasion by the larger repertoire theaters but not what anyone would call an audience favorite.

When I worked with the designer Es Devlin on a production of Meredith Monk's *ATLAS*, she recounted a remark from a British actor that has stuck with me: "The audience will go with you to hell and back," the actor told her. "But the bus has to say 'Hell' on it." In other words, if you can signal to an audience where you're taking them, you'll be amazed how openly they consent to coming along. The road can even be circuitous and nonlinear, full of scenic byways and detours. But in the end, you'll be surprised how far you can take them.

So my revised production put the destination on the front of the bus: during the overture, the curtain rose on the tiny puppet theater I had originally saved for the ending, with the six children coming out one by one. They brought with them small, inanimate puppet versions of all the characters we would later see embodied by the singers. I was worried this would make the production less interesting: neutralizing a central mystery and rendering the Finale moot, returning to an already-seen image rather than presenting a final twist. But whatever the production may have lost in mystery it gained in clarity. The children's voices mocking the original German and repudiating the text's racism were now embodied, and those moments landed with this new audience as they hadn't at the premiere. With spectators knowing where I was taking them, they clearly enjoyed the ride much more. When the children reappeared at the end, the image proved satisfying rather than redundant—not unlike Ingmar Bergman's shot of the young girl at the end of his *Magic Flute*, reminding us that everything we just saw was a child's fantasy.

Through this *Magic Flute* experience, I was able to finally articulate what real ambiguity means to me: *highly specific choices (a marionette, a kitchen) in an unexpected relationship to the music, the text, and all the other artistic decisions, creating an experience that can't be reduced to one meaning.* Ambiguity needs to reside on the macro level of a complex composite, rather than on the micro level of an individual decision, where it can read as indistinct and vague. This kind of ambiguity opens up new directions and unexpected relationships to the source material. It demands a degree of clarity and commitment—strong, clear decisions that accumulate, becoming something greater than the individual ideas, and not easily explainable.

// // // // //

AT THE FIRST PERFORMANCE OF the revised version, Matthias asked me if I was going to take a bow. I opted against it, mostly because I didn't relish reliving the experience of opening night. (Why poke a sleeping bear?)

But when this audience rose to their feet to cheer—yes, a standing O in Germany!—the booing of the premiere felt fully exorcised. Maybe I got the last laugh on the production after all?

In any case, I should have taken that second bow.

Frankfurt, Germany

John Cage's *Europeras 1 & 2* premieres, an indeterminate performance drawn from the entire range of European opera. In a radical act of repurposing, all the music is woven together from preexisting scores of the standard repertoire. "For two hundred years the Europeans have been sending us their operas," Cage famously says. "Now I'm sending them back."

1987

Houston, Texas

Nixon in China, music by John Adams, libretto by Alice Goodman, and directed by Peter Sellars premieres at Houston Grand Opera.

See PLAYLIST

La púrpura de la rosa by the Spanish composer Tomás de Torrejón y Velasco, with a libretto by the great Spanish writer Pedro Calderón de la Barca, becomes the first opera to premiere on an American continent. In its celebration of the birth of the Spanish monarch and in its depiction of a Greek myth as its story, Velasco's artistic achievement is overshadowed by its cooperation in the entrenchment of Spanish cultural hegemony.

Jean-Baptiste Lully's *Alceste* opens the new Palais Royal in Paris. When Louis XIV grants Lully the exclusive privilege of producing opera throughout France, he ushers in the country's new aesthetic monopoly. A new type of opera emerges that will eventually be called *tragédie lyrique*: closer to the declamatory style of French spoken theater than Italian opera, and striving for a complete balance of operatic expression.

Lima, Peru
1701

Paris
1674

THE LIBRETTO

The word *libretto* translates as "little book"—as if the role of the author needs any further diminution in the eyes of the audience, who tend to focus on the composer. Although opera is collaborative, we often attribute the work primarily to the composer—it's Strauss's *Elektra* or Verdi's *Otello*, with no mention of the formative influences of Hugo von Hofmannsthal or Arrigo Boito. The convention is so ingrained that I fall into the trap myself throughout this book!

The librettist doesn't efface themselves to make way for the composer; they offer a powerful piece of poetry that holds its own with the music. Rather than follow formulaic structures of the well-made play or the effective screenplay, libretti create new forms based on the myriad musical forms the composer may wish to apply. They take full advantage of opera's strangeness and singularity. The ideal text is an inspiration for interdependence.

1724

The Roman classicist and poet Pietro Metastasio writes a libretto entitled *Didone abbandonata*, which will be set by sixty different composers over the next century.

Metastasio becomes the exemplar of a new form later known as *opera seria* ("serious opera," as opposed to the empty bombast of so much other opera). He rejects the operatic landscape of his time as beholden to spectacle, content with nonsensical plots and characters. He turns to Aristotelean notions of dramaturgy to rein in a theater gone wild: ennobling rather than lascivious subject matter; unity of time and place, to restrict opera producers from over-the-top scene changes; and, wherever possible, a happy ending.

Metastasio later becomes the imperial court poet in Vienna's Burgtheater and oversees the staging of operatic works. As is so often the case with reformers, he settles into a form of conservatism and rigidity: what at first brings fresh possibilities soon reiterates its own status quo.

Christoph Willibald von Gluck's *Orfeo ed Euridice* opens in Vienna. **See PLAYLIST**

If the threat of stage spectacle overwhelming dramatic logic motivated Metastasio to rethink the libretto, Gluck in his time wants to make sure the perceived excess of star singers showing off vocal acrobatics is reined in. He forces the focus onto music and language, serving as his own stage director to ensure the singers don't take liberties. Variation in orchestration and the more active engagement of chorus emphasize the music's ability to capture dramatic changes.

His reform involves a fair amount of "looking back" to opera's origins, since the "beautiful simplicity" he is after was already a central tenet of Monteverdi's *Orfeo*. Although he has the reputation of a great reformer, Gluck himself admits, "I have not deemed discovery of new things praiseworthy in itself when not called for naturally by the expression and the situation."

1762

Charleston, South Carolina

1735

John Gay's *The Beggar's Opera*—mostly a stage play but incorporating popular ballads and the operatic music of George Frideric Handel—is a sensation that launches a new genre called "ballad opera."

A ballad opera called *Flora* becomes the first opera to be produced in the colonies of North America—and British cultural hegemony finds a foothold in a key center of the transatlantic slave trade.

London

1728

THE FINE ARTS Theatre
OPENING NOVEMBER 6
Matinees · Wednesday and Saturday

THE BEGGAR'S OPERA BY Mr Gay

THE FIRST AND BEST MUSICAL PLAY
1728 — 1921
DIRECT FROM LONDON AFTER ITS TWO YEAR'S RUN

1792

New Orleans

The Théâtre St. Pierre opens with plays, comedies and vaudeville. On May 22, 1796, the first documented staging of an opera in New Orleans takes place: André Ernest Grétry's *Sylvain*. Opera in the Francophile city flourishes.

Vienna

Mozart opens a curious Singspiel at Emanuel Schikaneder's Theater auf der Wieden. In its mix of "high" and "low" entertainment, *The Magic Flute* continues to inspire adoration and confusion.

see PLAYLIST

1986

X: The Life and Times of Malcolm X by Anthony Davis, Thulani Davis, and Christopher Davis premieres at the New York City Opera.

HYBRIDITY

In his documentary on the history of jazz, Ken Burns recounts the unexpected impact of a tenor singing Rossini in New Orleans. For Black artists, barred entry to the opera house, the voice they heard wafting onto the streets spurred them on to mimic the sound with cornet horns. The "singing" of the jazz trumpet was born, with opera layering into an intoxicating mix of voodoo ritual and Congo Square drum circles to create America's truest musical expression.

It's an uncomfortable image of separation that still feels true today: the opera house came to America as a fortress closed to real cultural exchange, with musical inspiration as hierarchical and "top-down." Since then, jazz, popular music, and opera have followed divergent tracks in this country. How different opera could have been in this country if those tracks intersected and the boundary between genres was more porous: if the theater was open to everybody, and if those cornet players were invited to participate in an exchange with the Italian import. What would have happened if they intentionally explored the potentiality for fusion and transformation? How much vigor did opera lose when it preened its exclusivity inside the theater while the music of the street continued to captivate the world?

Lorenzo da Ponte—the librettist of three of Mozart's masterpieces—opens the Italian Opera House for his New York Opera Company. At 84 years old, da Ponte is a tireless educator and advocate for Italian culture in his adopted country; it's due to his efforts that Americans still identify opera as an Italian art form. This theater is the first building dedicated to opera in the city, and although it only lasted two seasons, it became a precursor to the Academy of Music and the Metropolitan Opera.

New York
1833

TRADITION & INNOVATION

My favorite anecdote from John Cage: a European composer asked Cage, who was living in Los Angeles, "Isn't it difficult for you writing serious music so far from the center?" (Meaning, presumably, Europe.) Cage replied: "Isn't it difficult for you writing serious music so close to the center?" $\rightarrow$

1981

Inspired by the Black tenor Charles Holland's performance of the aria "O Souverain" from Jules Massenet's 1885 opera *El Cid*, conceptual artist Laurie Anderson uses the melody to create a song that captures the alien allure of American culture. "O Souverain" becomes Americanized as "O Superman," as Anderson transforms her speaking and singing voice with the hypnotic deployment of a vocoder. The song becomes a surprise popular sensation worldwide, reaching number 2 in the UK singles chart.

See PLAYLIST

O SUPERMAN

EP · 45

LAURIE ANDERSON

1975

A watershed year for opera on film: Ingmar Bergman's cinematic adaptation of *Magic Flute* and Jean-Marie Straub and Danièle Huillet's *Moses und Aron* set the benchmark for transforming opera from one medium to another.

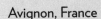

Bayreuth, Germany

Patrice Chereau's centennial production of Wagner's *Ring*, with Pierre Boulez conducting, explicitly draws out the Marxist underpinning of the work and provokes the frightening ire of staunchly traditional "Wagnerians" incensed at the liberties taken in this retelling of the original. In Germany, the operatic elite draws a skirmish line to distinguish *Werktreue*, an elusive concept of being true to the work, and *Regietheater*, productions where directorial license is paramount.

1976

Avignon, France

On the same day that Chereau's *Ring* production opens, *Einstein on the Beach*, a new opera by composer Philip Glass, director Robert Wilson, and choreographer Lucinda Childs premieres. With no conventional narrative form or characters and running five hours without intermission, it remains one of the most original "mold-breakers" in opera's history.

See PLAYLIST

Los Angeles, California
1969

San Francisco, California
1965

The premiere of composer Harry Partch's last stage work, *Delusions of the Fury*, a music-theater piece based on Japanese Noh drama and performed on instruments invented by the composer.

See PLAYLIST

Self-described as a "a philosophic music-man seduced into carpentry," Partch feels compelled to build an array of instruments that extends the traditional Western scale, in pursuit of micro-shadings within the traditional 12-tone system. His works (which he prefers to call "ritual" rather than "opera") strive for total integration: he expects each performer to sing, dance, play instruments, and take on speaking parts.

Re-purposing a record of Puccini's *Madama Butterfly* lying about in the studio of the San Francisco Tape Music Center, composer and sound artist Pauline Oliveros incorporates the famous "Entrance of Butterfly" scene into a two-channel composition. The eight-minute work, *Bye Bye Butterfly*, marks an early milestone in the history of electronic music.

See PLAYLIST

As Oliveros puts it, the piece "bids farewell not only to the music of the nineteenth century but also to the system of polite morality of that age and its attendant institutionalized oppression of the female sex."

Paris
1829

Gioachino Rossini's *Guillaume Tell* premieres. It turns out to be Rossini's last opera, although he continued living nearly forty more years. For some, Rossini marks the pinnacle of opera, with its emphasis on *bel canto* singing. (*Bel canto*, like the word *opera* itself, is only retroactively used to describe a singing style—and later an era— where beauty of tone and virtuosity outweigh content and drama.) The demand for new operas is so high that composers are pressured to churn out new titles as quickly as can be—even if that means repurposi old music or overlooking serious lapses in dramaturgical development

1964

NBC Opera Theatre televises its final production: Donizetti's *bel canto* classic *Lucia di Lammermoor*. The intrepid initiative to broadcast live performances, in an effort to bridge "high" and "popular" cultures, brought opera into homes starting in 1949.

1956

Maria Callas appears on *The Ed Sullivan Show* performing "Vissi d'arte" from Puccini's *Tosca*, singing directly into the camera and offering an Oscar-worthy performance. Opera was featured in more than 1,000 episodes and "brought opera to 80 million living rooms," according to Robert Merrill.

TRADITION & INNOVATION *(continued)*

← Cage prioritizes the *peripheral*, just as innovations in other fields often begin from an outlier position. The most exciting and original operas in America did not start at major opera houses; they emerged from composers who did not wait to be invited into the establishment to find their own voices. This industriousness is a hallmark of the most experimental of American composers—Robert Ashley, Meredith Monk, Harry Partch, Pauline Oliveros, Lou Harrison, Philip Glass, Julius Eastman, to name just a few intrepid artists who either created their own ensembles or their own instruments to realize their ideas. Of those names, several have successfully infiltrated "the center"—which regularly happens to those on the periphery. In time, they become tradition.

To anyone who fears that tradition is suffocating opera, the answer is clear: keep the pipeline to the periphery open, and both sides will receive the oxygen they need.

6

THE USE-LESS ART

THE ECONOMICS OF OPERA

WHEN DETROIT OPERA REOPENED ITS THEATER IN 2022 with my production of *La bohème*, the company was still grappling with one of the unspoken truisms of the pandemic: "Opera is nonessential."

Whatever mask of self-importance opera wore prior to Covid-19, it was ripped away and replaced with KN95s. If we thought the work we were doing offered meaning and value to people's lives, the shuttering of every opera house and the stacks of canceled contracts made one thing clear: it wasn't valuable enough. I certainly don't disagree with the measures taken to protect the safety of artists, staff, and audiences, but it was eye-opening to see how easy forgoing opera was for many; some even seemed relieved that the duties of enduring resolutely unentertaining evenings faced indefinite suspension.

As we cautiously planned *Bohème*, fearing a new viral surge all the while, Covid tests suddenly became scarce. An article in *The Atlantic* cited Dr. Walid Gellad's concerns that tests were being wasted on frivolous pursuits: "We don't want our limited testing supply tied up by people who just want to know [their status] so they can visit their friends or go to the opera." To drive the point home, Gellad's quote became *The Atlantic*'s Instagram tile, turning the disparagement of opera into a meme.

It was hard for those of us who make our living or derive deep meaning from opera not to take this personally. My own way of grappling with a sense of superfluousness was to somehow make a virtue of it. I grew to understand that opera, like all great art, is inherently use-less.

That is sure to sound insulting, especially in our consumer culture, where everything must have a use, including us. (Especially us.) Our entire way of being is so centered on consuming that even use-lessness has its use: as a diversion, as rest in between our useful stints as a working cog in the machine.

Use-lessness should not be confused with meaninglessness; as discussed in Chapter Four, opera has an overwhelming capacity to hold meaning in multitudes. And it is opera's very resistance to reducibility—to meaning just one thing—that frustrates any discussion of function. Plenty of unintentional, potentially useful consequences may emerge from our encounter with a work of art: a change of perspective, a new understanding of an emotion that confuses us, a resolve to be more politically engaged. But that's different from having a prescribed *use*, in the Brechtian sense of art acting as a hammer to shape the world with. A useful tool is one-size-fits-all and a means to an end, and the more we judge art based on its intended result, the closer it gets to the kind of consumerist view that art is better at subverting than serving.

In 1933, the French playwright and theoretician Antonin Artaud wrote a bracing manifesto entitled "The Theater and the Plague," which I reread during the Covid lockdown. Artaud describes a plague as having a disintegrating effect on both the body and society—but also possessing a beneficial power of revelation and transformation beneficial to humanity. Describing the chaos brought about by a plague, Artaud writes, "The dregs of the population, apparently immunized by their frenzied greed, enter the open houses and pillage riches they know will serve no purpose or profit. And at that moment the theater is born. The theater, i.e., an immediate gratuitousness provoking acts without use or profit."

Art is not a tool; it's not a medium for something else to happen. It contains its own totality. To call it *use-less* is not to dismiss art but to celebrate it. And despite all efforts to position itself at the height of the cultural hierarchy, opera is the most use-less art form of all: the most complicated, the least commercially viable, the least reified. It is the telescope-as-kaleidoscope, an instrument built not for the purpose of clear vision but for the proliferation of possibilities. To reduce opera to a function is to miss what makes it inimitable.

To love opera means to love its impracticality.

// // // // //

AS AN ENORMOUSLY EXPENSIVE ENDEAVOR that exists only in the moment of its performance, opera faces an impossible economic position in this country. Most arts organizations here are nonprofit entities, equivalent to charitable organizations held afloat by grants and donations from private patrons. These worthy causes are given the privilege of not paying taxes for their quixotism—that is, for pursuing a mission instead of chasing profit. Naturally, what may appear as a legislated generosity toward organizations defying the demands of the marketplace is ultimately a classic capitalist move, where a contrasting perspective is co-opted to strengthen hegemony. If alternatives to capitalism can be regulated and codified, then the dominant system can continue effectively unchallenged. Artists working in this alternative, noncommercial sector are expected to take on the ethos of poverty and sacrifice demanded by the company; we must stay in our place and remain grateful, never demanding improvements to how we work or what we earn.

Nonprofit status, a designation that predates the U.S. Constitution, has seen little development since the Revenue Act of 1917 encouraged donations by making them tax-deductible. And because American opera companies operate exclusively in this nonprofit mode, categorized with homeless shelters and soup kitchens, they go on the defensive. They are forced to prove they have a function in our society—or, in classic nonprofit speak, they "serve the community," an arrogant euphemism for offering handouts to the deprived. For a use-less art form like opera to demonstrate a quantifiable quotient of usefulness requires elaborate workarounds.

Education departments have proved the most successful workaround. There is much to admire in the way organizations have filled the void of American arts education, through programming that runs parallel to what happens onstage. And, as one of the most effective demonstrations of usefulness, an education department becomes the easiest part of the company to fund. But once opera seems relevant as a service, what happens to the art? To put it bluntly, the works themselves start becoming secondary, a parasite on a useful organization. Because they have so little ability to sustain themselves, opera productions need to be as financially contained as possible. How could you possibly justify spending so much money for an art with *no prescribed use*?

But arts organizations face a paradox that humanitarian nonprofits don't: they are also subject to the same pressures as their commercial counterparts. An opera company competes with charities on one side and the profit machines of Broadway and Hollywood on the other. This situation became evident to me when an executive from MGM Films came to see my production of Christopher Cerrone's *Invisible Cities,* presented by the independent company I founded in Los Angeles, The Industry. We scheduled around twenty performances for a limited audience of 200 per show. The executive, who confessed to "hating opera" but loving this production, admitted that he couldn't understand how a company like mine worked. "You would have to run for years before you start seeing a return," he correctly observed. However, there was simply *no way* we could see a return; even if we extended and ran for years, the cost of any one performance was way higher than anything we could earn on ticket sales. (We would have had to price the tickets at $2,500 apiece just to break even, rather than the more accessibly priced $50 we were charging.) "I don't get it," the executive said, "how are you supposed to make money?" I explained how my company's nascent nonprofit status worked, and that nothing about the endeavor was geared toward a profit margin; donations from foundations and individuals made up the difference between costs and revenue. The executive kept pushing: "But why would anyone invest money if it's a losing proposition?"

That's when I understood that even for people savvy in the business of producing art/entertainment, our work is perceived not as a social service like a nonprofit's but rather as the equivalent to other commercial enterprises. This executive operated among people investing in films or musicals as an altruistic alternative to the stock market: if you lose money, at least you've supported artistic creation along the way. Once again, art becomes *useful* as a commodity, with the surplus benefit of signifying an investor's values—an intangible way to mitigate any potential loss. Opera, orchestra, dance, and nonprofit theater companies work entirely differently from the dominant commercial model; there are no investments, only donations, an inevitable financial loss.

The most pernicious aspects of commercial art-making impact opera's mission-driven work. Chief among them: the expectation that all commercial live art must obey the dictate of "giving the audience what it wants." This manifests itself in the traditionalist perspective that defines most American opera companies, where "what the audience wants" usually means presenting opera the way they have come to know and expect it. The audience, the assumption goes, wants their powdered wigs and their livestock during triumphant marches, and they will grow irate at any creative intervention. They won't want to see *Bohème* in any way other than how they have always seen it. Thus the prevailing mandate at most opera companies is to pacify the tradition-bound.

While Hollywood films spend millions on market research and test audiences, opera companies don't tend to listen to a broad cross-section of society when it comes to making artistic decisions. They listen primarily to the voices of the donors who keep the organization alive, and to the company's board of directors—a governing body of powerful volunteers, required by U.S. tax law, usually comprising a company's most generous donors. In other words, our government's mechanism of nonprofits, devised to support selfless sacrifice for the common good, has created unspoken oligarchies within our democracy. An opera company's constant fear is the ever-present possibility that displeased donors, disliking what they see onstage, decide not to renew their generous donations next year. So the showbiz mantra "Give [the audience] what [it] [wants]" is better articulated as, "Give *[the entire population of this city]* what *[a small percentage of wealthy individuals] [knows]*."

What organization, under that kind of pressure, would venture something risky? Lucky the opera company whose largest donors are truly selfless; who donate not to attend galas or patron lounges; who don't attempt to influence the artistic output; who realize that they donate to maintain an institution and not to see only what they know and understand. Lucky . . . and rare.

A new opera written today faces the strongest pull of a company's commercial yoke. In desperate attempts to prove "relevance," companies tend to develop projects based on success in other media. You can almost see the marketing copy now: "If you liked the film *The Silence of the Lambs*, you'll love it as an opera!" Noble examples have certainly resulted from an earnest interest in transporting the work of one genre into another—but they are often accompanied by pandering and cynicism, as if chosen for their marketing potential rather than artistic merit. The mantra in this case would be: "Give the audience what they wanted at the movie theater, but slower, longer, more expensive, and less entertaining."

It's difficult for a new opera to capture the exegesis of the moment; the long gestation of the creative process can always make it seem behind the times. A three-year process to commission and produce a single opera would be considered "lightning speed" in today's opera world. Compare that with the rapid turnaround times composers were expected to adhere to in, say, the early nineteenth century—Gaetano Donizetti, who completed sixty-five operas in fifty years, would often sign contracts requiring him to produce four operas a year—and you can begin to understand why so many large-scale operatic commissions today tend to be over-thought, overwrought, and lacking in the spark of spontaneity that makes great art. Unlike theater, literature, or the visual arts, opera can only respond to major currents in social life with a significant latency.

My reaction to this conflicted state of opera, especially since Covid, has become: Why do we so desperately pose as the equivalent to commercial forms of entertainment instead of simply being who we are? Opera has never adhered to the beauty standards erected by mass media. It fits uneasily, if at all, with the rapid demands of the attention economy. It feels completely out of place with how we consume other art. So a perceived competition with the conformity and profitability of commercial art can only be at opera's expense.

The "American way" of producing opera, with its emphasis on glamour, glitz, and showbiz economics, defeated the late, great opera impresario Gerard Mortier, a Belgian producer whose 2007 appointment as General Director of New York City Opera was over before it began. He withdrew from the position in 2008, before his first season, when he realized how much resistance his vision of opera would face within a mold predicated so strongly on marketplace appeal. I was working at City Opera at the time, and I've never forgotten how he responded to doubts about his program's appeal to the tried-and-true operagoer. "We cannot merely offer the audience what it thinks it wants. Instead, we have an opportunity to give them something they never even knew they needed." I've never heard the true mission of this art form articulated better.

Opera in America now sits in the crosshairs of our consumerist machine. No wonder it struggles at the same time for relevance (from the marketplace perspective) and financial feasibility (from the charitable/cultural perspective). Seasons are based either on the assumption of what an audience will buy (i.e., Hollywood commercialism) or on the worthy purposes of a charitable organization (i.e., works primarily created for one, and usually only one, designated use). No wonder the art form feels so directionless in this country—and no wonder every company tries to justify its own existence through signs of usefulness.

There must surely be a way out of this gulf between the nonprofit and the commercial.

A couple of theater companies—the New York Theatre Workshop and Public Theater in New York City—have hit on a hybrid producing model, where works first developed in a nonprofit way go on to a commercial production on Broadway and then on tour. The profits earned from the most successful shows (like the musical *Hamilton*) are channeled back into the nonprofit arm to support other endeavors. This is an intriguing avenue for opera to consider, although there is an aspect of it that I haven't figured out: what part of opera could be leveraged for profit? If opera is the art form most resistant to reification, that also means it has the least to offer toward monetization.

Instead, I now believe that opera's only hope is to somehow escape both modes. If the nonprofit mode has reduced the actual art to a secondary activity, and the commercial mode requires dependence on the latest fashion, then we must discover a different way to cultivate the peculiar use-lessness of opera if we want to see it thrive.

Changing opera's business model may seem like a back-end concern, but the confused expectations around opera's place in America's entertainment market is directly impacting the art-making. It will take creativity and imagination to figure out a new way forward, and it will require artistic minds to get involved in the nonartistic aspects of creating opera.

// // // // //

FOUNDING AND RUNNING MY OWN nonprofit opera company has turned me into more of a salesman than I anticipated. I was aware that some administrative effort would be a necessary evil for facilitating my artistry. Little did I know I would become a round-the-clock hustler for the vision I was trying to bring into the world. Artists in the live arts today, lacking the patronage of a museum or other institution, are somehow expected to be both a charitable self-sacrificing saint (in the nonprofit mode) and a no-holds-barred entrepreneur (in the commercial mode). I'm sure that demand has silenced the best artists, the ones who could have truly changed our perception of the world. I'm also sure it has led to the ascension of artists savvy at working the system but who may have less to offer.

Thinking of this irresolvable tension, unsure where exactly I am on that spectrum between worlds, I'm reminded of producing *Hopscotch* with The Industry—an opera we tended to call "a mobile opera for 24 cars." The gist of the piece was that four audience members at a time would drive through Los Angeles experiencing the operas in twenty-four geographically conditioned chapters, sharing a car with performers and undergoing a round-trip drift through the city. (I will discuss the piece in more detail in Chapter Nine.) To make something like this happen, I would need to rally an enormous troop of support for the project—not just financial support or civic support but also in-kind support, like *pro bono* use of technology that would otherwise be out of reach for an independent, small-budget company.

So I put on my salesman hat and drove to Las Vegas to attend the world's largest technology convention, called the Consumer Electronics Show, or CES. I went there to follow up in person on conversations I'd started with a company that specialized in real-time video streaming with no delay. The technology, pioneered for major sporting events, held the key for realizing one of my dreams for *Hopscotch*: I wanted each scene taking place around LA to be streamed back to a central location, allowing a secondary audience (not in cars) to watch the pieces simultaneously as they happened throughout the city. I wanted a zero-latency stream to capture real time as truthfully as possible, screening exactly what was happening all over Los Angeles with precision. One scene in particular involved a phone call between two women, each in separate cars, where I hoped a delay-free live stream could offer the sense of a proper dialogue between them from a vantage point beyond both vehicles.

The technology that can accomplish this feat, used regularly for broadcast television, entails a highly specialized use of satellites in space rather than more conventional communication lines (read: *very* expensive). Any hope of achieving this within our budget required the enthusiastic buy-in of a company who could get on board with our nonprofit mentality. There was some reason to believe this was possible. The audio company Sennheiser had provided generous in-kind support for *Invisible Cities,* and they agreed to help us with *Hopscotch* as well. Sennheiser not only showed genuine curiosity about the projects' technical challenges, they also justified their donation as research. The meaningful exchange I had with them made me optimistic going into my Las Vegas meeting.

Granted, the setting was not exactly right for this kind of pitch:

massive commercial forums such as CES are clearly meant for high-level partnerships far beyond the stakes of small nonprofit arts organizations. In a showroom buzzing with salespeople and aglow in rapidly changing LED screens, like Times Square and the Wall Street stock exchange compressed into one jumbled exhibition hall, I sought out the company specializing in zero-latency streaming. I had been hounding their president for weeks via e-mail, finally receiving what I should have known was a brush-off: "I'm too busy to talk now, but if you come to CES, I will be happy to hear more about your project." I could see the disappointment in his eyes when I introduced myself and reminded him about our correspondence. Now he was forced to sacrifice lucrative time to listen to a profit-less idea for a "mobile opera." Seeing no escape, he sat down with me and let me pitch him on the project. I wasn't far into my description of the project before I noticed the quizzical, eyebrow-raised stare I had come to expect whenever I tried describing my work-in-progress. But when I got to the part about a simultaneous stream of twenty-four cars with no delay in sound or video, he stopped me and asked with considerable consternation, *"Why are you doing this?"*

I was completely caught off-guard; no one had ever asked me that question. I stuttered some tried-and-true platitude about the role of art in society, but whatever words came out failed to mask the insecurity provoked by his question. The meeting didn't last much longer and ended with a handshake and that classic American rejection: "Good luck to you!"

The drive between Las Vegas and Los Angeles is long and monotonous; at night, when you can't see the desert landscape around you, it can feel as though you're hurtling into an endless black hole. It's a perfect setting for replaying something over and over in your head. In this case, it was *"Why are you doing this?"* In the hyped-up, accelerated commercial environment of that conference, I was compelled to reach for a purpose, something easy to understand and translate into marketable value, for the very impractical thing I was pursuing. Even if the mismatch of perspectives was easy to shake off, the question wasn't. Why *was* I doing this?

Maybe driving allowed me space to meditate on that question, but it was on the road that I turned over something like an answer. I thought back to a scene in Leos Carax's surreal 2012 film *Holy Motors,* one of my favorites and an inspiration for *Hopscotch.* The film follows a man who gets in and out of a white limousine throughout the day, taking on various guises and performing in different film genres at each destination. The film's stylistic shape-shifting is bewildering and unpredictable, gleefully resisting logical reduction at every turn. His faithful driver engages with him in existential dialogue throughout, and at one point she asks him, "What do you do this all for?" His simple, perfect reply: "The beauty of the act."

I wish I had remembered it in Las Vegas when I was confronted with that same question. What better way is there to summarize an artist's reason for doing what they do? If we leave meaning in the hands of the spectator rather than the artist ("The death of the author is the birth of the reader"), then it should be the spectator—not the producer and not the creator—who should decide what "use," if any, an artwork can offer. Ideally, the spectator might realize that the search for usefulness is a knee-jerk reaction our marketplace economy tries to cultivate in us. Let art offer us an escape, a precious pocket in time where that voice is silenced.

Opera's use-lessness is, to some, the reason for its absurdity. I think it is opera's absolute incongruity with everything around it that opens up pathways of possibility—precisely when our consumerist sense of reality wants us to believe that no new possibilities exist. This is why I consider opera a rebellious, misfit art and not a standard bearer; in its lack of a singular use, opera can offer alternatives to any structure limiting our understanding of the world. Each individual spectator can decide on a work's meaning and value to them; let artists concentrate instead on the beauty, the audacity, and the boldness of acting in the face of use-lessness.

7

TOWARD AN
ANTI-ELITE OPERA

IS OPERA A STANDARD BEARER OR A PALLBEARER OF THE status quo?

Most aficionados subscribe to the former—the notion that opera, in its grandeur and refinement, represents a pearl of cultural production. Going to the opera, as *Pretty Woman* illustrates, signals classiness and affirms that everything is in its right place.

I have never looked to opera for affirmation of anything, certainly not for recognition of my taste's superiority over anyone else's. But among a typical audience at an opera, you can usually find no small number of people seeking precisely that kind of confirmation. They prefer to preserve opera as a signifier for self-serving virtues rather than a viable and contemporary mode of expression. That reduction of opera to its economic signifier—despite all use-lessness—is suffocating the art form and keeping it from realizing its possibilities. What a terrible thing to happen to work with so much still to say.

Advocating for opera's use-lessness is an offensive against one of its most common historic uses: for the adornment of authority and the entrenchment of the existing social hierarchy. As a private event in the Italian courts, opera offered a spare-no-expense theatricality that projected the power and wealth of the work's supporting patrons. Spectacle was a form of political justification, and extravagance became self-serving. The equating of display and dominance seeped into opera's DNA.

But as opera morphed from private to public entertainment, the pageantry stopped affirming a powerful patron and instead started adulating the audience. The spectator's elevated position, their own superior status, became the locus of the work's glory. Abbate and Parker describe early opera settings, especially regal interiors, as "flattering the audience by involving them in a world of unabashed magnificence." Even today, operatic spectacle holds up a sycophantic mirror to its audience, fulfilling their desire to see themselves reflected back in opulence. (Maybe this is the reason audiences still applaud the scenery when the curtain rises.)

That's opera as standard bearer of the status quo. What if opera were its pallbearer instead?

Is it even possible to imagine the art form today, created through the surplus wealth of philanthropists, as *challenging* our understanding of the state of things? For defiance and resistance to earn a place in the genre's identity, the opera world will have to kill, once and for all, any association with a concept that seems central now: *elitism*.

Most everyone's first experience with opera brushes up against some form of elitism, harking back to Parsifal's chastisement for "not getting it." For me, the jarring experience of attending the San Francisco Opera as a student at UC Berkeley still casts a shadow over how I think about opera. Back then, I had to take a grimy BART train to the Civic Center Station and walk through an unhoused community gathered on the street. The cacophony of sights, sounds, and smells never failed to make me deeply pessimistic about the state of our society (was it irony or accuracy that led to this plaza's being named the civic center?). After making my way through a truly gruesome spectacle, I arrived at the opera house, whose architecture demands you ascend a grand stairway flanked by columns to enter the theater (named the "War Memorial Opera House") and escape from real life. Its gold and velvet interior reinforced the feeling of a gilded cage, physically and aesthetically protected from the outside world. At twenty, having taken the train and walked the street, I couldn't connect with a space that so flagrantly displayed its callousness. Opera aspires to integrate every imaginable art and craft. Yet attending one, with the jarring shifts of reality, can make you feel fractured, incongruous, and isolated.

On one particularly egregious evening, the opera I saw was Alban Berg's *Wozzeck,* an emotionally devastating work from 1922 about an impoverished couple and the social mechanisms that gripped them in a cycle of crime and destitution. The title character, in a tormented first aria (SEE PLAYLIST), sings:

> *We poor folks! Look, Captain sir, money, money—try setting someone with no money on the moral path! Each one of us has their flesh and blood! Sure, if I were a gentleman, with a hat and watch and monocle, I would speak nobly.... I've always wanted to be virtuous! There must be something beautiful about virtue, Captain sir. But I'm just a poor guy! Our kind is unlucky in this and the next world! I think, if we made it to heaven, we'd have to manufacture the thunder!*

As Wozzeck sang, I found it hard to concentrate: the elegant older woman next to me couldn't sit still and repeatedly shook her arms to adjust her golden bracelets. The jangling added unwanted percussion to the score and covered Wozzeck's singing . . . though she didn't seem to be listening anyway. I had my issues with the performance—the clichéd stylization of the stagecraft and the hollow, routine acting—but the hypocrisy of the experience, especially after traversing a dystopian streetscape of shameful civic neglect, marked a breaking point for me. The evening is fixed in my memory as a critical inspiration for getting involved in opera as a director. Berg's musical realization of his poor couple's inner world could actually do so much to motivate us all to imagine a better, more just society. But that night, his opera's potential couldn't be heard over the clang of expensive jewelry and the dissonance with our world.

I may not come from wealth myself, as a first generation American and the grandchild of Holocaust survivors. But I have no chip on my shoulder with regard to successful individuals, especially those who give their money away to make art and culture happen. For all I know, the list-less woman with the bracelets may have been a benefactor of the opera. Maybe she even underwrote that night's performance. Or perhaps she was tired after a long day trying to improve San Francisco's "civic center."

It's the *catering* to wealth that causes the problem. Companies beholden to the well-off self-select a position of fear. Unwritten rules govern the art: Nothing onstage must challenge our patrons' position, nor must anything rattle the wealthy. Bend the programming to what they find familiar, comforting, and reassuring. This mentality has tipped the scales toward one population, toward elitism, and away from any other potential audience.

Opera in America has every incentive to adhere to the status quo—mostly for a sense of security that those paying the company's bills will continue to do so. But the illusion of predictable stability lulls people into laziness. Companies and producers settle into a clear-cut transactional attitude between the art and its patrons. Soon, the operas being selected and the ideas behind the productions are viewed through the lens of whether the benefactors will give a "thumbs up" or "thumbs down" with their checkbooks. Opera's potential as a critical or transformational voice faces myriad barriers long before the first rehearsal.

The effect on artists and the art itself is profound. The pressures a producer feels to please the people paying for an artwork almost invariably trickle down to the artists themselves. When they show up to a first rehearsal of a new production, will they be encouraged to strike out in new directions, to give voice to a fresh perspective that might not immediately appeal broadly? Or will they be urged to position their work within the trajectory of acceptable expression, laid down by the endless repetitions of canonical works?

It's useful here to compare Berg's opera about the poor and down-trodden with Puccini's opera that is, ostensibly, also about poverty:

La bohème, populated by starving artists outwitting the one percent of nineteenth-century Paris. One of these works remains the most popular opera of all time, while the other is still considered "challenging." Puccini cloaks his beggars in luxurious and seductive sounds, arias and duets that are ravishing and live in your head for days. Singers' voices are borne on a pillow of orchestral sound with vocal lines frequently doubled by the string section. Despite poverty, sickness, and death, Puccini's music embodies the affirmation of an ultimate harmony, and productions of *Bohème* invariably transform the characters' poverty into luxury. Rodolfo and Marcello are meant to reside in a tiny, ramshackle garret with no heat and past-due rent. But on the typical stage, their living quarters are usually blown up to seem like the most enviable penthouse in Paris. All in all, their hardships are portrayed as pleasantly and warm-heartedly as possible, and even the suffering seems sweet.

Berg's vision of poverty, on the other hand, is an expressionistic swirl of orchestral colors that often confronts the singers with an antagonistic field, a fitting mirror of an individual's struggle against a cruel society. Wozzeck dies by drowning in his last scene, but from his very first aria he is frequently swimming against an overwhelming sonic tide. Unlike Puccini's comforting blanket of sound, Berg wrote music that perfectly fits Adorno's image from *Minima Moralia*: "The splinter in your eye is the best magnifying glass." Puccini's score is a fitting capstone to the nineteenth century's development of opera, while Berg's score marks a radical advancement of musical language, taking opera in new directions in the twentieth century.

The comparison can stand for much new work that wants to be socially engaged or critical. Even as producers put a lot of resources into the development of a new work, they encourage creators to strike a chord in the pleasing direction of Puccini. The more a new opera is meant to sound like an old one (read: from the nineteenth century), the more it's likely to please the people who are paying for it to happen. Social critique remains in the realm of the written word, to be read in the supertitles but not viscerally felt in the music. Few composers today are encouraged to move in Berg's direction—not specifically in relation to atonality, which at this point is over 100 years old, but in the spirit of pushing musical language forward and finding an analogous musical expression for uncomfortable truths. To discover new and different aural ideas that express the need for an altered perspective of our society.

A prime example of a completely new-sounding opera is *X: The Life and Times of Malcolm X* (1986), music by the prolific and polyglot Anthony Davis to a libretto by Thulani Davis and a story by Christopher Davis. Surely a work on such a revolutionary subject can't be expected to fit easily into the accustomed language of opera! Just as Malcolm X introduced powerful new language to articulate America's racism, Davis's score expands opera's vocabulary. Its New York City Opera premiere showcased a large and mostly Black cast, with a full orchestra augmented by an eight-piece improvising jazz ensemble. The fiendishly difficult score veers from high modernism through R&B—not like a mindless turning of the radio dial, but as a dizzying enactment of double consciousness. A virulent aria for Malcolm X closes Act I by turning the spotlight on the audience (SEE PLAYLIST). "You want the story, but you don't want to know," he sings. "My truth is, you've been on me a very long time, longer than I can say! As long as I've been living, you've had your foot on me, always pressing. . . . You want the truth, but you don't want to know!" It's hard to imagine anything less "flattering" to the traditional opera audience than this searing indictment of our complicity with systems of oppression.

Davis's vocal writing is demanding and virtuosic, with unpredictable and unrelenting rhythms. His musical ideas seem built on repetition, but they are constantly shifting in volatile ways, embodying an idea of Black music that the poet Amiri Baraka called "the changing same." The concept is far from a detached aesthetic idea; it embodies the specific cultural perspective, the "exact replication of The Black Man in the West," Baraka described in his 1966 essay "The Changing Same (R&B and New Black Music)." The interplay between individual performer and collectivity Baraka writes about could just as easily describe what Davis's opera is really about: not just the famous man who became Malcolm X but his entire "life and times." "We want different contents and different forms because we have different feelings," Baraka writes. "We are different peoples."

Inviting this worldview into the narrow world of opera, into the hallowed halls of Lincoln Center, was a gutsy endeavor. But since its premiere, *X* has rarely been heard from again. Mounting a new production became my top priority when I became Artistic Director of Detroit Opera in 2020. Not only because the subject matter had taken on renewed urgency in the heat of the racial reckoning of that summer. Not only because Detroit is a predominantly Black city and Malcolm X's footprints there are still fresh in the ground. But because the music, like the human life at the work's center, confronts the status quo. At the opening of our production, directed by Robert O'Hara, the company's traditional operagoers were challenged by the score's "changing same" style. Not so the Black members of the audience, many of whom reported attending an opera for the first time. And the attendance was record-breaking: *X* was the first sold-out opera performance in Detroit since 2005, when the company premiered a new opera based on Toni Morrison's *Beloved*.

In its scale, *X* is a grand opera to rival the largest works in the repertoire. But in its deft handling of explosive subject matter and uncompromising musical character, *X* carries none of the elitism we ascribe to the canon. It remains to me an example of what a new piece should be, the epitome of an anti-elite opera.

// // // // //

A REDDIT THREAD WITH THE prompt "Why is opera considered elitist?" offers some hilarious illuminations:

> *"Pulls out gilded opera glasses:* Because those with such opinions are cretins."
>
> "I don't know, but it's certainly nice to have an entertainment where you don't have to mingle with hoi-polloi."
>
> "Because nobody likes it, so the entitled people enjoy the fact that they have a differing opinion."

Some users, opting for a less humorous commentary, blame "exorbitantly expensive" opera tickets: the art form is elitist because only the wealthy can afford to enjoy it. But opera's admission prices are not particularly outrageous when you compare them with sporting events, Broadway musicals, or stadium shows. In fact, most houses sell tickets at a much cheaper cost than the average baseball game. Price is quantifiable, but far harder to quantify is the *attitude* of elitism that permeates opera.

If a certain snobbery emerges from a conspicuous coddling to the wealthy, an elitist attitude can also be felt among the so-called aficionados, opera's most discerning and erudite spectators, separated from the plebeians in their cultivation and knack for distinguishing the good from the bad. While a "less educated" audience may enjoy a performance, the cultured connoisseurs need to flaunt their wisdom and status. They are the first to be outraged at the liberties taken by the stage director, or disgusted at how an artist pales in comparison with the great singers of the past. They quickly and loudly point out a singer's vocal issues—sometimes real, sometimes imagined—and compete to be the first to shout "Bravo!" in exaggerated Italian diction after an aria.

The true enjoyment of art demands above all an open mind and open heart. I thought of this at a 2022 blockbuster exhibition dedicated to Vincent van Gogh at the Detroit Institute of Art, which featured seventy-some of his paintings on loan from all over the world. I stood in front of a well-known image of an undulating landscape I'd studied in an art history class and had last seen in Amsterdam ten years earlier. But I noticed a shift in my perception, as that painting was now affected by at least three factors simultaneously: the paintings directly to the left and to the right; the works in Detroit's permanent collection I had passed on my way to this temporary exhibit; and the hurly-burly of Detroit itself, the world beyond the museum steps that everyone brought inside with them. And that's saying nothing of more transient points of contact, such as the national news that morning, or the irrelevant thoughts currently coursing through my mind. The composition on the canvas had not changed in 150 years; and yet it signified something unique based on those contemporaneous factors—some controllable, like the exhibition's curation, but mostly indeterminate.

As I stood in front of Van Gogh's familiar painting again, old academic habits of viewing instinctively kicked in. I assessed and categorized form and color, contextualizing the work within a rationally organized and well-rehearsed historical trajectory. But now I found myself attempting to silence that learned voice; instead, I tried viewing the painting with something closer to naïveté. What happens when I just show up, forgetting everything I know about the painter, the work, and art history? It was like seeing the painting for the first time: I was able to imagine the blank canvas, with every line and color pursuing something unknown. The anticipatory standpoint of searching, rather than knowledgeable reflection, became the painting's dominant angle. The artist's vitality and imagination suddenly became overpowering, and the painting held an immediacy and resonance I never could have expected.

The satisfaction that comes from viewing art with the experience of acquired habits invariably involves self-congratulation: *I* have studied this, *I* can understand it, *I* can appreciate it. This is what it means to desire confirmation in art rather than seek a discovery. If we believe that confirmation is the ultimate destination of understanding art, we get lulled into a false sense of superiority, becoming elitist. For those of us who have invested a lot of time in some form of "art appreciation," there is an *unlearning* required to approach a painting with a clear mind. Now I try to wipe the slate clean each time I engage with an artwork. I imagine the blank canvas, the block of clay, the empty timeline, the empty page, or the empty stage; everything added or taken away is a choice commanded not by foresight but by intuition. The work itself, rather than my ability to appreciate the work, becomes the focus.

Many Americans uncomfortably equate education with elitism. But education is not the problem; it can offer invaluable tools for becoming both more perceptive and more receptive—especially useful skills when approaching challenging work. But when that education blocks the actual presence of the work, we fail to perceive the myriad ways it can show us what we don't already know. There's a story about Berg giving a pre-performance lecture for *Wozzeck* that I love (even if some claim it isn't true). He allegedly delved deeply into the musicological details of his score, discussing its formal dimensions and various technical intricacies in minute detail for almost an hour. He then concluded by saying, "Now forget everything I just told you and simply experience the work." That still remains ideal advice for a "difficult" work like *Wozzeck*.

I would have made one suggestion to Berg: give your lecture *after* the audience has experienced the opera on their own terms, by which time—ideally—their curiosity and desire to learn will have been awakened. With their own experience as the central reference point, the lecture could reveal what was happening beyond their impressions. If they listen to the work again afterward, they will appreciate Berg's mastery in a way that deepens their personal connection to the piece. If listening inspires them to a third or fourth or fifth viewing, they would likely find Berg's elucidation drifting further and further away. Rather than repeated viewing for the sake of mastery or confirmation of what they have learned, an audience returns to relish the prismatic and ever-unfolding light of repeated exposure.

If the experienced spectator does not advance past the self-congratulatory stage of art appreciation, a performance that doesn't meet expectations can only be an affront. This is why you often see opera aficionados so disproportionately enraged at the mere thought of a production diverging from their learned understanding of a work; they see red in vociferous self-defense of what they have mastered. Any comment thread online provides ample examples of over-the-top wailing about directors destroying operas by conceiving them differently. One of my favorites has to be a comment on a *Daily Mail* article reporting on my production of *La bohème*: "I do not want to be on this planet anymore." (A commiserating reader replied, "I hear you!")

It is this grandstanding, much more than the ticket price, that makes opera appear so pompous. If there were some way to curb the aficionado's displays of arrogance, the shift of energy in the auditorium would make for an entirely different experience. What can feel forbidding may instead seem inviting and inclusive. At the very least, the oxygen in the house would certainly circulate better without so much hot air.

// // // // //

IT WASN'T SO LONG AGO that opera singers were featured on mainstream television, like *The Ed Sullivan Show* or *The Muppet Show*. The *Looney Tunes* send-up of Wagner remains for many as much opera as they've ever experienced. The director Peter Sellars shared with me a childhood memory of a handyman pulling up to his home in a pickup truck...with the Met Opera broadcast playing on his radio. Opera's position in culture didn't use to be as remote as it feels now.

It's easy to view this situation cynically, as though the bejeweled televised appearances of beloved sopranos like Beverly Sills and Leontyne Price represented a mainstream co-opting of opera to sell an image of upward mobility, so important in postwar American society. But when Leonard Bernstein or Maria Callas appeared on prime-time television, they did not reduce classical music to a mere signifier, as *Pretty Woman* does; rather, passionately performed music by the best interpreters of the time infiltrated households around the country at no cost. *The Ed Sullivan Show*, a popular variety program that, in the estimation of the *New York Times*, "defined American taste" from 1948 to 1971, featured opera on over a thousand episodes. Sills called the experience of singing on the show "staggering" when she considered that "more people would hear you sing than heard Caruso in his whole lifetime."

There's no silver-bullet answer for why opera has lost its footing in the popular imagination in the decades since. Some claim that the proliferation of specialized channels for entertainment has made it difficult to have unexpected encounters. While an *Ed Sullivan* devotee may have tuned in for the Beatles and discovered *bel canto*, the myriad options vying for a contemporary consumer's attention make accidental exposure far scarcer—and surely the algorithmic filters that shape our hyper-personalized experience of social media have made the problem exponentially worse. Others blame a diminished presence of the arts in schools. A 2008 report by the National Endowment of the Arts stated that "all 18-to-24-year-olds, no matter what their socioeconomic status as children, were less likely to have had a childhood arts education than the 18-to-24-year-olds of 1982." The same study laid out data to prove that "arts education has a more powerful effect on arts attendance than any other measurable factor." (In which case, I should stop encouraging art lovers to forget their education!)

We can speculate on what happened *to* opera as American culture has changed, citing so many doom-and-gloom statistics. But what about opera's own culpability in the loss of its popularity? It's hard to look at companies today and not sense a voluntary removal from all contemporary conversation, as they retreat behind red velvet curtains and fill fewer and fewer of the plush seats. Lincoln Center in New York embodies this remove both socially and architecturally. In the 1950s, to realize the dream of a central performing arts complex on the city's West Side, over a thousand working-class Puerto Rican families had to be displaced. And exclusion remained the dominant tone of the resulting venues, where fortresses of imposing archways and columns, far removed from Broadway, implicate the visitor in a similar "ascent" from the street that San Francisco's War Memorial enacts. The complex seems to be looking down its nose at the city's riffraff and offering sanctuary to an arts-initiated elite.

Carnegie Hall, meanwhile, is located right in the heart of New York's bustle; pedestrians might pass it by without even noticing. And even if blaring ambulances have nearly ruined my experience of extremely quiet moments in a Mahler symphony, there's a natural energy and vitality in this hall that's much more difficult to muster within the travertined compound of Lincoln Center. That certainly explains why Carnegie Hall remains New York's musical mecca, while the initial aspirations of Lincoln Center have called for significant overhauls and renovations over the last two decades, with an eye toward a more inviting inclusivity.

The conversation around opera's and classical music's remove from society is often pitted as a tension between "highbrow," "lowbrow," and "middlebrow" cultures—a hierarchical image that betrays the elitism of those drawing the distinctions. What elitists would term low or popular culture circulates broadly, while opera and classical music remain a refuge for a (dwindling) few. But when opera companies are in panic mode, they inevitably grasp at trying to appeal to a lowbrow culture they clearly disdain. In attempting to lure a younger, sexier demographic to the opera house, whether through sarcastic and pithy language or photoshoots of singers in leather jackets in front of spray-painted back alleys, most marketing efforts demonstrate a tone deafness to the real culture on the street. They usually only ever serve to reinforce a division.

But if it does work, and the communication around an opera feels intriguing or enticing enough for someone to give it a try, what happens when a newer audience actually arrives at the opera house? Most likely some variation of the *Parsifal* performance described in Chapter One: a feeling of being left out by the ritual. And if the production mimics the kind of rote repetition the Knights of the Grail undergo, the promise of the alluring marketing will feel like a bait and switch.

"What makes it so difficult for our culture to be communicated to the people is not that it is too high, but that it is too low," is how the French philosopher and activist Simone Weil articulates the difficulty in connecting philosophy (what she calls "our culture") with the working class, in her posthumously published book *The Need for Roots*. In watering down everything that makes a work highbrow—opera, let's say—and making it palatable to "the people," we patronize those we subconsciously prefer to keep beneath our stature. This is akin to believing that the uninitiated need things dumbed down to understand them, while the aficionados, like colonizing missionaries, stoop to spread the light. (The success of Davis's *X* in Detroit proved the opposite: that an uncompromising aesthetic can speak intuitively to its intended audience.)

To counter this condescension, Weil proposes "not popularization, but translation, which is a different matter."

> It isn't a question of taking truths—of already far too poor a quality—contained in the culture of the intellectuals, and then degrading them, mutilating them and destroying all their flavor; but simply of expressing them, in all their fullness, in a language which, to use Pascal's expression, makes them perceptible

to the heart, for the benefit of people whose feelings have been shaped by working-class conditions.

A crucial distinction here is that the "translation" is not one-directional, from above to below. Culture itself benefits from this encounter.

The search for modes of transposition suitable for transmitting culture to people would be very much more salutary still for culture than for the people. It would constitute an extremely precious stimulant for the former, which would in this way emerge from the appallingly stuffy atmosphere in which it is confined, and cease being merely something of interest to specialists. For that is all it is at present—a thing for specialists, from top to bottom, only more degraded the nearer you approach the bottom.

Weil could easily be describing the current state of opera, the "stuffy atmosphere" of opera specialists a perfect description of too many nights at the opera house. But what I find remarkable in her thinking is that acts of translation, while necessary, involve no loss or diminishment whatsoever. If "the subject dealt with is the human condition," she argues, the greatest art will speak *more directly* to those with a personal experience of the emotions the work explores. "What an intensity of understanding could spring up from contact between the people and Greek poetry, the almost unique theme of which is misfortune! Only, one would have to know how to translate and present it."

"Translating and presenting" is precisely what the opera director's work can do. A production can come across as belittling and affected—a self-conscious updating of sets and costumes to draw a too-simple analogy between past and present. Or it may unlock the work for an audience of any experience or education level. A democratic respect for the audience sets the bar high but always aims to *engage*. The pathway of translation is an arduous one, but each production demands that the interpreters walk it.

This attitude remains a minority opinion at the higher level of opera management. At a board meeting following my production of *La bohème* in Detroit, a kind board member who did not like experiencing the piece in reverse order asked a question I knew others had been thinking. "An audience may not know anything about *Bohème* before seeing this one, and now they may never know that Puccini intended it to go the other way. Isn't it our responsibility to offer a reference to those who want to experience the opera the way it was intended?"

I appreciated his generous interest in understanding more about something he initially rejected. I prefer this dialogue much more to how another board member reacted: she was allegedly so disgusted by my "hanging a Picasso upside-down" that she resigned from the board. Had she thought to engage with me about the production, I might have helped her understand that comparing Puccini and Picasso denigrates both, because the two art forms are different. One is a finished work, a marker of time unchanged other than by the degradation of the pigments and the canvas. The other, as I argued in Chapter Four, is an open-source text that demands our interpretive intervention.

To the more curious board member, I explained my disagreement with the notion that our role is to offer reference points or an objective reanimation of an opera. Every re-creation can at best realize inherited assumptions of how we think performances used to be. And even if air-tight documentation existed detailing how a work was originally performed, we are no more beholden to those instructions than we are to restricting ourselves to candlelight for illumination. If we are looking for references, we should consult our phones, tablets, and laptops, which provide limitless access to past recordings. These reference points—landmark performances, world premiere productions, and so on—can be called up instantaneously for further study and research. Live performances, appearing contingently in our time and in our community, should contribute translations that bring works closer to us, so they become "perceptible to the heart."

We don't talk about elitism in those rooms of power, where a company's board meets to exercise good governance. Maybe because a sense of belonging to an elite ideal is part of what propels people to volunteer for these positions in the first place. That particular board meeting, in the wake of a performance that was meant to be celebratory and conciliatory, felt like a stand-off between defenders of tradition and the vanguard of what was now taking place. In the terse discussion, one board member joined in via phone. Although she wasn't visible, her slow and careful voice betrayed a woman "of a certain age." "I'd like to share my experience of this *Bohème*," she proclaimed, and a hush fell over the room.

As she began, I was expecting the worst. "I have repeatedly tried to get my granddaughter to come with me to the opera, and after convincing her that this production of *Bohème* was going to be different, she reluctantly agreed." The woman was very well spoken and knew how to tell a story; we hung on her every word. "I was skeptical myself as to how this concept was ever going to work," she continued, "and when the performance started and Mimì died in the first twenty minutes, I thought, 'There's no way my granddaughter is going to understand what's going on.' So at the end of the performance, I asked her what she thought of the production." The woman took a dramatic pause, and we all leaned in.

"She . . . *loved* it!"

// // // // //

THERE IS ANOTHER KIND OF elitism that we don't talk about—not in boardrooms, production meetings, or design presentations: the elitism of seeming to burn resources on extravagant productions, all while our natural climate is literally on fire. It's a kind of "Let them eat cake" attitude that constructs an entire universe for a mere five performances, before it all ends up on the junk heap.

How can we justify the excess of opera when the world is in survival mode? Humans have steadily and inexorably made the planet uninhabitable—so why are we expending our precious resources on something so ephemeral? In our daily lives, we are called to conserve more, to participate in sustainability, to tiptoe on the earth rather than leaving deeply entrenched footprints. How do those necessary (and perhaps too late) correctives resonate with the extravagance we see onstage—not to mention the wastefulness the audience purposefully does *not* see? There is an elitism in flaunting excess, as if opera deserves a bigger piece of the natural resources pie than anyone else.

Who am I to talk, you might be thinking, since many of my productions might appear to be single-handedly responsible for deforestation? But opera at its most epic can also, paradoxically, create conditions for people to think differently. Opera can't teach, but it can always inspire. Engaging with new ideas, new sounds, and new visions may motivate a spectator to seek solutions for problems that seemed intractable, whether it's homelessness, racism, or the climate crisis.

Our relationship to the land was a central theme of *Sweet Land* (2020), a world premiere opera produced by my Los Angeles company, The Industry—and which made it only halfway through the performance run due to the Covid shutdown. Before public gatherings of any kind were prohibited, we hastily came together one last time to film the piece and to preserve something of what we'd created. While I'm grateful for this record, the video version for me is disappointing for missing the central character: *the land.* The experience of the fictional opera always relied on the constant reminder of the real land that was underfoot and the real stories that resist the dominant national narrative of "Manifest Destiny." Its staging was never intended to be experienced walled up and removed but was instead porous and influenced by the natural and unnatural environments surrounding us.

Sweet Land essentially told diverging stories of the encounter with, encroachment upon, and attempted erasure of a mythic Indigenous population, whom we called the "Hosts," by an equally mythic group of colonizers, the "Arrivals." The conceit was for the audience to be split, one watching the story of the Arrivals invading and violating the land by building a train, the other group following the story of a potlatch after the Hosts uneasily welcome the Arrivals. The two audience groups sat together to witness the landing of the Arrivals before diverging into those two tracks. An intermediary, liminal space we called the "Crossroads" brought the audience back together before they diverged again to experience a revision of the first narrative they saw. The train, once completed, leaves the insatiable Arrivals disgruntled; as they set off for the next promised land, they leave behind bones and ghosts scattered on a poisoned, industrialized land. Meanwhile, the feast has turned into a meal at the forced wedding of a last remaining Host woman with a crude Arrival, each of whom remembers the past very differently. In the end, both audience groups returned to where they had started. But no one had the same perspective on the piece called *Sweet Land*. Their experience itself became a crucial aspect of the narrative, as the forking paths re-created the diverging and partial views of historical events. It became impossible to talk about *Sweet Land* without foregrounding your individual experience of it—a fitting metaphor for the humility we need in order to talk about our national identity.

Perhaps the most remarkable aspect of *Sweet Land* was the intersection of voices that created it. The jobs usually taken by one artist were shared by two: two composers, Raven Chacon and Du Yun; two librettists, Aja Couchois Duncan and Douglas Kearney; and two directors, me and Cannupa Hanska Luger (who also created the fictional characters' regalia). Each pair played on the Arrival-Host dynamic in at least two ways. Indigenous artists (Raven, Aja, and Cannupa) worked alongside artists who had arrived in this country through some form of migration (Du Yun, Douglas, and me). And each pair consisted of one artist with experience creating opera (Du Yun, Douglas, and me) and one brand-new to the territory (Raven, Aja, and Cannupa). Even then, all six of us had to work together on co-articulating our ideas so that music, text, dramaturgy, and visual representation could resonate. We took opera's inherent collaborative nature to the next level, which Aja and Douglas discussed in a dialogue we printed in the program.

> AJA: The collaboration, the breadth of it, made so many wondrous and nuanced things possible.
> DOUGLAS: You can see how opera can create an ecosystem in which collaboration becomes sustaining. . . . There is

something about that collective creative possibility that's just powerful. Add to that what happens when you have collaborators who are trying to make something that could have a sociocultural impact; collaborators you can engage with questions in a very serious way. You might not always agree, but you feel there's real discourse happening even in just making the damn thing.

It was great to read the librettists' thoughts after our work was complete. Beginning the project was, naturally, a much trickier proposition. To discover what could have been (and sometimes was) an uneasy path toward consensus, the six of us articulated the values we wanted to hold and guide every decision in the production. Among those values, a mindful expenditure of natural resources felt particularly important for a production about indigeneity and the widespread attempts to exclude Native perspectives from the story Americans tell about ourselves. We selected the site for the production—the aptly named Los Angeles State Historic Park, a narrow parcel of land downtown where Yaangna, the most important Tongva village in the region, was once situated—and reaffirmed our commitment to treading lightly on this land.

But in the frantic run-up to the opening, the material realization fell out of sync with our professed values of preservation and mindfulness. The set designers—also a duo, Tanya Orellana and Carlo Maghirang—were tasked with creating spaces that spanned a huge area while honoring the land's history. They designed three ambitious spaces—for the "Feast" track, the "Train" track, and the gathering space where the piece began and ended—with long tunnels snaking through the park that connected them. Like good collaborators, Tanya and Carlo extended and enriched the ideas brought up by the six creative team members. But they faced almost insurmountable obstacles in realizing both their designs and ecological mindfulness. Anything we built had to sit self-supported on the land, because preservation purposes forbid stakes in the ground deeper than eighteen inches. We also committed to gifting all the set's materials to a local arts school for its reuse. A worthy aim—but requiring us to construct the sets to be adaptable, which stressed our already tight build schedule and a budget that didn't account for that extra care.

It's hardly unusual with The Industry that a set is still being finished as the first audience members are arriving. In this case, our first audience comprised invited members of Tongva, Tataav'am, and Chumash tribes for a free community preview. As people started approaching the very land we wanted this opera to hold sacred, all I could see were screws, sawdust, and splinters scattered through the grounds. The project we imagined as a laying bare of the mechanism of colonialism was undergirded by a reenactment of colonialist carelessness with the land. It felt like a defeat. I shared my conscience pangs with Cannupa, who suggested that the only solution was to acknowledge our shortcomings up front. So after a ritual invocation by a Tataav'am elder, Cannupa and I both greeted the audience and recognized the production's heavy footprint on the earth.

The moment was sobering—and when Covid hit, things got worse. The chaos of our mid-run cancellation forced us to dismantle the sets rapidly and under the most unsafe conditions imaginable. The two-by-fours and planks we planned to donate were rendered mostly useless through haphazard disassembly; most of them were thrown away. Beyond the cruel irony of another plague silencing Indigenous voices, the improvident use of the earth's resources made me worry that there was no escaping the pernicious influence of America's founding spirit of exploitation.

In the early phase of the pandemic, accompanying the shock of the world shutting down, I sat with a sense of failure around this project. I wondered whether opera had any hope of pursuing alternatives to wastefulness. But a year later, I received an unexpected call from Marvin Schober, an energetic manager at the Department of Water and Power who oversaw the utility's recycled water program. He had worked closely with us in the year before *Sweet Land*'s premiere to help us find a solution for the Crossroads, an improvised musical interlude reuniting the audience in an open field. The Crossroads offered the audience a meditation on the land: by sitting on it, feeling the crisp bite of the February air, and experiencing the discomfort of not knowing what to look at or how to engage. We imagined projected images revealing layers of history—but instead of projecting on hard surfaces, which would distract from the natural environment, I wanted the images to crystallize and disappear as if airborne. The artist Alex Schweder and projection designer Hana Kim collaborated on the idea of a mist system that would allow images of livestock and industrialization to seem as if they were emerging from the dark night and disappearing into the sky. That ghostly trace would also prepare the audience for the opera's final scene, where they returned to their starting location and heard voices whose disparate texts were projected on the industrialized landscape around the park.

How could we create a mist effect—requiring a lot of water *in a drought*—without being wasteful? The park, it turned out, had an elaborate system of reclaimed water as part of its sprinkler systems, distinct from the potable water in the drinking fountains. We would need to work with the Department of Water and Power to figure out the safest way to use this water for something other than what it was originally designed for. When Marvin heard what we wanted to do, he became incredibly engaged. "I've never done anything like this before!" he enthused. But he also warned us that reclaimed water was highly unsanitary. If we could find a safe way to keep the water at a remove from the audience, he would authorize our use of it. Although the original design had the mist surrounding the audience, with the projections covering a 360-degree field, using reclaimed water was more important than achieving an "immersive" effect. After all, the real immersion we were after was not into an illusory art installation but rather the reality of the land. In frequent negotiations with our production manager Mariana Perez-Seda, we reached a consensus: the mist wall became a backdrop for the singers, far enough from any contact with artists or audiences, but still powerful enough to give the effect of ghostly projections floating in front of the downtown Los Angeles skyline.

Marvin's call a year later broke the news that The Industry was going to be recognized as "Customer of the Year" by his department. *Sweet Land,* they claimed, was a model of creative adaptation and art's resourcefulness. The award (in the shape of a drop of water, of course!) put all the collaborators' efforts into perspective. *Sweet Land* had not just been an irresponsible act of wastefulness but also an example of how green thinking will require the same creativity that artists deploy in every project. Nothing lets us off the hook from striving for a more mindful use of every resource.

In process and in structure, *Sweet Land* was perhaps the most anti-elite project I've ever participated in. Why this is such an anomaly in the opera world is, perhaps, best articulated by Cannupa, in the dialogue that we printed in the program:

> CANNUPA: It's funny, because within my normal art practice I have been thinking about the importance of art existing as a verb rather than a noun. Art as a noun is how it becomes controlled: it becomes a commodity, sheltered in edifices in every major city to box it up and put everything in their place. I keep thinking about that in relationship to opera itself: why has it become this elite form, when those original projects simply brought artists together to create a narrative and communicate to their community about the problems of their society? Opera existed as a verb that happens in a place; and the audience completed the work by embedding the ideas within the community. The only way to control that is to objectify it. So you build a house for it, like a museum—and then you're beholden to those who paid for it. And a process of objectification begins in a colonial fashion until it becomes opera as we experience it today.

// // // // //

ELITISM IN OPERA IS SYSTEMIC, and identifying elitism in the opera house will not be difficult as you experience the art form for yourself. Yet an anti-elite attitude is growing in the field, with *X* and *Sweet Land* only two examples of what that looks like. Here's a guide for identifying others.

PRINCIPLES OF ANTI-ELITE OPERA

- *Exclusivity* is not a virtue; *inclusivity* is.
- Acknowledging that conventional spectatorship breeds acceptance of the status quo, newer works must challenge and avoid well-known musical and dramatic conventions in favor of new directions, new sounds, and new voices.
- "Dumbing down" insults the audience. The opera's creators and producers don't rely on any assumed knowledge of the spectator.
- In classic works, historical indecencies are not relativized or apologized for but actively called out and revised.
- In newer works, the opera's subject matter originates from "the ground up." No celebration of privilege or power.
- Translation and engagement are encouraged; condescension and arrogance—toward the artists and members of the audience—are shamed.
- Rather than schooling the audience on correct and incorrect modes of spectatorship, the opera house is hospitable and inviting, encouraging the spectator to make the experience their own.
- In the lobbies and on the stage, opera is actively decoupled from fantasies of economic advancement. Instead, the possibility of social and spiritual advancement—accessible to everyone—can once again become opera's true aspirational character.
- A mindfulness around the use of natural resources must inform every choice, from the audience experience to the rehearsal conditions to the material creation of a production. Where can our taking be offset by giving?
- Perform opera outside the opera house. In parking garages, in escalator corridors, in park grounds, and in automobiles. Opera can happen anywhere.

The final principle has been a particular passion of mine, and one I feel is still a nascent development for opera. The next chapter will explore site-responsive works beyond the proscenium arch of an opera house.

Before turning to that, let me conclude this chapter by considering a final form of elitism: that of the artist. It's a dicey topic to address, since I've been considered by some a snob just by way of my devotion to opera. But let's look at one of opera's most surprising meditations on anti-elitism, Arnold Schoenberg's great, unfinished biblical epic *Moses und Aron* (written 1932, first performed in 1957). Schoenberg depicts the prophet Moses feeling a direct and overwhelming connection to divinity—but not to the world he lives in. He never sings but kind of speak-sings instead, as if he belonged in neither an opera nor a play. Because his blinding insight sets him apart from the people he is meant to lead, he must rely on his brother Aron to communicate his truths. (Aron, completely at home in the world of opera, sings with a heroic tenor.) The dilemma at the heart of the opera becomes an allegory for the artistic process: the truth can be harsh, severe, and forbidding, while art offers a seductive disguise that allows truth to become perceptible. That disguise, however, can also be a corrupting force, as Aron's alluring singing voice stirs the people into an orgiastic frenzy around the iconic representation of a golden calf. The irreconcilable difference between the brothers remains at a stalemate. Moses's final line—"Oh Word, you Word that I lack!"—serves as a devastating but appropriate conclusion to an incomplete opera.

Moses und Aron remains an unpopular work. Instead of capitulating to "what the audience wants," Schoenberg committed fully to his vision at the potential expense of pleasing his public. "Since I can't reckon on a performance of the work for a few decades," Schoenberg acknowledged in a letter, "I didn't feel obliged to avoid difficulties in the choral and orchestral parts!" It remains a benchmark in the history of opera—Anthony Davis cites it as one of his major inspirations, with the punishing vocal writing for Elijah Mohammed in *X* carrying echoes of Schoenberg's Aron. But *Moses* is considered box-office poison by any company with the resources to pull it off. When the Metropolitan Opera revived Graham Vick's excellent production in 2003, an employee told me, "You could fire a cannon into the auditorium and not worry about hitting anyone."

It's easy to interpret the opera as autobiographical, with Schoenberg allegorically represented as Moses and Alban Berg, his pupil, as Aron. While Schoenberg never broke any of the rules he laid out for his compositional technique, Berg's more liberal handling of the same techniques speaks with a surprising directness to an opera audience. In *Wozzeck* and his own unfinished opera *Lulu* (1937), Berg found seductive and empathetic costumes to drape around his mentor's advanced musical ideas. The unrelenting rigor of Schoenberg's music still alienates many listeners, and a performance of *Moses und Aron* is a rarity. Berg's music, while not as popular as Puccini's, finds far more frequent performances.

I don't know how Schoenberg grappled with his "disciple"'s popular success. Did he consider Berg's work a betrayal? Was he jealous? It's tempting to consider Schoenberg/Moses taking an elitist position, detached from the populace and parroting a Reddit user's comment: "It's certainly nice to have an entertainment where you don't have to mingle with hoi-polloi." I have heard people reverentially claim that Schoenberg's music is so advanced that humanity has not yet evolved far enough to appreciate it. In his appropriately titled essay "How One Becomes Lonely," Schoenberg accepts the messianic fate of being ahead of his time:

> While composing for me had been a pleasure, now it became a duty. I knew I had to fulfill a task: I had to express what was necessary to be expressed and I knew I had the duty of developing my ideas for the sake of progress in music, whether I liked it or not; but I also had to realize that the great majority of the public did not like it. I remembered that all my music had been found to be ugly at first; and yet . . . there might come the promise of a new day of sunlight in music such as I would like to offer the world.

Schoenberg truly sounds like Moses in this essay, standing alone "against a world of enemies." Yet Moses's remove in the opera is not presented quite so heroically. The character is much more ambivalent: his severe truth isolates him more than it inspires others. Aron may have pushed selling his brother's sacred ideas too far, but if he had not taken on the burden of what Weil called "translation," the divinity Moses hoped to transmit would have remained locked away.

The path toward translation is narrow and easily corrupted. But it may be the only way to avoid the isolation of detached exclusivity. Devotion to whatever we discover as divine will not be enough; we still have a responsibility to our fellow humans. This, too, is explored in the allegory of *Moses und Aron*: if music is a dialogue between a musician and a listener, then a new musical language that fails to communicate betrays a monologic arrogance. Even as opera explores the limits of human perception, with expanded vocabularies for music and drama, the essence of what we do must be grounded in *contact* and *connection*.

In short: in imagining anti-elite opera, we must imagine Moses and Aron's collaboration as happy.

8

BREAKING THE FRAME

OPERA BEYOND THE OPERA HOUSE

HERE'S A CONFESSION: MY ATTENTION WANDERS A LOT when I'm sitting in a theater. I can't keep myself from looking around. I inventory the lighting grid, try reading my program, observe things I'm not supposed to, and throw sideways glances at the audience members around me to see how they are reacting to what's happening.

Conventional wisdom would either chide me for my lack of focus or blame the performance for not being compelling enough to hold my attention. People who sit behind me might assume I'm restless or bored senseless. But that's how I prefer to engage with the event in space: not with laser-focused attention on what happens on the stage but taking in the *whole world* of a performance, naturally including the audience and the architecture. I'm still listening and imagining and dreaming along with a production as it unfolds; I just may not be looking at what the director wants me to see.

Little wonder I feel such a connection with John Cage: his work proves that anything your concentration alights on can become a perfect catalyst for engaging the world. Realizing the potential of what we don't notice is, for Cage, art's true province. His most famous work, *4′33″*, asks musicians to sit at their instrument for four minutes and thirty-three seconds, performing the work in three movements without playing a note. Sometimes called a "silent piece," Cage's work creates space for all the music we choose to drown out, everything left out of the narrow cone of concentration that demarcates learned listening from the world at large. The coughing and rustling of the audience, the hum of the air conditioner, the thud of a dropped program all make up the piece, the score, the music. If concentration, like the word "concentric," implies a zeroing in on a fixed point, a piece like *4′33″* offers an escape from our otherwise narrowing minds.

I find it enormously freeing to let my mind drift and take in everything as I watch an opera or listen to a concert, and I must admit to being that kind of reader as well: a word, a phrase, an idea sends me into unexpected territory. I don't stop reading, but the text fades into the background of my mental activity, as new ideas inspired by the words push to the forefront. I may occasionally miss a crucial plot point or a particularly deep thought, but my mind's wandering is woven into the fabric of that book in a way that transcends the literal; the meaning of the words recedes, and my mind meanders among the ideas presented to me. Music—inherently, wonderfully nonliteral—can prompt this drift even more powerfully, so that I feel more deeply connected to what's transpiring. I may not be aware of the composer's clever inversion of the movement's second theme in the woodwinds, or whatever. But when I stop trying to understand a piece rationally and let my mind wander like a river over new terrain, I am allowing the music to help me explore how I think and feel. Then it becomes about my experience, and therefore the development of my consciousness.

Why are we forced to attend a performance of classical music as if we're schoolchildren with a stern disciplinarian as our principal? Why have we reduced spectatorship to a constricting of our attention to a single point, where *everything* speaks? Why do we sit still in the dark and ignore the myriad impressions surrounding us?

Opera today demands complete concentration, an expectation so out of step with the rapid pace of our "attention economy" that it must be a contributing factor in the art form's decline in popularity. But it wasn't always this way. Abbate and Parker list the "alternative activities" French operagoers participated in during an opera performance in its heyday: "gambling, chess-playing, eating, talking, ogling one's fellow attendees, and, in the so-called *loges grillées* (shuttered boxes), quite possibly things a gentleman never mentions." Sitting silently with single-minded attention paid to the stage was "not the historical norm." Yet now—precisely in an era of extreme attention deficit—opera stubbornly demands your unwavering absorption. If it's difficult to focus your mind on one point for ten minutes, how much harder is it to sit for hours with only the activity onstage to occupy it?

Even after nearly thirty years of attending operas, I have not developed the skill of keeping my mind focused on the stage throughout a performance. Yet by embracing an *escape* from that focus, I've learned to love opera more. I'm sure I would never have devoted my life to the art form if I couldn't also imagine it taking place beyond the boundaries of the opera house.

We have grown accustomed to engaging with live performance in a way that feels cinematic, something happening within a frame. That frame was probably lifted from theaters, where for centuries the portal we call a proscenium arch separated the world of fiction from the world of reality. From the spectator's perspective, the frame precedes the scene (the literal definition of *pro-scenium*) and masks the machinery that creates stage illusion. Almost all operatic performances take place safely behind this archway that creates a picture of a faraway, floating world.

If you visit Renaissance and Baroque theaters today, with their impressive proscenia emblazoned with the names of the generous benefactors who built them, you can't help but notice how awful the sight lines are from anywhere but a lavish central box. The proscenium often stands in some viewers' way. What would be an impossible frustration for audiences now was nothing out of the ordinary back then: only royal personages could expect perfect visibility. Not only were sets designed to emphasize the noble box's centrality—employing a perfect vanishing point of perspective that could only be appreciated at the center of the space—the entire theater was built to remind everyone who was in charge. Horseshoe-shaped balconies, terrible for viewing the stage, were fine for catching a glimpse of the stand-ins for divinity in the central box.

The vanishing point in these theaters was less about an organizing center for the composition on the stage. The very real center of attention was in the auditorium: the seat of power.

The proscenium arch is therefore a silent contract with the audience, and attending theater becomes a rehearsal for being in the world. The space where we view a representation of society prescribes a mode of reality, not so much for the world behind the proscenium, the world of fiction, as for the society in front of the proscenium (*pro-proscenium?*), the world of the audience. And just as society was built on a rigorous system of hierarchies, the architecture of the hall visually reinforced that hierarchy as natural and right. Today the problem is not the proscenium but the accumulated archeology of assumptions it has come to represent. It orients a well-rehearsed understanding of our position in relation to our community, and signals a promise that what transpires beyond it will correspond with our expectations.

Aristocracies and monarchies may have waned in most countries that produce operas, but the architecture of auditoriums has remained surprisingly consistent. The proscenium arch has become less prominent in newer theaters, but it's rarely eliminated; a theater losing its proscenium would be like a ship losing its anchor. Instead, proscenia draw less and less attention to themselves, to the point where they are now usually an invisible given (like all ideology). Baroque proscenia were so ornately decorated that even if you could only see the stage from an oblique angle, the space surrounding the performance was still something to savor. Since then, theaters have increasingly followed guidelines of neutrality, the more to focus exclusively on the performance.

Wagner's Festspielhaus in Bayreuth, opened in 1876, began a process that has resulted in drab auditoriums bereft of all ceremony. Wagner even went so far as to build a series of fake gray proscenia to push the eye even further into a funnel, emphasizing the drama onstage as an impossibly faraway universe. To ensure concentration, house lights in the auditorium are dimmed, maybe extinguished entirely, as a preemptive strike against an unfocused public expecting to "see and be seen." But though the social pleasures of theater are denied to Wagner's audience, the awe-inspiring effect is worth it: when a performance unfolds on the Bayreuth stage, you easily fall into an illusionistic space that can feel like a private dream, as the world around you disappears into darkness.

With models like Bayreuth, it has become bad taste for a new theater to draw any attention to itself. Theater has become a space yearning to disappear, inviting the audience to forget where they are and lose themselves in a fictional universe. Every other space we inhabit contains history and potentiality, while theaters have become a void and a nowhere land. Those who watch a performance as I do can easily feel suffocated in these environments, as our inclusive concentration feels forced into a flue. The art alone can rarely succeed in holding our interest for long, when everything surrounding it is rendered invisible and unworthy of attention.

What would opera look like if it were given opportunities to engage all its many dimensions: activating the performing space, changing the spectator's position, maybe even inviting their active participation? What if the house lights didn't go down? What if you were allowed to take pictures or video? What if you could get up and move around during the performance, taking it in from different angles?

To reach its full potential, opera is going to have to explore the world beyond its conventional frame.

// // // // //

THE URGE TO ESCAPE THE framework of the proscenium became increasingly urgent in the twentieth century, beginning with Antonin Artaud. Before writing "The Theatre and the Plague," Artaud completed his first manifesto for a so-called "Theater of Cruelty" in 1932, which demanded a different social contract from the one mirrored in the hierarchies of traditional theater:

> We abolish the stage and the auditorium and replace them by a single site, without partition or barrier of any kind, which will become the theatre of action. A direct communication will be reestablished between the spectator and the spectacle, between the actor and the spectator, from the fact that the spectator, placed in the middle of the action, is engulfed and physically affected by it.

Artaud's ideas and emphasis on action spurred generations of theater artists to think differently, especially in America. The founders of the New York–based Living Theatre, this country's first experimental theater collective, called Artaud "that madman who inspires us all" and "the philosopher, for those of us who work in theatre, whom we can reach toward most quickly." Staging "poetic dramas" as Dionysian group rites meant to provoke a revolution, the Living Theatre mixed media and broke the boundary between artist and spectator in search of Artaud's "direct communication." By the 1980s, the collective was using participatory techniques to rehearse and directly involve the spectator in the action.

"Action" was also a key word for the American experimental artist Allan Kaprow, who considered the action paintings of Jackson Pollock a harbinger: all the arts would escape their traditional frame and extend into space. The flung paint making up Pollock's compositions created an "instability" where "the artist, the spectator, and the outer world are much too interchangeably involved," as Kaprow wrote in a 1958 essay on the artist. The scale of Pollock's paintings engulfed the viewer the same way Artaud wanted: "the entire painting comes out at us (we are participants rather than observers), right into the room." Kaprow followed Pollock's lead in exploring art as something spatial and experiential. "We do not come to look *at* things," he asserted in an essay accompanying his exhibition in New York's Hansa Gallery. "We simply enter, are surrounded, and become part of what surrounds us, passively or actively according to our talents for 'engagement.'" (The title of this essay, "Notes on the Creation of a Total Art," could have been cribbed from Richard Wagner.) Kaprow became most famous for what he called Happenings, performance art predicated on a lack of separation between audience and performer. "These events are essentially theater pieces," Kaprow noted in 1961, "however unconventional. That they are still largely rejected by devotees of the theater may be due to their uncommon power and primitive energy, and to their derivation from the rites of American Action Painting."

With Kaprow as his inspiration, the director Richard Schechner conceived of an "environmental theater," which sought to envelop the audience in the world of a drama. For his 1983 production of Anton Chekhov's *Cherry Orchard* in India, Schechner placed the audience in a different environment for each act: inside the estate for Act I, in the cherry orchard for Act II, participating in the party for Act III, and outside the estate for the farewells of Act IV. Rather than disappearing into darkness as in Bayreuth, Schechner's spectators were always on the move and visible to each other. In an interview for the *India International Centre Quarterly,* Schechner defines environmental theater as an outgrowth of art's move "from the framed painting to the collage, to the environment, where the whole room is designed." Comparing the effect of environmental theater with folk rituals like India's *Ram Lila* festival, Schechner points out the anti-elite potential of immersing the audience in the work.

> It touches on inclusion; and an extreme example of inclusion is participation. In other words, the proscenium theatre and much of classical theatre . . . functions on the basis of exclusion. You, as an audience, are invited to watch somebody else do something; and they are in a different space—actually and conceptually. Two rooms with a wall removed: you're in one and they're in another. You are not really included, nor does theirs extend out into your world, or yours back into theirs, except in some sort of metaphorical or allusive way. *But, in the environmental theatre, the audience is part of the world* [italics in original].

Schechner's experimental techniques have since become familiar, even over-exposed. Immersive experiences are all the rage, from theaters to galleries to commercials. Everywhere, that is, except in opera, which remains ensconced behind the frame of the proscenium arch. Why?

The answer is primarily a question of acoustics. To the shock of most first-time operagoers, most operas perform unamplified. I often find myself correcting audience members after a performance in the 2,700-seat Detroit Opera House: "No, the singers were not miked. What you heard were their natural voices projecting over all those instruments, all the way to the back of the auditorium." This certainly provokes amazement and admiration—but most contemporary audiences, accustomed to amplified theaters, are not always aware this is so. That means an enormous amount of effort is being expended to preserve a way of performing that may not even register with the audience.

It's truly astonishing to experience a glorious unamplified voice fill a theater. The acoustic space allows the great earlier operas to take you on a journey of light and shadow, loud and quiet, with an extraordinary sonic range that is impossible to achieve with microphones. I love the unamplified quality of operas, especially in houses that are more humanely built, with fewer than 2,000 seats and where silence has a chance to carry true power.

But keeping opera an exclusively unamplified phenomenon has come at a cost. Sound's directionality is probably the biggest impediment to the creative ideas of directors and designers. Since optimal aural conditions always take precedence over perfect positioning, singers end up moving downstage and facing fully forward. In many theaters, just turning slightly profile threatens to disconnect a singer's sound from the audience—the reason you see so many performances defaulting to "park and bark." Imagine a play where the actors are never in profile, never upstage, and always front and center when speaking; that's often what you experience in the unamplified spaces where opera happens. You can see why an "environmental" performance that maintains a nonamplified tradition becomes an impossibility.

Opera, then, is experienced through two frames: the hall's proscenium, which frames our eyes, and the hall's natural acoustics, which frame our ears. Without these two absolutes, many aficionados will not consider what they are seeing "real opera." Natural acoustics have become their fetish—and a particularly sadistic one when a singer's voice is required to fill a 4,000-seat theater without support. As thrilling as acoustic singing often is, the pursuit of that sensation has pitched the entire operatic enterprise toward achieving the largest possible effect, regardless of whether the performance is Wagner's gargantuan *Götterdämmerung* or Britten's tiny chamber opera *The Turn of the Screw*. Singers who can fill the expanse of a football field without a microphone *and* bring subtlety, delicacy, and alertness to the drama are exceptional... and exceptionally rare. An opera house's architecture locks in much of what companies search for: volume, precision, and willingness to move in sync with the seemingly unmovable machine that runs the show.

Those who dare tamper with natural acoustics face a wrath out of all proportion to reality. The first company I worked for was New York City Opera, which took the ingenious step of deploying a state-of-the-art acoustic enhancement to the notoriously dead sound of its Lincoln Center home, the State Theater. Built for George Balanchine's New York City Ballet in 1964, the theater was designed to mitigate the noise of dancers' footfalls. What makes for a wonderfully "quiet" experience of ballet turns into catastrophic conditions for opera. So in the late 1990s, Paul Kellogg, City Opera's General Director at the time, added spatial microphones (though none for the singers) and hundreds of inconspicuous speakers to give the natural sound a chance with the architectural design. The enhanced effect was as natural as could be. I had the opportunity to listen to stage rehearsals with and without the sound system operating, and the difference was uncanny: the same music could feel muffled and tired without the system, or direct and present with the system functioning. This boost helped City Opera fulfill its mission of nurturing young American talent. Without that support in the inhospitable acoustics of the hall, most still-developing artists would have struggled to establish a connection between themselves and the public.

The innovation Paul Kellogg spearheaded should have been applauded and adopted by every opera company with an outsized theater. But they might have been gun-shy after seeing the reaction this acoustic enhancement unleashed. A headline in the *New York Times* about the system, "Meddling With Opera's Sacred Human Voice," says it all. Or nearly. The article quotes the editor of *Opera News* (a magazine published by City Opera's larger Lincoln Center competitor, the Metropolitan Opera) laying out the intractable rules of opera: "It's an implicit contract with audiences that there will be no amplification of any kind and that they will hear the voices as God made them." There was hardly a *Times* review of a subsequent City Opera performance that failed to chastise the theater for this acoustic sacrilege.

Beaten down, the company dismantled the sound system ten years later, attempting to rectify the acoustic problems with a costly renovation to the State Theater. Three years after returning to a hall that now offered an unadulterated experience of natural acoustics, City Opera folded for good in 2013. I suppose the message is: *no* opera is better than acoustic enhancement?

Kellogg's innovation should never have provoked such a scandal. Amplification is not a panacea for everything that makes opera lack immediacy; and it's true that artless amplification will flatten out sound, reducing the highs and lows for general audibility. But there's no reason to demonize what an enhanced extension of sound can do to further the evolution of the art form.

After all, the holy acoustic fortress of opera had already been breached, frequently to revelatory effect. Houston Grand Opera introduced amplification with two pieces specifically written for enhanced voices in the 1980s and 1990s. The world did not collapse—rather, those operas proved to be two of America's most astonishingly original works for the art form. In Meredith Monk's 1991 masterpiece *ATLAS,* the intrepid voices of the ensemble were able to employ extended vocal techniques with extraordinary subtlety. Monk's musical language is inextricably linked with a physical language of gesture and dance, demanding a new kind of performance that is not inherently compatible with the rigid style many opera singers have been trained to master (to be fair, most singers have never been invited to explore such a freedom). What would have happened to her audacious composition if she had been forced to comply with the demands of an unamplified opera house? In Houston, microphones not only extended the distance a human voice could be heard but expanded possible vocal techniques. A new music, and a new dramaturgy, emerged in an opera that still feels like no other ever written.

Five years earlier, in the same theater, John Adams amplified his voices for *Nixon in China,* heightening the crucial nonreality of the work. All of Adams's subsequent operas similarly require an imperceptible acoustic boost for the singers, which allows his interpreters so much more freedom. Singers can sing conversationally rather than "barking"; conductors don't have to worry about covering the singers and can let Adams's astonishing orchestrations really shine; and directors can place singers wherever they choose, even facing directly upstage, for maximum dramatic impact. Adams's sound designer, the composer Mark Grey, expertly brings the voices right to the threshold of being noticeably amplified. The effect is natural and seemingly effortless—and rather than taking away from the singers, the miking enables them to more fully inhabit their roles without worrying about volume.

American soprano Renée Fleming, whose voice effortlessly fills the Metropolitan Opera without ever losing subtlety of expression, performed the role of Pat Nixon in a 2023 production at the Paris Opera. When asked about singing with a microphone, Fleming told the *New York Times,* "I don't think it's helpful to the art form to insist that there never be any enhancement on the stage. There's a huge difference between a subtle enhancement . . . and full-blown amplification. I appreciate it, especially because a lot of what I'm doing is way upstage. And many set designers don't want to be forced into building boxes all the time to help us with the acoustic." Twenty years ago, this kind of comment would have sparked outrage, and a more ego-driven singer may have denounced the microphone as insulting. If the rigid resistance to amplification is indeed breaking down, that's an encouraging sign for opera.

Then again, in the same year that Fleming sang Pat Nixon, my use of light enhancement to stage a much older opera provoked irrational ire among traditionalists. As the sound system was getting dialed in during the production's piano dress rehearsal, the company's general director pulled me aside to proclaim his outrage over the amplified voices: "This is an opera house!"

Nevertheless, microphones have definitely helped opera, theater, and music venture into environments outside the theater. Schechner's use of microphones for his *Cherry Orchard* production meant that all spectators had access to what was spoken, even if they found themselves in an unpredictable relationship to the performer. In opera, a highly sophisticated sound system at the Bregenzer Festspiele in Austria allows nearly 8,000 spectators at a time to take in spectacles on an open-air "floating stage" on Lake Constance. One of the most powerful set designs I've ever seen was for a production of Verdi's *Un ballo in maschera* that couldn't have happened anywhere but in Bregenz: an enormous skeleton jutted out of the lake, holding open an oversized book where the fateful drama played out. Part of the set's potency came from its completely "unoperatic" setup: no proscenium, no orchestra pit, and no off-stage wing space. I remember feeling awed by the scale of that audacious image, but couldn't help wondering, "Where did they put the orchestra? And what happens if it rains?"

When I eventually worked at Bregenz, assisting the British director Graham Vick on his 2009 production of Verdi's *Aida*, I discovered that the live orchestra plays safely in a separate building, perfectly in sync with the singers outside on the lake. At the first stage-orchestra rehearsal, I marveled at how audio and video monitors allowed the conductor to maintain real-time contact with the performers, as well as keep big ensembles and choruses together. The complex series of speakers all around the lake allowed for a vividness of sound that never felt artificial—and the sound design always guided your eye to look exactly where the singers were staged. State-of-the-art sound technology not only made new experiences like this possible, it created an effect so natural that you never once thought about the sound design. (As Mark Grey once told me, "You only ever notice sound design if it's bad.")

We now find ourselves daily in environments with higher and higher volumes—in cinemas, arenas, theaters, nightclubs, even restaurants. In opposition to that trend, there is surely something attractive about the nostalgic space of unadulterated sound that opera offers. The right repertoire and the right theater can still provide audiences with a magical escape. Opera proudly (or stubbornly) keeps audio levels lo-fi and unidirectional—even as the scale and ambition of the art form actually lend themselves to full immersion in sound and image. So as our ears have adjusted to new levels and new ways of listening, I can't blame audiences who attend a performance of music meant to be ear-splitting—the "Ride of the Valkyries" from Wagner's *Die Walküre* or the "Dies irae" from Verdi's *Requiem*—for walking away with the disappointed feeling that the music didn't have the visceral impact of the recording they'd heard in their car on the way to the theater.

Opera companies fear amplification for everything it might seem to take away. I can only see the possibilities it opens up—not just for new work like *ATLAS* and *Nixon in China,* but for great works from the past. At the Hollywood Bowl, a massive venue that seats over 15,000, a sold-out crowd gathered to witness a single performer with a single instrument playing a single work: Yo-Yo Ma playing the Bach cello suites from memory. For two and a half hours, the crowd sat silently in a kind of pure communication. The Bowl's pristine sound system allowed every nuance to be savored half a mile away; never for a second did you believe there was anything mediating your experience of this music. Thanks to a technological miracle, a miraculous performance was shared with an unprecedented crowd. Epic scope and intimacy merged for something ineffable, reaching operatic heights.

// // // // //

BEYOND INTRODUCING AMPLIFICATION to expand our acoustic frame, can more be done architecturally to encourage new ideas in opera outside the visual frame?

The conductor and composer Pierre Boulez made a notorious suggestion. As a thinker and performer, Boulez had few rivals in twentieth-century music; I like to think of him as a philosopher of sound. On the one occasion I got to meet him, at a lecture on Wagner he gave toward the end of his life, I was shocked to encounter a self-effacing man of effortless humor. The decidedly elderly crowd was charmed by the smiling raconteur—as if he had nothing in common with the hot-headed revolutionary who had tried taking the New York Philharmonic in a thoroughly modern direction after Leonard Bernstein. The younger Boulez was a firebrand, probably best known for one battle cry: *Blow up all the opera houses!* The fact that this incendiary statement remains his best known surely speaks to a deep-seated desire, even among aficionados, to witness such a conflagration.

But what did Boulez really mean? If we look at his statement in full, we see that the target of his attack is the architecture:

> Only with the greatest difficulty can one present modern opera in a theatre in which, predominantly, repertoire pieces are played. It is really unthinkable. The most expensive solution would be to blow the opera houses up.... But don't you think that would be the most elegant? ... Or one can play the usual repertoire in the existing opera houses, Mozart, Verdi, Wagner, up to about Berg. For new operas, experimental stages absolutely need to be incorporated. This apparently senseless demand has already been widely realized in other branches of the theatre.

Monk and Adams may have shown how a conventional theater, with its proscenium arch, does not have to be a limitation to new thinking; creativity and state-of-the-art technology can still escape the vanishing point of a traditional experience. But for original work, Boulez's point remains urgent: new music demands new modes of engagement and new configurations of encounter. Altering the relationship between spectator and performer is hard to achieve within the separation enforced by the proscenium arch. To create new work inside the theater will necessarily involve a "blowing up" of all expectations—at the very least, a subversion of all the limitations the architecture of opera houses now implies.

The Industry in Los Angeles was born from a wish to discover what new ideas might emerge away from the proscenium arch. The resulting work, taking place in spaces that were not built for a theatrical purpose, is sometimes called "site-specific" or "site-responsive." Following Artaud's dream, the division of artist-spectator disappears in site-specific productions; a different relationship offers an unexpected encounter with a work. There are many similarities to Schechner's environmental theater, although the phenomenon is probably as old as theater itself. "From grizzled medieval tradesmen re-enacting the death of Jesus on a muddied cart trundling through the streets of York to bespectacled '60s avant-garde artists huddled in the back of sweaty bookshops, there has never been a time when theater has only happened in theaters," Andy Field wrote for *The Guardian* back in 2008. "It would be fair to say that the idea of sitting down in a purpose-built auditorium of plush red velvet seats arrayed in a number of tiers is a relatively new one."

For my Industry productions, I prefer the term *site-responsive*. Rather than a background, the location is a character itself, and the productions search for connection and dialogue with the found environment. This process brings immediacy and history to the surface—since, unlike the "invisible" space of the theater, the site is an inextricable partner in the performance. There's a powerful tension in the juxtaposition of a devised fiction with the silent witnesses of history that haunt every space, including (maybe especially) those sterilized locations some call "non-places"—parking lots, escalator corridors, abandoned lots. How can a fiction, embodied in a performance, shake off a space's layers of routine experience and uncover what might be sleeping under the concrete?

Attempting to escape the narrow perspective of the vanishing point, my projects for The Industry became increasingly expansive in their use of space—leading up to *Sweet Land,* as described in the previous chapter. The company's first production—and in many ways the inspiration for starting the company in the first place—was Anne LeBaron and Douglas Kearney's "hyper-opera" *Crescent City* (2012). I spearheaded workshops of this brilliant and original piece twice at New York City Opera's laboratory for new operas called Vox. But the work-in-progress, with its electronica-driven score (for amplified voices, naturally) and a manic, fragmented narrative, resisted everything associated with operatic institutions and the proscenium arch. The operatic field didn't know how to engage with the amorphous, undefinable entity Anne and Douglas were creating. That reluctance gave me the impetus to start a company in Los Angeles for developing precisely the kind of work that otherwise would not find a home. And the sprawl of the music and text made it clear to me that the new work did not belong in a conventional theater.

Site-responsiveness was not yet an idea I had fully developed when I started The Industry. The non-proscenium site for *Crescent City* was a fairly straightforward "non-place," a temporarily vacant 15,000-square-foot warehouse in Atwater Village. In some ways, the space took a backseat to the art that filled it—not drastically different from the drab auditoriums that draw no attention to themselves. There was no *responsiveness* to the warehouse, and the result was much more in line with Schechner's environmental approach to *Cherry Orchard*. But right from the beginning, my goal was to escape the proscenium arch and change opera's spectator-artist relationship. So the audience had to choose between four distinct ways of seeing the work: a fixed seat on the perimeter of the warehouse, each one offering a unique perspective and with video relays filling in what was happening out of sight; a fixed seat on an elevated platform looking down on the whole performance from a zone we jokingly called the "Skybox"; a fixed seat on custom-made beanbags that were part of the set/environment; and a walking path that let you move freely during the performance, continuously changing your relationship to it. The performance was the same for everyone, but a spectator's experience ranged from most detached (in the Skybox) to most immersive (on the beanbags). There was no true hierarchy to the experiences; no seat could really be considered better or worse than any other. In our non–opera house, each spectator had a partial view and a wholly individual access point. The audience became collaborators in their own experience.

The production was excitingly chaotic, but the results were not entirely satisfactory. The modes of spectatorship still felt prescribed, even if simultaneous and multiplied. I began to think of spreading opera across multiple spaces; to offer even more indeterminacy in the audience's engagement possibilities; and to let a different location truly shape the work, not merely serve as an alternative to the opera house.

That exploration began with Christopher Cerrone's *Invisible Cities* (2013), based on the 1972 novel by Italo Calvino. As with *Crescent City*, I had championed this work at Vox and again witnessed the operatic field struggle to place Cerrone's intimate and haunting work in the context of an opera house. Calvino's novel takes the reader on an imaginary travelogue through fantastical places, like cities built on seashells or stilts, framed by a series of dialogues between Kublai Khan and Marco Polo. Their conversations involve philosophical and often cryptic musings on semiotics, the shortcomings of language, and a mistrust of external reality. With only a trace of narrative, *Invisible Cities* traverses a circuitous route with endlessly forking paths; it's as concise as ancient wisdom but contemporary in its worldview.

Like the novel, Cerrone's adaptation resists operatic treatment in all the obvious ways. My immediate impulse was to situate the work in Los Angeles's Union Station, with the opera hidden among the comings and goings of normal citizens. Rather than surrounding the audience in the constructed world of *Crescent City*, *Invisible Cities* immersed us in a heightened awareness of the everyday.

All train stations have an air of romance about them, but the best and most beautiful ones transcend their functionality and become an existential expression of life's transience. Union Station possesses a grandeur defying any charge of irrelevance in the ultimate Car City that is Los Angeles. (It's not unusual to meet Angelenos who aren't even aware that a train station *exists* in their city.) Unlike LA's other Art Deco gems built by John and Donald Parkinson—City Hall, Bullocks Wilshire, and the Memorial Coliseum—the station's elegance feels charged with nostalgia. It's easy to imagine yourself a traveler from the East Coast in 1939, pulling into Los Angeles as if it were the end of the world, and feeling like you've arrived at Shangri-la: Spanish architecture, tessellated tiles, vast space, palm trees. It was the city of the future, with the largest network of public transportation in the country offering its citizens unbound freedom. The optimism in 1939 for what the city might become still speaks in the tiles and archways. It's a perfect site for illuminating one of Calvino's thoughts: "Futures not achieved are only branches of the past: dead branches."

Union Station is nevertheless hardly an anachronistic holdover. It's still used as a transit hub, and public transportation is becoming an increasingly viable and environmentally necessary option for a city in need of alternatives to clogged freeways. Ambitious plans for expansion, including high-speed rail, had moved the station back to the forefront of the city's imagination when I decided to do Cerrone's opera there. Union Station at an important moment of transition reminded us that Los Angeles itself is in a constant state of becoming. Cities are not fixed images but fluid entities that morph according to their inhabitants. We must believe that the time we invest in a city shapes its very geography, in both tangible ways (building a house, skyscraper, or freeway) and intangible ways (acts of kindness, crimes, fashion statements, car accidents) that over time become tangible. Spending time in the station allows us to meditate on and perhaps even perceive this fluidity.

This, ultimately, is what a site-responsive work seeks to do: to put the aura and identity of a location in direct relationship with the ideas explored by a work of art. A production of Cerrone's opera for a proscenium theater would require the creation of designs and mechanisms to realize and communicate the work's themes; in Union Station, the building itself just spoke.

Like *Crescent City*, amplification was a requirement for *Invisible Cities*—but this particular site allowed us to take a step beyond straightforward miking. The entire opera would be heard through individual wireless headphones, untethering the audience from any one seat or perspective. Directionality of sound was no longer an issue: the headphones allowed the audience to move among various spaces, inside and outside the station, and always remain connected to the live performance happening around them. Sometimes a spectator might "find" the singers among the crowds at the station, and sometimes they would ascribe singers' voices and their stories to the faces surrounding them. Who was a singer or dancer, and who was merely waiting for their train? Headphones made possible a new experience of opera.

I loved the use of headphones for being so commonplace; I use them nearly every day, and certainly anytime I am traveling. Headphones have made the detachment of sound from its source a familiar occurrence. Music that only we can hear detaches us halfway from the physical space we inhabit and opens a private doorway into reality. As you move through your environment, you're simultaneously somewhere else—inside a cocoon of sound, supernaturally close to its heartbeat. Your personal soundtrack transforms the space around you. A train station is a radically different place for the commuter listening to the blunt dread of Carl Orff's *Carmina Burana* than it is for the passenger listening to the cool complexity of Miles Davis's *Kind of Blue*. Any potential meaning they glean from the interplay of private soundtrack and public space is no less truthful for being purely coincidental. Headphones thus offered an exciting solution to the problem of representing Calvino's cities: they allowed the imaginary cities to live as images in an audience's imagination.

I've had some unforgettable experiences with headphones as an artistic tool: Janet Cardiff's haunting walk around Central Park, where prerecorded memories coexisted with the present-day life of the park; Merce Cunningham's EyeSpace, where each audience member was given an independent MP3 player to hear an individually randomized selection of Mikel Rouse pieces to accompany a choreography that was the same for everyone; and Back to Back Theatre's play *Small Metal Objects*, where a drug deal takes place among unwitting commuters and headphones let the audience in on their real-time conversations. When you factor in the "silent disco" phenomenon—headphone-wearing ravers dancing to music no one else can hear—it's clear that headphones have been disrupting trends in all forms of artistic experience for some time.

For opera, a genre where the human voice is so essential, the possibilities opened up by the headphone experience are limitless. When I called Cerrone to pitch the idea, I half expected him to hang up on me, but he responded, "Funny enough, I've been thinking of myself more and more as a composer for headphones." I was relieved but on reflection not surprised: the beauty of his music depends on an almost impossible intimacy. You truly want Kublai Khan and Marco Polo to be whispering in your ear to achieve the magic of Cerrone's *pianissimo* vocal lines.

Thinking in a site-responsive way expanded our understanding of opera. A thematically resonant space spurred us to reexamine all the art form's most central tenets, such as voice, vocal production, technological intervention, and audience experience. My subsequent projects for The

Industry have sought ever new forms of responsiveness. In *Hopscotch* (explored in depth in the next chapter), the story was splintered into thirty-six different chapters, many of them experienced in cars and on the streets of Los Angeles. In *War of the Worlds* (2017), a co-production with the Los Angeles Philharmonic that adapted the notorious Mercury Theatre radio play by Orson Welles, voices from Walt Disney Concert Hall were broadcast to three defunct air-raid sirens near parking lots in downtown Los Angeles—with voices from those locations streamed back to the hall, creating an uncanny two-way communication inside and outside the auditorium. (A project I could have never conceived of before experiencing the detached orchestra at the Bregenzer Festspiele.)

These productions offered every audience member a freer sense of spectatorship, one of drifting attention and making choices. Outside the traditional theatrical space, they resisted the framing supplied by so much other media. There is no single path, and spectators can let their imaginations wander. Out in the open, where frameworks don't exist, a sense of activity becomes a precondition. It's a spur that can generate endless new routes for opera to take.

// // // // //

THE ELITIST AND THE AFICIONADO will likely scoff at what I'm describing: "That's not opera, that's just gimmickry."

I'm all too familiar with the accusation. Any time I've tried to do something different with a production, it's been routinely dismissed as an attention-getting stunt. But I have never undertaken an experiment or deployed a technological novelty without considering it an essential contribution to a poetic reading.

Every artist exploring new terrain has a bigger picture they are pursuing, beyond the aesthetic result. Artaud, in the preface to his essential collection *The Theater and Its Double,* claims his theater is a form of Nietzschean protest: "A protest against the senseless constraint imposed upon the idea of culture by reducing it to a sort of inconceivable Pantheon . . . A protest against the idea of culture as distinct from life. . . . This leads to the rejection of the usual limitations of man and man's powers, and infinitely extends the frontiers of what is called reality."

The Living Theatre's experiments, more socially and politically driven, were rooted in an anti-authoritarian vision for American social and political life. The group started, according to their website, as "a company of actors who want to bring about the Beautiful Non-Violent Anarchist Revolution." Julian Beck, a painter and one of the company's founders, articulated the organization's mission as a poem: "To call into question / who we are to each other in the social environment / of the theatre . . . / to set ourselves in motion / like a vortex that pulls the spectator / into action, . . . / to cry 'Not in my name!' / at the hour of execution, / to move from the theatre to the street / and from the street to the theatre."

Allan Kaprow likewise emphasizes the bigger picture that drove him to create Happenings: "They are a moral act, a human stand of great urgency, whose professional status as art is less a criterion than their certainty as an ultimate existential commitment." Best of all, perhaps, is Schechner's ultimate aim. "What we have done, in a certain sense, is what modern science and modern philosophy have tried to do," he explains in the *India International Centre Quarterly*. "In other words, extend the horizon of what we can see—not to deny that there is more than we can see, but to put as much as we can see into our consciousness—literally to expand our consciousness."

I deeply resonate with Schechner's aim, and I find myself pursuing a similar extension of the sensorial in opera. In our everyday lives, we are reduced to one viewpoint—the world we see, hear, and relate to our inner life—and the conventional theater space mostly reproduces that mode. Environmental and site-responsive stagings expand the "horizon of what we can see," sometimes making it impossible to experience the work as a complete world. The partial view of a site-responsive performance can bring about a reckoning with reality, along the lines of our experience with *Sweet Land*; or it can point to a much larger world beyond what we know. We stretch our concept of a single vision of reality; we never lose our subjectivity in the process, but we are made aware (sometimes painfully) of its limitations.

I have felt first-hand how challenging it is to make the proscenium arch feel unexpected and multidimensional, especially in comparison with the much freer work I've done with The Industry. If the hierarchical architecture of the theater prescribes a social contract, that contract is ripped up when we perform outside a theater space. In new experiences, the audience must figure things out for themselves rather than relying on what they've come to find familiar. Suddenly, so much more is possible.

As my directing work oscillates between theater-based and site-responsive productions, I must admit to feeling more at home outside the theater. The work that I believe most fully represents my worldview offers alternatives to the vanishing point of our perspective. I nevertheless endeavor to bring what I learn "offsite" back to the apparatus of opera, to explore how this old infrastructure can still welcome new ideas. That seems to be the way to question the old social contract. The architecture can remain intact; it's our expectations that will need to be blown up.

9

CASE STUDY:
HOPSCOTCH IN LOS ANGELES

I want to live life like a book you can start anywhere,
that you find has no beginning
and no end.

—SARAH LABRIE, from the libretto for *Hopscotch*

CÉSAR DIED FOUR MONTHS BEFORE *HOPSCOTCH* OPENED in 2015. He was a loyal friend and a trusty companion in my first five years in Los Angeles and accompanied me on so many journeys. He carved out a personal space for me to think or sing, never judging how badly. And when we were alone, like on the open road that stretches through Joshua Tree, he gave me a sense of freedom and possibility. He was my first car—a silver 2003 Mini Cooper.

I acquired him from a couple who nearly cried when I drove him off. He got his name from the guy I was infatuated with at the time. When the car's power steering died five years later, I also felt like crying when I faced trading him in, in such a diminished state. It sounds like the ultimate example of fetishistic materialism, but I couldn't help but identify with César the Car. Like a mechanical spirit animal, he reflected me and framed my vision of my adopted city. Saying goodbye was closing a chapter in my life; five years of memories and emotional journeys were shedding their material shell.

Maybe it's only in Los Angeles that cars feel like an extension of your being. I learned to drive in Chicago, but it was in LA that the state of driving struck me as compelling. The fluidity between your inner world and outer reality creates a surreal state not dissimilar to the one induced when you listen to music: external stimuli internalized into something completely personal, where the event in the present moment and the field of individual associations interpenetrate.

Site-responsive stagings can make us aware of our limited perspective, and could there be any better symbol of a limited perspective than the protective bubble of your vehicle? When we view the city through a windshield, there's a constant danger of dissociation from our environment. The philosopher Paul Virilio claimed that "what goes on in the windshield is cinema in the strictest sense"—a sentiment that implies an unnaturally detached view of the world around us. That confusion of real and virtual worlds, the tension between freedom and myopia centralized in the experience of driving, became one of my fascinations and led to the creation of *Hopscotch* as an opera taking place in cars. On the heels of *Invisible Cities,* where the music in our headphones transformed our perception of the train station's reality, I wanted to continue exploring how music in real time could subvert an alienated experience of our everyday.

Hopscotch also began as a kind of dare. I was sitting in the atrium of the Cleveland Museum of Art with my friend and close collaborator Jason H. Thompson, taking a break from technical meetings for a 2014 production of Janáček's *Cunning Little Vixen* with the Cleveland Orchestra. This was six months prior to *Invisible Cities,* which was in a bad way: we had much more money to raise, and more important, we were undergoing an arduous process of trying to secure the use of Union Station from LA's Metro Transit Authority. Their willingness to allow this indescribable project to proceed—instigated by a company with only one other project under its belt—was anything but certain. And even if we won them over, many technical uncertainties had yet to be tested. Was the project even possible?

Jason and I decided to hit a reset button. What could we imagine doing that was more difficult than *Invisible Cities* and would allow us to gain some perspective on the train station experience? No sooner had he suggested, "What about cars?" than we had drawn a ring of arrows on a napkin indicating the opera's structure: cars that travel from point A to point B, shuttling the audiences on discrete journeys that formed a loop within the city. At the center of the ring was a circle—a central axis for the entire project.

Invisible Cities, occupying only one location, suddenly seemed so much easier. I could go back to Metro with renewed energy because I had one-upped that challenge. During the final stages of the opera at Union Station, the car concept took hold in a way I knew I would have to see through to its completion. Two and a half years later, *Hopscotch* took place on the streets of Los Angeles, with twenty-four cars zigzagging a path around the city and shuttling four audience members at a time through a nonlinear experience.

I'm sure that if I'd merely heard about *Hopscotch,* I would have written it off as a gimmick. Whenever I emphasized the logistics, the enterprise came across as a superficial stunt. In a career of projects that resist definition, I still have never created anything so "hard to explain" or reduce to an elevator pitch. Which I take to mean that it is the fullest realization of the ideas of opera outlined in this book. *Hopscotch* involved more disciplines—from architecture to animation and actual life on the street—than any other project I've worked on. It remains my most complicated experiment in destabilizing the relationship between artist and spectator. And to my surprise, it ultimately became a genuine spiritual exercise, holding out the hope that somewhere there is a center where everything connects.

// // // // //

SINCE THE EXPERIENCE OF *HOPSCOTCH* is nearly impossible to explain, let me try and re-create the perspective of a ticket buyer.

You are given GPS coordinates of where to go, and at the appointed time a car pulls up to meet you and three other audience members there. A stage manager opens the door for you and announces a chapter number. You climb into the car and proceed into one moment of a larger narrative. The cars are various types of limousines, allowing for four passengers to share a space with singers and instrumentalists, who themselves are always interacting with singers and sounds positioned outside the car.

After driving for ten minutes, you arrive at a destination simultaneously with another car carrying four other passenger-spectators. The doors are opened for you, and the two sets of audiences swap cars. Your new chapter is announced with numbers as your guide—if your first drive was Chapter 18 and the new one is Chapter 2, you could position both experiences in the story's chronology. New artists, performing music and text by a different composer-librettist team, bring a new segment of the story to life as you continue to move through the city.

A performance consisted of eight "transfers"—six drives and two sites—until, roughly ninety minutes later, you end where you began, completing one route of a possible three that made up the full piece. An audience could travel just one route and experience the entire piece in microcosm; "completists" needed to attend three times to see all three routes.

The audience was intentionally *not* in the driver's seat, partially because the city looks completely different to a passenger than it does to a driver. But also because each chapter required a renegotiation between the audience and the work. As they entered some cars, passengers would find themselves sitting next to singers performing as if they were alone—a "fourth wall" view that ignored the presence of onlookers, despite the strange intimacy of sharing a confined space. The spectator was an observer, not necessarily a participant. But in other cars, there was direct interaction. (In one scene, for example, a fortune teller asked the audience members to pull a tarot card, and based on their choice, the singer and violinist in that car instantly called up one of eighteen possible short musical portraits.) If you entered a car and found yourself submerged in the environment of the drama, it wouldn't be long before everything changed, and you were forced to find your footing all over again.

Perhaps the most serious disruption to the conventional understanding of opera was the multiplicity of composer-librettist voices. Each time you got into a car, the musical/dramatic treatment would shift, as the baton was passed to different voices. The composers, all Angelenos, were Veronika Krausas, Marc Lowenstein, Andrew McIntosh, Andrew Norman, Ellen Reid, and David Rosenboom; the librettists were Tom Jacobson, Mandy Kahn, Sarah LaBrie, Jane Stephens Rosenthal, Janine Salinas Schoenberg, and Erin Young. Even with so many authorial voices, we featured additional music by Philip King, Odeya Nini, Lewis Pesacov, and Michelle Shocked. We never aimed for a cohesive unity subsuming these authors; instead, each voice was allowed to behave interdependently, aware of what others were doing but carving out their own identity within the larger framework.

Musically, sonically, experientially, the performance was one of constant disruption and disorientation. While a loss of familiar bearings was the basis of exploration for my first two projects for The Industry, *Hopscotch* pushed the idea to an extreme with its constant repositioning between artist and spectator. I have since attempted to bring this sense of disorientation to opera houses. In *Bohème,* for example, in addition to its reverse order, a newly created character would occasionally interrupt the musical flow (see Chapter One). For the Lyric Opera's *Proximity* in 2023, a triptych of three independent composer-librettist teams, I opted to "shuffle" the works: a scene from one work gave way to a scene from an entirely different musical-dramatic universe. In *Comet/Poppea* (2024), two different operas separated by nearly 400 years, with music by George Lewis and Monteverdi, perform simultaneously—clashing, overlapping, interrupting each other, and sometimes even harmonizing. But all those experiments seem a contained microcosm compared with the commotion of *Hopscotch.*

When I consider *why* I strive to achieve such disorientation, I have to resort to an automotive analogy: *to dismantle the autopilot.* I've spent a good portion of this book attacking an autopilot approach to opera, from the thoughtless repetition of how operas are traditionally performed to the machine-like operation of houses that mitigate risk at the expense of new creative expression. I've also looked at how audiences have been conditioned to attend opera in search of confirmation for what they already know, from familiar music, familiar stories, and a familiar experience. The entire field can seem to operate on some form of autopilot, resulting in a numbing mindlessness that prevents us from taking unfamiliar paths or scenic routes, or activating our own agency.

"Living on autopilot" has become a common metaphor for a detachment from self-awareness. We can (uncannily) drive ourselves home safely even while more directly engaged in talking or listening to the radio. But psychologists, therapists, and philosophers fear that contemporary society encourages us to spend the majority of our day on some form of autopilot; some neuroscientists even believe that such an approach to life has shrunk our capacity for self-awareness to a duration of only seven seconds at a time. To expand that duration, we need to escape the daily habituation of autopilot behavior—and for opera, that means constantly disrupting an automatic way of experiencing the work.

No single artist involved in *Hopscotch* could ever lapse into autopilot. We all had to negotiate changing conditions, especially those that were beyond our control—like how unexpected traffic might require some improvisation! Each one of us was pushed to achieve something we weren't entirely sure was even possible—and this uncertainty, which crystallized for me in *Hopscotch,* has become a goal for any project I now undertake. Whether it's asking singers to fly through the air singing Mozart or to interact within a green-screen environment while performing Wagner, I find opera exciting only when singers are asked to discover places they never imagined they could go, regardless of the repertoire being performed. For *Hopscotch,* artists performed the same ten-minute scene twenty-four times a day while undertaking some audacious stunts: singing while standing up in the back of a Jeep driving down a dirt road; rappelling down the concrete bank of the Los Angeles River; playing the violin while crossing a busy street; or climbing a tall chimney to perform a solo trumpet line hundreds of feet away from the audience. In each case—even those that didn't involve daredevil activity—the rehearsal process required us to work through uncertainty and doubt to a place of mastery. It's awe-inspiring to watch a performer surmount something they imagined impossible, to the point where it becomes an integrated part of their performing selves. It may be *the* most inspirational aspect of experiencing opera, which (when not on autopilot) can be the most audacious and superhuman artistic activity we humans have yet come up with.

// // // // //

"THIS BOOK CONSISTS OF MANY BOOKS, but two books above all. The first can be read in a normal fashion and it ends with Chapter 56. . . . The second should be read by beginning with Chapter 73 and then following the sequence indicated at the end of each chapter."

This is how the Argentinian author Julio Cortázar recommends that his readers navigate his great 1963 "anti-novel" *Rayuela* (*Hopscotch*). If you read Cortázar's narrative in nonchronological order, you shuttle from Chapter 73 to Chapter 1, then 2, 116, 3, 84, 4, and so on. The last two chapters, 58 and 131, end up pointing to each other, creating a closed circuit in place of any kind of conclusive ending. The physical act of reading, where linear front-to-back thinking is reinforced by the book's weight gradually shifting from your right hand onto your left, and by your bookmark as guidepost to where you are in the novel's trajectory, is disrupted in a way that I find enjoyable. You're at a permanent midpoint, never seeming to advance or retreat. No beginning, no conclusion, but endlessly in the middle. *Rayuela* prefigured *Choose Your Own Adventures*, my favorite books as a kid, where young readers are confronted with a choice at the end of each chapter that takes them through a maze of narrative permutations.

My original plan was to adapt *Rayuela* for Los Angeles and for cars—an impulse that had everything to do with its playful, nonchronological approach and almost nothing to do with its plot, which follows bohemian Latin American artists living in Paris. The one plot point that intrigued me in considering an adaptation of the novel was a game played by the two central characters, Oliveira and La Maga. In a resolutely pre–cell phone era, the two wandered separately on "round-about routes" through "the tangled ball of yarn which is Paris," to see if they could serendipitously find each other. Inevitably, improbably, they always do manage to meet, hardly a surprise to either of them, since they both professed a belief that "casual meetings are apt to be just the opposite." The rest of the novel is comprised of dialogues and "nonaction," or the refusal of action, which would have made opera an uncomfortable fit. But a drift through Paris of two lovers, testing the boundaries of chance and fate, held the kernel of a beautiful idea for an operatic experience.

The hide-and-seek Cortázar's lovers play resembles what the French philosopher and artist Guy Debord developed as a *dérive,* or a "drift." A *dérive* became a strategy to shake habitual patterns of urban living, as a small group of inhabitants take an unpredictable, rapid journey through terrain routinized by regimented social passage. Their hope is to somehow get lost in a city that has become too familiar, to discover what is alien in the terrain or what patterns invisibly control the flow of citizens. Along the way, a "possible rendezvous" with someone they don't ordinarily encounter becomes part of the game. But the most important factor is a "letting go" of those predetermined goals that create a tunnel view of our surroundings. Focusing on destination over journey cuts us off from the myriad possibilities that surround us at every street corner.

Although the *dérive* originated in a Paris on the brink of the major social unrest of the 1960s, Debord's strategy seems tailor-made for twenty-first-century Los Angeles. LA living hinges on a point-A-to-point-B habit, with the fear of soul-crushing traffic keeping people within a confined radius of comfort. Debord was apparently inspired to create the *dérive* after studying the predictable pattern of a young woman's movement through the 16th Arrondissement; a map of her daily life formed a triangle between only three points on any given day. It's easy to imagine countless Angelenos never straying from a similarly closed circuit. Even those of us who love the city must deal with the consequences of an urban plan built on the exclusive reliance of cars. It becomes hard to resist the deadening isolation of a life on autopilot when we experience so much of life this way. In his essay "Theory of the *Dérive*," Debord leans on a quote from Karl Marx, who observed that "humans can see nothing around them that is not their own image; everything speaks to them of themselves. Their very landscape is alive." Driving can offer freedom and connection (at least the physical connection of two geographically distant points), but it can all too easily alienate us from our own surroundings, turning vibrant centers of communal possibility into a sun-filled backdrop for narcissism.

And so, even more than Cortázar's novel, the *dérive* became the major inspiration for *Hopscotch*. By suppressing destination and routes—forcing drivers into the passenger seat and allowing audiences, four at a time, to experience "unexpected rendezvous" along the way—the elaborate mechanics of opera boiled down to a twenty-first-century "drift." For Debord, a new relationship between an individual and the city could emerge through the *dérive*. An increased awareness of artificial borders might "give rise to new objective conditions of behavior that bring about the disappearance of a good number of the old ones."

What might happen to our experience of Los Angeles after engaging the city with this kind of fluidity and potentiality? And how could music and opera participate in coaxing such a change of perspective? Could it draw even hardened audience members toward a transfigured vision of our communal lives?

// // // // //

JULIO CORTÁZAR'S ESTATE REFUSED US the rights to *Rayuela* without giving a reason. This actually came as a relief: other than the *dérive*-like game the two lovers play, the rest of the novel would stubbornly resist adaptation. But then the question became "Okay, but *what* story? And would we need a story at all?"

Hopscotch is a case in point of an opera with a *de-centered narrative*, where plot becomes secondary to the totality of the experience. In fact, that totality *became* the narrative—in this case, an open-ended, jumbled, sprawling one. Spectators could not resist creating their own narratives built on the impressions around them. What was real, and what was part of the production? How would personal associations with individual streets or neighborhoods intersect with the chords, the concepts, the characters presented in each chapter? Achieving this level of openness was my principal goal, even as narrative still played an essential supporting role.

A light trace of narrative encouraged an audience to seek out connections from chapter to chapter. There was something to hold on to, even if the scrambled chronology made the story seem more like a Rubik's Cube. Disparate scenes in and out of cars that *weren't* pointing to something larger—that is, without thematic cohesion and without dots to connect—would never have made for a satisfying artistic experience, neither for us nor for the audience. *Hopscotch* without a narrative span would have likely turned into an art-adjacent stunt—a pleasant (and sometimes unpleasant) lazy river ride through the city. Quickly forgotten upon completion.

To develop a narrative distinct from Cortázar's, writer and dramaturge Josh Raab gathered the creative team together for a series of exploratory exercises over several months. We started to define what the opera would explore, and then extrapolate situations (in a nod to Debord) that could bring those ideas to life. Through those conversations, we drew up a thematic map, which had three major hubs: "Life experienced as continuous or disjointed"; "The changing relationship between inner life and external world"; and, maybe most directly connected to Cortázar, "The search for a center." Each theme offered offshoots—but all three pointed to the center, toward a box labeled "LOVE."

We all wanted to make sure each scene (or chapter) was influenced directly by the streets the audience would be traveling—without ever resorting to simple historical illustration. Landmarks, neighborhoods, street names, and histories became "givens," found subjects rather than found objects, shaping the story. A statue of the legendary Mexican singer Lucha Reyes in Mariachi Plaza, for example, inspired the name of our main character—and Reyes's most famous song, "Por un amor,"

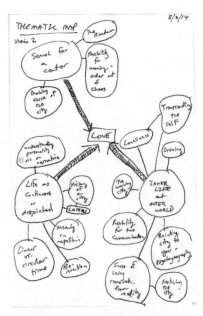

A thematic map preceded the writing of *Hopscotch,*
with three cycles and a central axis establishing the
form of the performance.

ended up weaving through the score of *Hopscotch,* as a kind of talisman
for her circuitous destiny.

The Lucha of *Hopscotch* is a performer—a singer like Lucha Reyes,
but also a puppet maker who performs with her best friend, Orlando.
Lucha's car crashes into the motorcycle of Jameson, a brooding and
brainy scientist, which marks the ominous beginning of a catastrophic
marriage. After the two are married, Jameson drifts further and further
away, obsessively researching the location of consciousness in the brain.
Troubled by her husband's erratic behavior, Lucha receives a phone
call from an unidentified old woman who offers mystifying advice: "A
thousand streets lead to one great road, and no gate blocks your way."
Jameson eventually vanishes under unknown circumstances, leaving
Lucha to career through nightmarish states of loss—until she recalls
the woman's message, which sets her on a path toward larger acceptance.
Orlando, having suffered his own painful losses, reunites with Lucha,
and the two fall in love. They resume their artistic collaborations, now

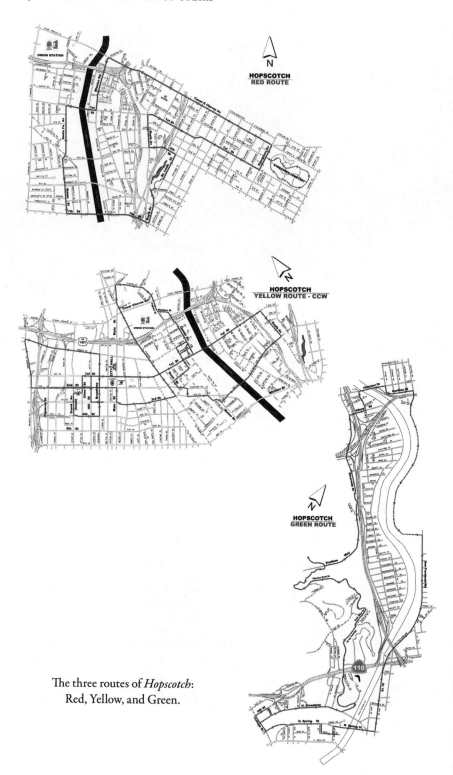

The three routes of *Hopscotch*:
Red, Yellow, and Green.

brilliantly successful, and live out peaceful days. On the precipice of death, Lucha finds her way to a phone and sings to her younger self: "A thousand streets, a thousand streets . . ."

Even a simple story like this one was bound to be challenging to comprehend, and the confines of a car severely limited the range of possible actions. Although some chapters involved key plot points—usually taking place at sites, where audiences left the car and explored a part of the city—the drift through the city lent itself better to emotional or psychological states of being than to narrative. (The same can be said, of course, for many of the best operas!) Traditional opera uses recitative to move the plot forward between the more reflective and musically memorable arias; for *Hopscotch,* ten short, animated chapters (created by five different animators) were made available online to audiences in advance. On a practical level, these videos provided audiences a baseline understanding of the story. But on a more interesting, conceptual level, the various styles of animation prepared them for an experience that was not going to be homogenous: style, language, and aesthetic varied wildly, with our three characters and their interwoven stories as the only through lines. The animated chapters, numbered like the other chapters (1, 3, 5, 10, 13, 16, 23, 27, 30, and 34), served as narrative tent poles. Attentive, sleuthing spectators could position what they were experiencing live through the number chronology.

(A perspicacious/obsessive audience member might realize that *Hopscotch* was incomplete. One number was missing: Chapter 21, the point in the story where Jameson's disappearance would have been explained. Not many people caught this particular trick—but it allowed us to ensure that the narrative stayed open-ended.)

Legibility was additionally challenged by the inconvenient fact that performers could only be in one place at any given time. To trace the trajectories of the three characters through multiple stages of their lives—from childhood to old age and death—we would need multiple singers portraying them. Costume designer Ann Closs-Farley used colors to help us identify them: Lucha always appeared in a yellow dress no matter her age, and Jameson always rode his motorcycle through LA in a black leather jacket and white T-shirt. I've seen this tactic work brilliantly in film—hilariously in Luis Buñuel's *That Obscure Object of Desire*, where a Frenchman's mercurial love interest is portrayed by two different actresses; or profoundly in Todd Haynes's *I'm Not There*, where four different actors portray seemingly irreconcilable sides of Bob Dylan's identity. To the question of whether audiences would understand that every performer they saw in a yellow dress was playing the same character, I pinned my hopes on a theory that underpins all my productions: If you can state the rules of your particular game, accepting them becomes an audience's agreement to play along.

Having multiple performers depict our three characters, while pragmatic, was also core to the concept: each character "contained multitudes," and they were portrayed by singers of different cultural backgrounds, ages, and genders. All of us contain myriad versions of ourselves, a sentiment that became part of the libretto. Lucha increasingly falls in love with an expansiveness she finds within herself, while an anxious Jameson wonders, "How do you know you are in love with me, when there are so many you's and so many me's?" For Jameson, his split personalities indicate a continuously fractured reality, full of disjointed chaos; he obsesses over T. S. Eliot's line "Hell is the place where nothing connects with nothing," and likens that place to Los Angeles. For Lucha, lack of continuity doesn't mean an absence of center; she rewrites Eliot to claim, "Love is the place where everything connects with everything."

In the disjointed experience of the narrative—which may have begun with a heartbroken Lucha, followed by an older, wiser Lucha in love with Orlando, followed by Lucha as a young artist, and so on—the audience had to take a leap of faith that Jameson could not: the belief that there *was* a center to everything. And, at least for *Hopscotch*, there actually was a center: a bespoke pavilion equidistant from all three routes that we called the Central Hub. An audience could visit the Central Hub for free and experience all twenty-four live performances simultaneously: a live feed from each car, in some cases manipulated by an audience member, was beamed back to this location on individual monitors. With headphones and an individual remote control, audiences could tune in to whichever chapter they wanted and jump freely around the narrative on their own.

As a practical matter, the Central Hub guaranteed the work was not limited to an exclusive car ride. Any audience member who only attended one route could see the missing chapters (or rewatch chapters they'd experienced) with a free visit to the Hub. But the pavilion also served as an aspirational center of the work, where its various sprawling strands intersected. The Hub was the place where "everything connected with everything," or as our thematic map preferred it, LOVE.

At the end of each performance day, we performed Chapter 36, titled "To Find a Center," as a Finale. Singers and instrumentalists from each chapter began an incantation of daily rites ("To get the transmission looked at, to get the hair trimmed, to listen to the messages . . .") in their isolated cars as they drove toward the Central Hub. As each car arrived, they joined the other performers, improvising on the various modes that wove throughout the performance. If you were watching the piece at the Hub, the singers you were seeing on screens out in the city suddenly began sharing space with you one by one, until you were immersed in cascading waves of sound. Passengers emerged from an encounter with a solitary voice into a harmonically dense field, waves of sound punctuated by the chimes of crotales. The very disparate, sometimes lonely, sometimes scary, sometimes exuberant rides that had been happening in individual cars converged and made one circle: a center.

The Central Hub embodied another recurring theme of the piece: escape from a physical sense of time. The pursuit of a circular rather than linear experience of time echoed throughout the narrative. When Lucha and Jameson are fully in love, they experience time "not as a river but as a web." In a later chapter, on her own, Lucha wonders with a quiet anxiety, "Is all time simultaneous?" And the chapters depicting the elder Lucha calling her younger self enact a supernatural loop in time. Yet the route taken by each car, which felt contiguous and sequential in real time, was actually a circular path, ending exactly where it started. The linear experience was the illusion, the result of not knowing where you are going, while your true movement through the city traced a circle.

At the (circularly constructed) Central Hub, time really *was* simultaneous. Narratively, the entire story was happening in the same instant; experientially, twenty-four different situations around Los Angeles could be viewed at once. (This is why I chased the company offering zero-latency transmission, as described in Chapter Six, in an attempt to outsmart our illusion of time. I don't, however, think that would have satisfied the representative's question of "why I was doing this.")

The Hub was no small logistical feat on its own. Everywhere else in *Hopscotch,* we worked with the city's existing architecture and infrastructure; but we had to build the Hub and invent its infrastructure. That task was taken up by Constance Vale and Emmett Zeifman, two young professors at the Southern California Institute of Architecture—the experimental school in downtown's Arts District that enthusiastically lent us their large parking lot to house the project. Constance and Emmett engaged their students in designing the temporary pavilion, clad with discarded billboard material, and ensured its functionality.

The Central Hub's artificiality was a reminder that a unified state was always an aspirational one. But to me, this was like opera. With its high level of artifice, its distance from our perception of reality, opera is best suited for conceiving and speculating on sounds, images, and ideas of another way of being. The more outlandish the work, the more powerfully it inspires spectators to be that change.

// // // // //

FOR A PIECE THAT BEGAN as a dare, *Hopscotch* pushed us to the brink of the possible. With Jason as production designer, we kept imagining more and more challenging situations. What if we projected images onto downtown's 2nd and 3rd Street tunnels—but only for the audiences in the cars, not for anyone else in the tunnels? Or traversed the narrow dirt path by the Los Angeles River and then had the singers venture into the river's apocalyptic concrete channel? How about placing a lone trumpeter on the top of an old water tower for the audience to hear (and see) off in the distance, playing in time with a scene happening on a different rooftop? The first person we hired to manage the production suggested we delay the project to make time for a feasibility study. "There's no point in a feasibility study," I responded, "because I can already tell you the project is not feasible. That's the whole point." (Unsurprisingly, she didn't stay on the job very long.)

There was a kind of lunacy involved in the making of *Hopscotch*, an over-the-top obsession that I think is characteristic of opera itself. Artists pursuing opera push themselves and their colleagues to preposterous lengths—for "the beauty of the act," as the protagonist of *Holy Motors* put it. Yet that sort of madness is missing in a lot of the opera I see, where respectability and good manners are points of pride. Opera would do better to cultivate more foolishness, more anarchy, more unruliness.

Every aspect of our production required audacity, especially in pursuit of the sites we wanted to include: iconic LA locations like the Bradbury Building, Mariachi Plaza, and Million Dollar Theater as well as nondescript spaces like an abandoned parking lot in Boyle Heights, unused loading docks in the Arts District, and a vista point in Elysian Park. The line between fiction and reality was constantly blurred for people we dubbed "unexpected audience members." But in a movie town like Los Angeles, where every corner is a backdrop for filming, our situations were rarely disruptive or alarming to bystanders. In most cases, they were written off as "just another film shoot." In a scene depicting Lucha and Jameson's marriage, for example, the performers ran up or down the grand stairway of City Hall with the audience watching from the car. At one performance, the singers made it to the top of the stairs and found Mayor Eric Garcetti addressing an assembly of staff members. He stopped his address to publicly acknowledge the couple: "Look at those two getting married in our building. Let's congratulate them with a round of applause!"

I constantly looked for ways to blur the line of inside-outside— letting the life of the streets infiltrate the seemingly hermetic sphere of the car. With antennae mounted on top of the cars and microphones on our singers, passengers found themselves "eavesdropping" on scenes taking place outside. In the accident scene, for example, where Lucha's car hits Jameson's motorcycle, the two actors played the scene intimately while the audience's car slowly circled them. The passengers inside could hear every word, "underscored" by live improvisation in the car by a beatboxing harpist I happened to see perform at the Hollywood Farmer's Market. In another scene on a different route, the spectators sat with an unnamed stranger who struck up a conversation with Jameson, riding alongside the car on his motorcycle. Jameson continuously circled the car as they navigated LA streets in real time, and at one point even "threw" his red notebook, a critical object in the plot, into the hands of the stranger in the car. (And mind you, like every other performer, the actors repeated this nail-biter on the open road twenty-four times a day.)

Because the text and score were written specifically for *Hopscotch*'s unusual parameters, each chapter influenced the music as it was being composed. For the entire operation to be synchronized, each piece had to run exactly ten minutes. In one scene that traversed Elysian Park, the drive took only five minutes, so we let the audience take a short stroll outside toward a vista point. Composer Andrew McIntosh wrote the scene in the car for two sopranos—one playing Lucha and one Jameson—and saxophone. But on the stroll to the vista, the saxophone merged with three other saxophones, creating a bewitching short quartet that remains, to me, one of the musical highlights of the entire work.

In every aspect, the project demanded a give-and-take attitude from each participant. What was available to us shaped everything we did, and nothing was used that wasn't in some way connected to the ideas. And all those ideas needed to find harmony with unpredictable forces: traffic, road closures, demonstrations, weather, flat tires ... the list goes on.

Artists (especially directors) are often viewed as control freaks. The theater might seem to provide a haven of control from a world in flux. You can dictate the ideal light, the exact shade of yellow, the perfect choreography of humans in and out of the space. But people often fail to account for the wild card of live performance, where cues misfire, actors forget their staging, or someone gets sick. Despite those "risk factors" (to my mind, the very factors that make up theater's electricity), many artists *are* drawn to the theater to exercise a sense of control over time and space—perhaps as a refuge for how little we control our everyday reality. *Hopscotch* is a nightmare scenario for that kind of artist; there was no way to control much of anything. Precisely for that reason, I found it a profound exercise for living. We all had to seek joy in the limits of our control.

Since I could only be in one place at a time, I would never know how things were running beyond what was broadcast at the Central Hub. I had to fundamentally trust the flow of what we had constructed, which meant trusting each participant. The level of cooperation required was staggering. My partner in the building of that cooperation was Elizabeth Cline, Executive Director of The Industry at the time, who was not just a great thought partner artistically but an expert overseer of the entire operation, from ticketing to permitting to post-show parties. Elizabeth and I forged relationships with organizations that offered the best chances for success, including government entities like LA's Parks and Recreation and the Department of Transportation (which generously agreed to biweekly meetings in the months leading up to the project); neighborhood associations like the Business Improvement Districts for downtown and Chinatown and the East LA Community Corporation in Boyle Heights; real estate developers who authorized the use of their properties for a project I'm sure they didn't quite understand; colleges like the Southern California Institute of Architecture and the University of Southern California, where students helped us think through the opera's thornier logistics; and commercial firms like Sennheiser, the sound technology company that donated their equipment to help us realize the inside-outside scenes.

Elizabeth called *Hopscotch* a "micro-economy" of Los Angeles artists, artisans, and technicians. Working closely with Elizabeth and me was Ash Nichols, the perfect person to take on the outsized role of production manager: Ash devised the chain of communication and oversaw the structure for making the performances run like clockwork. One technical director was not going to suffice for the project's myriad challenges, so we had two ingenious ones: Edward Carlson and Danielle Kaufman. Working under Ash was an army of stage managers (who oversaw the routes) and assistant stage managers (who supervised individual chapters). And then, of course, there were the twenty-four drivers.

In the early days of *Hopscotch*, I imagined our cars would be the classic Volkswagen Bus. We obviously needed a car large enough to house a group of audience members and artists, and the beloved '60s van symbolized the freewheeling spirit that I imagined this project embodying. "The VW bus had become the iconic image of the counterculture," wrote Jill Lepore in a 2022 *New Yorker* article. "You could go to concerts in it, or to protests. You could smoke pot in it, or fool around. You could sleep there, on the cheap. You could plot a revolution, or you could store your surfboard." But even for a project where nothing seemed too daunting, the idea of finding twenty-four of those now rare cars was a bridge too far. After much research (and frequent "Why are you doing this?"–style rejections), we managed to secure a partnership with a private firm called Wilshire Limousines. The request to their general manager, Michael Kushner, was formidable: we would need the *same* twenty-four cars every weekend throughout the fall, as well as for the rehearsals in the weeks leading up to the performances. We somehow made a deal that fit within our budget, and the company proved a trustworthy and dedicated partner—even after watching us mount projectors to the top of one of their limos.

At first I was concerned that limousines would signal the kind of elitism and exclusivity my company was founded to overturn. But Michael helped me come to terms with them when he explained that he rarely gets requests for limos anymore. His clients now consider them outdated, preferring to show up to red carpet affairs in a "real" status symbol like a large SUV. Limousines have surprisingly become a more accessible way to mark a social rite of passage, most frequently for teenagers celebrating proms, bar mitzvahs, and *quinceañeras.* Something about an out-of-time car as the vessel for a mobile, guerrilla opera had a paradoxical logic. And since it was truly our only viable option, we simply had to make it work.

It may seem hypocritical of me to advocate for opera to be less wasteful of natural resources and then initiate a project that could be considered a celebration of car culture. Yet in some ways, the "carpool" effect of the piece—riding alongside strangers, experiencing the city in a group—could be seen as promoting the kind of mass transit Los

Angeles used to enjoy before infamously dismantling it all to pave the way for cars. Likewise, Debord's group of Situationists advocated in the 1960s for a system of free taxi shuttles around the city to facilitate mobility while counteracting private transportation—an idea way ahead of its time, emerging again now as a possibility in smaller communities with the rise of self-driving vehicles. Compared with operas requiring huge sets to be shipped internationally, *Hopscotch*'s use of the available city infrastructure likely created a much smaller footprint. On the other hand, ours were twenty-four "use-less" cars that didn't "need" to be on the road, with gas and oil burning just "for the beauty of the act." So, as was the case for *Sweet Land,* if I try tallying up the environmental impact versus efforts in resourcefulness, the best I can hope for is a mixed result.

Then again, look at the massive assembly of artists, institutions, and organizations who gathered around the vision for *Hopscotch.* Even in fractured times, we sometimes succeed in finding ways to co-create together and to problem-solve collaboratively. Without restricting the opera to a "use," I believe there are lessons here that transcend the realm of aesthetics. Some people may have been attracted by the stunt of it all, but most everyone seemed devoted to this project because they were inspired to explore ways to live our lives differently.

Much of traditional opera revolves around the notion of diva worship. *Hopscotch* offered an alternative: what if it's the collective, rather than the individual, that can inspire us to awe?

// // // // //

WHILE *HOPSCOTCH* WAS OBVIOUSLY A huge departure from anything that could be accomplished in an opera house or with a conventionally organized opera company, I have nevertheless tried to deploy similar tactics in the traditional environment. The most prominent example was *Twilight: Gods,* a drive-thru adaptation of the last part of Wagner's *Ring* cycle as a response to the Covid lockdown. While Detroit Opera's theater could not be used, its parking garage could.

Audiences in six to eight cars at a time heard live performances of Wagner's epic (condensed into an hour-long exploration of dissolution and conflagration) as they slowly ascended the levels of the garage, by changing the dial on their FM radios. In the open-air top level, Brünnhilde was driven off to her suicide by a Ford Mustang. (What could be more Detroit than that?) The project was co-produced by Lyric Opera of Chicago, which presented the work six months later in the more foreboding and labyrinthine underground garage in Millennium Park. The work had completely different implications depending on the space (a vertical ascent with a constant view outside as opposed to a lateral movement through darkness) and time (at the heart of the pandemic and weeks before the 2020 election, versus the time of the cautious first vaccine doses and in the wake of an attempted insurrection). And the work itself was also different in the two locations: poetry written by two poets embedded in their community (Marsha Music in Detroit and avery r. young in Chicago) wove the piece together, contextualizing the same music in completely distinct ways. *Twilight: Gods* adapted to reflect the place where it was performing as shaped by local artists—a hallmark of what *Hopscotch* was all about.

Otherwise, experiences like *Hopscotch* are rare, both shamelessly unsustainable (the elements barely held together until the last performance) and brazenly unrepeatable (the chance of reassembling this behemoth seems ludicrous and unlikely to satisfy). It was not designed to leave behind deep footprints. A recording exists that preserves selections from its spectacular music—well worth hearing and performing in other contexts. But no video could truly encapsulate the experience. In place of any conventional visual documentation, we assembled an online scrapbook (www.hopscotchopera.com). The exact routes, a chapter-by-chapter breakdown of what happened and who participated, and the ten animations are all still there at the time of this writing.

Beyond that digital archive, *Hopscotch* has essentially ceased to exist. It was a work *of the moment*, and as such, follows in the footsteps of the very earliest operas: spectacular works defying genre divisions, written for a specific occasion, for specific artists, and with no eye toward posterity or preservation. They were provisional acts of collective imagination.

In the end, you just "had to be there"—a phrase I've often heard from people trying to explain their experience of *Hopscotch* to others.

As an overture to this book, I imagined a future where opera as we know it no longer exists. When opera houses are converted into shopping malls, what would a reborn opera look like? What would emerge from the unruly and barely explicable impulse to collectively create? If opera is the art of rebirth, works like *Hopscotch* could help us imagine what the art form might look like in that future. It obviously doesn't need to be performed in cars; that would be taking the opera's superficial aspects as the key ingredient. Instead, *Hopscotch* attempted to escape everything, in every way, that has kept opera fixed in well-worn patterns. If I were to enumerate those characteristics of *Hopscotch* that could point to a reborn and anti-elite future, the list would look like this:

- Opera as temporary, ephemeral, and provisional rather than eternal and unchanging.
- Opera as embedded in the city and communities that it performs in and for—as evidenced in the actual work being produced, rather than supplementary activity around the art-making.
- Opera as syncretic, investigating what is of the moment, such as technological possibilities.
- Opera beyond the framework and expectations of the proscenium-bound theater.
- Opera with an expansive sense of form.
- Opera as an *adventure*—consistently awe-inspiring and never-before-seen. Wherever the work is difficult, the creators and producers provide testimony to the idea that *the challenge is the pleasure.*

New York
1955

Bayreuth, Germany
1951

With her performance of Ulrica in Verdi's *Un ballo in maschera* (1859), contralto Marian Anderson becomes the first Black singer to perform at the Metropolitan Opera.

See PLAYLIST

But her best-known performance remains the one she gave at the Lincoln Memorial in 1939, after she was denied permission to sing at Constitution Hall for the Daughters of the American Revolution.

Following a prolonged closure after Wo[r] War II, Wieland Wagner reopens the theater his grandfather built with a radically abstract production of *Parsifa[l]*. Representative sets are replaced by emptiness and extraordinary lighting, which stops replicating a naturalistic "ti[me] of day" and starts reflecting the psychol[ogy] and atmosphere of the drama. His style becomes known as "New Bayreuth" and unleashes the outrage of faithful keeper[s] the Wagnerian grail, who band togethe[r] under the name "Club for the Faithful Rendition of Richard Wagner's Works."

OPERA & POLITICS

Wieland Wagner's move toward abstraction is conventionally read as pro[of] that music and theater can transcend politics. I think that misses the poin[t] entirely: what is astonishing about "New Bayreuth" is how an avant-garde approach can be deployed in such a politically effective manner.

Rather than a move toward "purity"—surely a fraught term after the Nazi genocide—abstraction offered a clear political repudiation of the past. Not even a decade had gone by since Bayreuth was the cultural center of Germany's Third Reich, with elaborate, conservative performances of Wagner's *Die Meistersinger* "entertaining" the troops with propaganda of German superiority.

London
1945

Benjamin Britten's grand opera *Peter Grimes* premieres, with his longtime companion and muse, the tenor Peter Pears, portraying the central character. A small fishermen's village becomes a petri dish for Britten to examine the consequences of pressure upon outsiders to fit into "respectable" society.

See PLAYLIST

1938

Wieland Wagner, right, with Adolf Hitler and his mother, Winifred, at the opening of Bayreuth in 1938. Wieland Wagner created the sets for the wartime festival performances of *Meistersinger*.

With the chorus "Va, pensiero" from his opera *Nabucco* serving an unofficial anthem for the Italian *Risorgimento*, Giuseppe Verdi enters the parliament of the newly unified republic and serves for four years. Thirteen years later, although disenchanted with politics, Verdi is named a lifelong senator by King Victor Emmanuel.

Wieland Wagner designed those Nazi-era *Meistersinger* productions as well, so he was deeply aware of the connection between visual representation and political agenda.) The political instrumentalization of Wagner shattered the facile assumption that opera and culture in general were only edifying and ameliorative, which is what Theodor Adorno meant when he said that poetry was no longer possible after Auschwitz. Not far from Wagner's theater, his music accompanied Jews and other "undesirable" members of society to gas chambers and executions.

Italy
1861

Vienna
1903

Secessionist artist Alfred Roller designs sets, costumes, and lighting for a new production of Wagner's *Tristan und Isolde* at the invitation of the Court Opera's director, Gustav Mahler. Rejecting the more pictorial approach of his time, Roller claims that "stages are not pictures but spaces, tailored to fit the work of the authors and the action of the performer." Roller's more symbolic, simplified, and nonnaturalistic approach sends shockwaves through the Viennese public—the press labels it "Lichtmusik"—which leads the ever-provocative Mahler to invite him back repeatedly for the next four years.

British actor and director Gordon Craig leads the Moscow Art Theatre's acclaimed production of *Hamlet* and publishes *On the Art of Theatre*, an imaginary dialogue between a playgoer and a director that speaks of a total unity of all theatrical elements. For Craig, directors are "the true artist of the theatre" who will bring about a true Renaissance of the stage. He was a ruthless innovator and a spiritual heir to Richard Wagner: In a London production of Purcell's *Dido and Aeneas*, Craig sought "to make illusion more complete" by filling the performance space with scents—sulfur during the witches' scene and perfumes while rose petals dropped on Dido.

1911

PRODUCTION AS A TEMPORARY ART WORK

Wieland Wagner famously stated that "every new production is an adventure to an unknown destination." A beautiful concept, which could be elaborated as such: "every new production, with a constantly changing collection of personalities, demands its own rules of engagement." Rather than approach each work with the rigid view of "how things are done," the most creative productions rewrite the rules, influenced by the people involved; the city the work is being performed in; and the time of its realization, which supersedes the time of the work's writing, each and every time.

1899

The Swiss artist Adolphe Appia publishes *Music and the Art of Theatre*, which lays out theories for the embodiment of a musical text. Appia advocates against the two-dimensional painted backdrops of his time and promotes uncluttered three-dimensional sets, illuminated with intricate lighting, where the performer can be more fully integrated into the image. Although he is unable to put his own ideas into practice for another twenty years, his writing inspires Roller—as well as Wieland Wagner and Robert Wilson many years later.

1932

Arnold Schoenberg composes Acts I and II of his magnum opus, *Moses und Aron*, in a new musical system he has invented. Act III is never completed and the work remains unfinished; it nevertheless receives a posthumous world premiere in Zurich in 1957.

See PLAYLIST

La Scala,
Italy

1926

Giacomo Puccini's final opera, *Turandot*, receives its premiere, even though the opera was never completed.

See PLAYLIST

Berlin,
Germany

1925

Alban Berg, a dedicated disciple of Schoenberg, premieres the opera *Wozzeck*. The work incorporates atonality and the half-spoken, half-sung style known as *Sprechstimme* into its bleak but dazzling expression of the inner lives of impoverished people. Georg Büchner's unfinished play offers the perfect vehicle for Berg, each episode of the drama a chance for him to explore a formally inventive idea.

See PLAYLIST

1911

Scott Joplin, a Black composer and pianist known as the "king of ragtime," publishes his opera *Treemonisha*. The work goes unperformed for more than sixty years.

Russia

The Futurist opera *Victory Over the Sun* premieres in Saint Petersburg. Written in the invented language of "zaum" and with stage designs by Kasimir Malevich, the opera—although vehemently rejected by the audience—becomes a symbol for the avant-garde art that accompanies the sweeping changes of the upcoming Bolshevik Revolution.

1913

Utah

In regional theaters in the American West, the Sioux poet and musician Zitkala Ša creates the *Sun Dance Opera*, depicting rituals that were banned by the Bureau of Indian Affairs. Ša keeps key moments in the Sioux vernacular but collaborates with William Hanson, who integrates her work into a conventional European context. Justifying the project while co-opting authorship of the work when the production is invited to New York after Ša's death, Hanson writes about himself in the third person: "This writer's ambitions were further augmented when he realized that the unrecorded aboriginal songs, the rituals, and the habits (the National culture) were doomed to oblivion in the natural processes which were rapidly allowing the policies of the white man to have complete power and domination of America. . . . The most efficient mode of transcribing and interpreting the culture was in OPERA FORM."

La Scala, Milan

1893

Verdi's final opera, *Falstaff*, has its world premiere, capping a career that encapsulates the full transformation of Italian opera from *bel canto* to verismo and beyond. After devoting his life to elaborate, grand tragedies, Verdi says farewell to the stage with a comedy, one that concludes, "Everything in life is a joke—and he who laughs last, laughs best."

See PLAYLIST

Bayreuth, Germany

1882

Wagner's final opera, *Parsifal*, premieres one year before his death. Because it was written specifically for the acoustics of his theater, *Parsifal* is forbidden from being performed anywhere but Bayreuth, a restriction that stays firmly in place for almost twenty years.

See PLAYLIST

Bayreuth, Germany

1876

Richard Wagner opens his Festspielhaus, an austere building on a green, rural hill that could easily be confused for a barn. Its hard wooden seats and unadorned walls are meant to focus the audience's attention exclusively on the operas as they unfold. The plain architecture serves as one of the instruments in the performance of Wagner's epic four-work cycle *Der Ring des Nibelungen*. The orchestra vanishes from sight; where opera audiences are used to seeing instrumentalists, the Bayreuth audience instead faces "a mystical abyss." Sound is now disembodied and emanates, rather than results from any human activity. With a performance time of nearly sixteen hours and music that sounds like nothing else ever written, *Der Ring* remains an unparalleled achievement in theater. Opera will never be the same again.

See PLAYLIST

THE ARTWORK OF THE FUTURE

Richard Wagner is the ultimate swerve in opera's history, a crater on the surface of the opera world. Inspired by the nascent Marxist movement and outlawed from Germany for his involvement in the 1848 Dresden uprising, Wagner's work has revolution written all over it. Drunk on the future, he imagined a new form that fused all the arts into a single entity—a *Gesamtkunstwerk*, or total work of art. Don't call them operas—well, at least he didn't. They were stage consecrations, festivals, or simply *Handlungen*, dramas. Opera as he knew it was a bloated and elite paean to a world order that had to be overthrown. Instead, this new, total work of art (as he describes it in his essay "The Artwork of the Future") "encompasses all art forms, employing each one as a resource, to destroy them for a totalizing purpose: the absolute embodiment of a fully realized human nature." →

THE ARTWORK
OF THE FUTURE (continued)

← For his *Ring* cycle, Wagner served as his own stage director and wrote all the words and music for a four-day spectacle (not to mention his involvement in the fundraising and producing of this first festival). His original intention was for the theater to be burnt down on completion of the first festival—part of the reason for its simple wood construction, and certainly why the final opera, *Götterdämmerung*, ends with a conflagration. Yet the theater remains operational today, performing only Wagner's ten major works. In her diaries, Wagner's widow, Cosima, implies that the theater couldn't be destroyed because of the heavy debt the family faced in the wake of the first *Ring* cycle's massive costs. Yet this logic seems questionable, especially considering how enamored King Ludwig of Bavaria was by an artist he named his "magician from Bayreuth." More likely, a gnawing sense of legacy, and its accompanying vanity, took hold. Someone like Richard Wagner comes along only once a century—would they really have burned a theater that Homer had built for the recitation of his epic poems?

But perhaps there was something more than self-preservation at play. In the months following the premiere of the *Ring*, Cosima's diaries depict an artist in deep despair. Wagner hated the scenic realization of his own work, which looked and felt nothing like the larger-than-life images depicted in the music. Listening to the opening and the first scene of the tetralogy's first opera, *Das Rheingold*, you get a sense of movement, freedom, and silvery sirens embodying the untroubled stream. Instead, in reality, Wagner had to make do with rather clunky contraptions holding up his sopranos in an absurd illusion of swimming in water. He failed to create a radical break from traditional theater: gravitational forces could not be overcome, and the proscenium reinforced a sense of a static picture more than an evolving stage reality that, like the "endless melody" of the score, would be constantly in motion, changing and becoming. So after the *Ring*, Wagner felt his notion of *Gesamtkunstwerk* needed to be rethought. "I made the invisible orchestra," Wagner remarked; "now I need to make the invisible theater."

Perhaps this is why, beyond even the consideration of posterity, he didn't follow his plans to destroy his building: not only had he failed to reach the endpoint he desired, but he discovered that an imagined endpoint was unrealizable. There was no such thing as the final artwork, just as there is no possibility of ever becoming "the fully realized human being." There is always room for transformation and always something new to explore. Wagner may not yet have figured out how to articulate the visions he transcribed onto paper, but he trusted that the future would discover new directions. Those new paths would also inspire composers—Mahler, Schoenberg, Strauss, Messiaen, Stockhausen, and Anthony Braxton, to name the most obvious ones—who would keep exploring the furthest boundaries of music-dramatic possibilities, not to mention visual artists and directors (like Wagner's own grandsons) who would explore their most resonant embodiments. Wagner may have wanted to become opera's final destination—the last stop in opera's evolution—but he realized he was destined to be a hub in never-ending cycles of human searching, a roundabout sprouting endless forking roads, connecting forward and backward in time. Wagner acknowledged this unquenchable drive to his children when he urged them not to follow blindly in his footsteps, commanding them instead, *"Kinder! Schafft Neues!"*—"My children! Create new things!"

That charge might well be his most important legacy.

UNRESOLVED PARADOXES

WHERE OPERA SPEAKS SPIRITUALLY

The unseen things are our masterpieces
The seen things are merely by-products.
—BEN OKRI

A PARADOX: WHILE LISTENING TO JOHN COLTRANE'S "The Father and the Son and the Holy Ghost," I almost failed to notice that the needle of the record player was stuck in a groove. The loop was perfect, so I let it play on for nearly an hour. I traveled far in that moment, as chance allowed the infinite to appear in finite time.

We describe our experience of time as an arrow, moving in one direction. All our communication and coordination rely on our agreeing to a measure of time divided into regular intervals: twenty-four hours a day, sixty minutes per hour, sixty seconds per minute. But music holds out a proposition: what if a group of artists decide to escape that regularity and commit to another experience of time—one that decelerates, or one that gradually speeds up?

All music, ultimately, is an organization of time, building off our personal metronomes: the beating of our hearts, the cadence of our steps, the ebb and flow of our breath. And through elongation or acceleration, music shows us how easy it is to slip out of a linear experience of time. Even if art is inextricably bound to the world and its materiality, music can shed light on hidden dimensions of reality, like those exposed by an infinitely looping record.

In opera, the illusionistic sense of progression—a beginning and an end, a "drama" of causality and forward motion—coexists with a cyclic experience of time: repetition, recall, a spiral motion. This is the core conflict of our perception of existence: a linear "tragedy" that runs from birth to death, and the spiritual potential of being, infinitely more profound than that superficial story. (Talk about a "time-curve!")

When we view opera as suspended time, we arrive at its proximity to ritual. The superficial and dispirited aspects of ritual, like the rote repetition young Parsifal witnesses, are often, so to speak, downstage— being the most immediately apparent. They can bury the powerful and often subconscious aspects of ritual focused on transcendence: those choreographed and communal actions that invite us to look beyond our narrow understanding of life.

What the elderly knight tells the baffled young Parsifal—"Here time becomes space"—should be true of opera. It should help us break out of our limited perspective on the world, which, like a flashlight in the dark, misses the vast majority of reality. If everyday life requires us to narrow our focus, art momentarily broadens that focus. Sometimes gently, sometimes irrevocably. Opera, working in many dimensions at the same time, is the art form best suited to the irrevocable mode—all the more so when we experiment with bending the seemingly most fixed elements of our reality: time and space.

When opera escapes time, we get to the heart of theater's metaphysical potential. The human voice, raised beyond everyday speech into singing, carries with it a communion with the realm of the spirit. Gary Tomlinson, in *Metaphysical Song*, refutes the long-held assumption that the earliest operas required excuses to justify characters' singing their thoughts (the characters needed to be singers like Orpheus, or the scene had to depict celebratory events where singing and dancing were expected, and so on). He argues that premodern operas, rather than attempting to make singing seem like a natural thing to do in a scene, depicted the sung human voice as capturing an *otherworldly* quality. The unnaturalness of singing opens up other realms beyond what we perceive in our daily lives. Orpheus and other mythological musicians were not the obvious choice of protagonists for this new form of music drama because it "made sense" that they would sing; instead, music allowed characters to traverse the border of this world and the next. "They affirmed the existence of higher orders of expression that are a supersensible part of the natural order itself," Tomlinson writes. The nature of a drama at the threshold of perception requires something other than speech. The rigor of musical training pushes our most intimate instrument to become a tool for connecting to other dimensions. "The voice could create correspondences, through the soul, to the harmonic concord of the cosmos."

In other words, a single human voice contains multitudes. Place that single voice into a theatrical space teeming with other voices and you have a dizzying, large-scale feat of materiality: bodies, objects, and lights in space, coordinated by a mutually agreed upon chronology. An enormous physical vessel to capture an experience of what Tomlinson calls the "supersensible"—that is the central paradox of opera, the immaterial expressed through entirely material means.

Thinking about ritual and the spiritual dimension of the live arts is a potentially sacrilegious notion for those conditioned by dogma. But theater as a metaphor for an illusionistic experience of reality is common in many spiritual traditions. Reading the Shvetashvatara Upanishad, I was struck by a reference to the creator of the world as "the great magician." This magician creates the entire material world as a series of images, sensual illusions that we need to look past to get to the true Self inherent in every creature. Only then do we realize that the material world is a distraction from the authentic reality inside each of us.

The theatricality of "the great magician" made me consider whether "the great director" wouldn't be just as appropriate: directors, like magicians, expend much energy on employing artificial elements to seduce the audience. But a magician's showmanship is not the director's end point: stagecraft is in service of the immaterial, the content that will hopefully be revealed through the artificial elements. Every new production confronts the director with the challenge of illuminating the indefinable inner life of a work through things coarse enough to be perceptible.

This is one reason opera can seem so utterly absurd. As long as there are singers, instruments, sets, and costumes that attempt to depict characters and dramatic situations, opera is imprisoned in the material world. Outside the theater, music can seem to speak directly to the soul. But as a component of opera, music's power is harnessed as a garb for theatrics—uncomfortably saddled with the narrative demands of drama. Doesn't opera ultimately rob music of its power, by reducing it to the servitude of some other master? In becoming material, music can often seem to calcify before our eyes. You notice the singer struggling for breath, the heaviness of the material set, the effort being made to enter into dialogue with a music that seems able to accomplish everything on its own. The *Turn of the Screw* problem discussed in Chapter Four isn't limited to Britten's opera but is a fundamental paradox of the entire operatic enterprise.

Even more challenging to inflect than Britten's opera are those that make the ineffable their subject matter. Take Wagner's *Tristan und Isolde* (1865), the ultimate work about the unresolvable tension between what is visible and what remains invisible. Ostensibly the story of an illicit affair between a king's vassal and the new queen, Wagner's three-act, five-hour epic is finally an expression of love as a cosmic force that obliterates any trace of ego. In Act II, an hour-long love duet examining the philosophical possibilities of individuals melting into some new entity gives way, almost comically, to action dispatched in thirty seconds. It's as if Wagner can't really be bothered with the narrative and prefers to focus on the way his music chisels out of air the most subtle gradations of a transcendental experience. I don't think *Tristan* should even be called an opera, since so much transpires that can never be expressed by the singers or production. This is what makes it the single hardest work in the traditional repertoire to stage: in the demand to find physical form for what the music expresses, performances inevitably revert to the material and the inescapable experience of traditional opera.

A similar paradox faces Debussy's *Pelléas et Mélisande*, with a libretto by the Symbolist poet Maurice Maeterlink. It's less an opera than a piece of poetry full of symbols and images, much of it rotating around Mélisande's voluptuous hair. Her lover Pelléas sings an ecstatic aria while losing himself in her hair, and in the next act her jealous husband uses that same hair to violently pull her in the four directions of the cross. On paper (as a libretto and as a score), these dreamy scenes are completely convincing, even devastating. But put yourself in the place of the poor stage director, who is charged with finding a visual realization for Mélisande's hair! Pierre Boulez, in his essay "Reflections on *Pelléas*," put it best: "The poetic themes in *Pelléas* often remain imaginary in character and their representation on the stage is marked by a heavy realism that contradicts their dream-like quality. . . . It proves in practice extremely hard to make this symbolism of hair-as-river, hair-as-erotic-symbol visually acceptable, even plausible. The poetic, imaginary vision is difficult to combine with a girl leaning out of a window and hair that is quite obviously a wig."

Especially in the case of operas like *Tristan* and *Pelléas*, staging an opera can seem like a losing proposition. Why do we foolishly continue inflecting works that can never reach a true inflection point? Yet that might be what I love most about opera: there is no such thing as a final, perfect production of any work. The gulf between the idea and its possible realization is fundamentally unbridgeable; it's precisely that tension between what can and cannot be depicted, between the material and the immaterial, that makes opera infinite and always incomplete. The quixotic struggle to make the immaterial material becomes the touchstone of opera's aspirational quality.

Yet here is the same paradox that religious communities face: having to invoke the invisible through purely visible means. Spirituality would be easy if we could get rid of material reality. In the case of opera, nothing happens without the wood of a violin, the breath of a performer, the metal that produces the exact bell-like sound the composer is imagining, and of course the organic tissue of each human participant. As much as we might wish we could escape into a purely abstract world where ideas alone can become searing events, we can't ever banish the theater's thingness. In fact, in an irony that can sometimes feel tragic, that materiality must be the messenger of the spiritual.

In Chapter Three, I argued that the emotional life of opera does not reside in the music *per se* but in the interpretation of that music, primarily through the singing actor. I believe the same is true of the spiritual life of opera, which does not reside in the music but only in the music as it's being made. Nevertheless, the first uneasy transposition from an immaterial realm to material reality begins with the composer. Before a piece can be performed, it must be notated—much to the dismay of many a composer, working under intense deadlines to deliver a tiny bit of access into the invisible arena they are attempting to articulate. In that process of notation, the composer takes the first steps toward transporting thoughts that resist all form into something performers can learn and reproduce.

In the liner notes for a recording of Arnold Schoenberg's music, the great conductor Daniel Barenboim sets up the perfect framework for appreciating the excruciating act of pinning music down to paper:

> Like all works of music, Schoenberg's pieces were initially present only in the imagination, in the mind of the composer. It had nothing to do with anyone else or indeed with the real world. When the composer has written it down it is already a reduction, and before one can talk about a performance at all, one has to consider the orchestra and the conductor who introduce these pieces into our physical world. . . . I can think of a sound in my mind, and it can last forever. But when I play the same sound on the piano, it dies away. For this reason, transferring

it from the cosmos, where it only exists in the imagination and the mind of the composer, to the real world is a decisive and complicated process.

What Barenboim conveys so beautifully is the art of translation at the heart of all expression. Interpretation is not only left to performers; the score itself is already an interpretation, the composer's—of something much vaster than our visible world. The music defies getting pinned down, but a composer wrestles with it anyway.

The conventional view of musical masterpieces considers the score a perfect realization, not the distillation of a larger vision. Thus, "as it is written, so shall it be done"—the interpreters become obedient servants of the handed-down scripture. The score is not a prompt for further investigation but a holy text to be painstakingly re-created. But there is so much more excitement, energy, and even profundity in considering the score an *approximation* at best—as Barenboim put it, a "reduction" of a work's true spirit.

Composers have used different tactics in trying to bridge the abyss between their immaterial ideas and the incompleteness of the notated score. On one end of the spectrum is Gustav Mahler, whose elaborately orchestrated symphonies are accompanied with idiosyncratic instructions: "*duftig*" (filmy, hazy); "*ersterbend*" (dying away); "*gesangvoll hervortretend*" (emerging full of song); "*immer fern und ferner*" (farther and farther away); "*bis zur Unhörbarkeit abnehmen*" (decrease to the point of inaudibility). His directions reveal Mahler to be something of a control freak, flailing against the impossibility of fixing ideas to a page. But as an artist more renowned in his lifetime for his conducting than for composing, Mahler must have known how much is lost once the music is offered to someone who doesn't share the same brain as the person who struggled to write it. That epic resistance at the outset of all his symphonies shows a man wrestling with how little of what he experiences can actually be expressed. The titanic soundscapes he still managed to create push as hard as possible against the limitation of a written language's communicability.

On the other end of the spectrum are the scores of Monteverdi—the open matrix of *L'Orfeo* and moments like "Addio Roma" from *The Coronation of Poppea*, which leave everything open to interpretation. Monteverdi's scores reveal a worldview where his role as composer was less central, where the oral tradition still mattered and the ephemerality of music was a given. Mahler's worldview considers the composer a creative god and the score his granite tablets, awaiting the interpreter prophets. The incompleteness of the score is clearly a matter of frustration for Mahler, recalling Moses's final line in Schoenberg's *Moses und Aron:* "Oh Word, you Word that I lack!"

Yet incompleteness is embraced by Monteverdi—the mark of his greatness, humbly viewing humanity as a cooperative condition. Rather than handmaidens for a composer, interpreters are a composer's collaborative partners. That notion has inspired the most interesting contemporary composers, even if it places their work in a precarious circumstance. Meredith Monk's *ATLAS* was written on the voices and the bodies of her original cast, and until my production in 2019, a fully notated score did not exist. Making a score was an essential part of ensuring the work's longevity, but the process wasn't easy for Monk, since the act of pinning down a performance in notation is antithetical to the spirit of her work.

The published score of *ATLAS* now, similar to Monteverdi's, consists of a set of spare instructions to facilitate future discovery. A performer who treated the musical lines with the kind of unwavering reverence Mahler demanded will not produce a satisfying performance. Robert Ashley's operas lacked fully notated scores as well, as he expected his performers to improvise large sections. Ashley considered this kind of openness the cornerstone of his work, according to his website.

> The collaborative aspect of the work follows principles I have used for many years in search of a new operatic style. The collaborators are given almost absolute freedom to develop characterizations from the textual and musical materials I provide. . . . The collaborators in all aspects of the work are free to interpret, 'improvise', invent and superimpose characteristics of their own artistic styles onto the texture of the work. In essence, the

collaborators become 'characters' in the opera at a deeper level than the illusionistic characters who appear on stage.

In that spirit, we can draw a connection between Ashley and the origins of opera—a fact that was not lost on the writer Kyle Gann, who reviewed his work for the *Village Voice*: "When the 21st Century glances back to see where the future of opera came from, Ashley, like Monteverdi before him, is going to look like a radical new beginning."

// // // // //

THINKING ABOUT MUSIC'S HOLINESS and the spiritual dimension of theater, I find myself returning to an image from José Ortega y Gasset's book *Meditations on Quixote*: "The individual cannot get his bearings in the universe except through his race, because he is immersed in it like the drop of water in the passing cloud." This is a profound skyscape that has haunted me ever since first reading it. The drifting cloud represents the nebulous aspects of our personality that we have no chance of outrunning, so formative in shaping our perception of the world that they become inextricable from our identity. Culture, race, nationality envelop us even in exile. Such notions have led me to consider how the Jewish heritage I carry in my DNA has shaped my philosophy of opera. Even more profoundly than a national identity, my religious upbringing has colored every aspect of how I approach my work. It surrounds me like a cloud, one that I ignore at my peril.

In Jewish tradition, the essence of God is so far beyond the scope of human comprehension that *any* act of representation is an affront to that sublime truth. Therefore, in stark relief to lavish cathedrals with the noblest representations of the Word made flesh, synagogues are for the most part pure architecture. No imagery for risk of idolatry, no architectural ostentation for risk of distraction from the human. And yet, somehow, so many Jews rush to participate in activities like theater, film, and opera. (Go figure!) Perhaps this is because Jewish thinking is rich in metaphor and emanation. Those qualities are ultimately what theater is all about. Any pretense of "direct representation," an event interchangeable with reality as we know it, is either hubristic or naive. The stage transforms something recognizable and commonplace into something strange and unfamiliar—what Brecht called theater's capacity for *Verfremdung,* or alienation. What we see exhibited before us is fundamentally unrealistic, but not untrue, or at least not inauthentic. ("Lying," as Oscar Wilde said, or "the telling of beautiful untrue things, is the proper aim of art.") Art can reflect life but not by mimicking realism. Symbol, metaphor, and abstraction offer an indirect and poetic path to a true essence.

Although Jews are often considered "people of the book," oral tradition played a major role in the creation of our sacred texts. The transition from oral to written tradition in Judaism was a controversial move in BCE times because it threatened to turn sacred teaching into something reified and fixed—the same anxiety faced by composers grappling with notation. In Judaism, the Talmud emerged: a massive collection of reflections and interpretations of the Mishnah text. The essence of the Talmud is the spirit of debate and discourse, and the dizzying flurry of voices that make up the Talmud allow the original text to remain a living and open-ended document. (The original "open work," if you will.) If anything could possibly embody the evolutionary and dialogic essence of Judaism, the Talmud would be it.

My study of Jewish scripture remains limited, but a lifetime of experiencing the world from the perspective of my heritage has naturally shaped my perspective of all texts. It's the cloud that surrounds the little drop of rain of my life. So it is, perhaps, inevitable that my view of opera is fundamentally Talmudic, involving the inexhaustible rereading and discussing of texts that we consider incomplete. Engaging with the Talmud means entering into a centuries-long, never-ending dialogue—and engaging with opera should feel the same. Even as the original libretto remains exactly as it is, there's always something new to be gleaned. The act of interpretation never obliterates the original but aims to unlock it. Our purpose is not novelty, nor do we expect to exhaust the possibilities with a final word. No ultimate reading exists.

Just as there are few definitive statements in the Talmud, I imagine my own transitory work on profound older texts to be at best a link in a long chain of dialogue. I'm picking up on a conversation, not at its beginning and not at its end. I'm inviting the future to participate. My work is done not for my own sake, but to perpetuate a line of inquiry that helps us grapple with the visible and the invisible.

The Talmud as the essence of dialogue must have impacted the influential twentieth-century Jewish existentialist Martin Buber. Next to Ortega y Gasset, probably no other writer has influenced my thinking as deeply as Buber, whose poetic 1923 treatise *Ich und Du* (often translated *I and Thou*) considers the loving encounter of two people a microcosm for a bond with a living divine presence. Instead of considering our surroundings as a world of opaque objects, Buber asks us to change our perspective and think of everything and everyone as a subject yearning for connection. He rewrites Genesis to proclaim, "In the beginning, there was *relationship.*" But clear and direct expressions like that are rare in Buber's writing, which favors prismatic and elusive language. Rhyme or the related sounds of his words create unexpected possibilities of meaning rather than logical sense. Like the best poetry, Buber's writing resists translation and demands a Talmudic discussion of what his original text may or may not mean.

In one passage of *Ich und Du*, Buber draws a direct comparison between his ideas and the world of artistic expression. *"Das ist der ewige Ursprung der Kunst, dass einem Menschen Gestalt gegenübertritt and durch ihn Werk werden will. Kein Ausgeburt seiner Seele, sondern Erscheinung, die an sie tritt und von ihr die wirkende Kraft erheischt. Es kommt auf eine Wesentat des Menschen an."* Or, in Walter Kaufmann's translation, "This is the eternal origin of art, that a human being confronts a form that wants to become a work through [them]. Not a figment of [their] soul but something that appears to the soul and demands the soul's creative power. What is required is a deed that a man does with his whole being." This is true of both the artist creating and the spectator receiving: both need to show up as "whole beings" to engage in dialogue with a new form. No one can do it alone, or half-heartedly.

Beyond the sheer beauty of his writing and the potency of his simple but profound ideas, Buber has affected me greatly because he embodies the essence of what I believe theater strives to achieve. What Buber later called "the dialogic principle," the world of relationships, represents the most important element of all in theater: *collaboration.* It is here, in collaboration—the ineffable meeting place of "I" and "Thou," wherever two or three are assembled—that the spiritual dimension of opera resides.

But isn't a director's role all about taking the lead? A hierarchical view of art-making is something our society can't seem to shake. The labor of many artists, artisans, and associates gets subsumed under the single name of the lead artist, an objectifying move at the opposite end of the Buberian dialogic. We applaud artists for a vision we call "uncompromising"—which might mean an unshakable resolve but could also refer to a stubborn ignoring of everyone else's experience. Opera, which can be the most tyrannical in its love of hierarchical structures, is perhaps the least appropriate platform for this kind of authoritarianism. The ground holding opera up is so unstable that no artist can possibly stand alone; each artist is inextricably linked to every other. No composer, librettist, director, or conductor can create anything that doesn't rely on the co-articulation and collaboration of many other voices. The right artist for opera embraces this tapestry, while the artist insisting on individual achievement will always struggle.

True collaboration, in the Buberian sense, requires a sense of spiritual strength. Artists must approach a work with both an extraordinary capacity for empathy and a determined discipline to express themselves. It was hardly a surprise, in my early conversations with the great writer and actor Anna Deavere Smith as we started to work together on *Proximity*, to discover how much Buber's work meant to her. After creating scripts from interviews representing different perspectives on a topic, Smith embodies those people she interviewed onstage, a solitary Black woman who takes on their language and idiosyncratic speech patterns. Smith's appearance as an individual reenacting a myriad of other individuals creates a panorama of shared humanity. She describes her work as an act of "radical hospitality"—extended to her often-traumatized dialogue partners but also, ultimately, to the audience. In theater, the spectator is our final and most important collaborator.

Collaboration is often confused with the chaos of a free-for-all, independence being the primary virtue. But the live arts simply don't work without consensus and give-and-take. We require *interdependence*, a word John Cage adopted as a principal methodology. Collaboration may present itself as a leaderless utopia, but in fact it *requires* a leader in order to avoid anarchy and incoherence. Collaboration needs to be nourished; it involves mutual trust and a patient chipping away at a work that is larger than any one artist. Collaboration is fundamentally anti-elite.

Interdependence has always been the most important aspect of my work as a director. The visual aspects of my productions of *The Magic Flute* and *Hopscotch* are examples of the most outward demonstration of a director's work. The more important aspect is invisible: mobilizing, activating, and inspiring the many forces participating in the production. Beyond the concept, designs, and characterizations, a director generates the collaborative atmosphere that enables everyone to unlock their very best work. Hand in hand with the conductor, who oversees the musical performance, a director coordinates all the elements, and leaves an undeniable yet undefinable fingerprint on the transformational process of coming together.

A rehearsal room full of fear, doubt, or obedience doesn't necessarily mean the resulting work will be poor. The archetype of the harsh teacher whose love of discipline sometimes tips over into abuse is deemed acceptable if the outcome is successful, especially in the rigorous field of music. Many directors, conductors, and impresarios, believing that the ends justify the means, thrive by instilling an atmosphere of terror, where exactitude reigns. If their "uncompromising" methods achieve miraculous results and showers of accolades, they are free to punish further. But that increasingly unacceptable approach fundamentally misses the higher purpose of bringing to life a work of art—which is not result-based but process-oriented. An environment of belonging and support transcends the final product. Any particular production disappears after the last performance, but an encounter with a symbiotic environment can change whoever participates in it, whether as performer or spectator. The work of collaboration is invisible and therefore spiritual—but it follows no dogma, and it resists all manipulation.

While anyone can learn the material craft of directing, there's no way to teach this crucial immaterial aspect. Directors reveal their authentic selves in the pressurized rehearsal room, and if collaboration is a posture, the other artists will always see through it. The director who wants to create a true space of belonging needs to fundamentally believe that the act of making theater is a rehearsal for living. Just as ritual is communal, theater is dialogic. It's an act of coordination in the midst of chaos, requiring focus and determination and *just the right application of force*. Intuiting when to push and when to let go, when to radically alter and when to accept, when to revise and when to recognize something can no longer be changed. Directors set the intentions toward greatness, toward the new, toward unseen horizons—and ultimately make the best of what they've got to work with.

My time in Los Angeles must be rubbing off on me, because I've come to view surfing as the best analogy for performance. Surfers have an instinctual understanding of large natural processes at work in their environment. To ride a wave, they learn to shift, listen to the water, and seek a path for beautiful and temporary harmony. They also know full well that they can never fully predict what will unfold beneath their board. Theater likewise provides a space for meditative thinkers who are also flexible doers. Or, in a less Californian metaphor, for those adept at harvesting, who allow time to ripen and nurture what has not yet emerged. Nature will take its course, but cultivation and discipline matter. The best fruit will soon be eaten, but the nourishment of both soil and soul sends limitless ripples into the future.

// // // // //

IN WHAT I HAVE DEFINED as a dialogic, Buberian art form—an emerging art form, an art form of unlimited paradoxes, an art form of multiplicity and potentiality—the self-satisfied artist will be doomed to eternal dissatisfaction. You are never self-sufficient in opera: everything you do is contingent on every other human being involved in your project, not to mention the contingencies of time and space.

If life is the sometimes harmonious, sometimes dissonant blend of different voices and meanings, we should see that multiplicity reflected in the art we create. No singularity of perspective or meaning, but instead richness, depth, and complexity.

How do you achieve that richness, depth, and complexity?

Through layering, by embracing diverse perspectives simultaneously. Letting paths unfold in all directions rather than restricting traffic to one direction.

And chiefly, by recognizing the collaboration that's at the center of all creation, engaged in a profound dialogue with the invisible. Meeting together in rehearsal rooms, in design studios and workshops, and in the theater—day in and day out, giving and taking, exploring what happens when one element is added and another removed. It doesn't always work. Collaboration is a challenge to the ego. In an American culture conditioned on rugged individualism, collaboration can seem antithetical. So the work requires patience above all, from all parties, as the right consensus slowly takes shape.

So have patience with the musician, dedicated to sound, constantly questioning the authenticity of a vibration in the air that evaporates into memory.

And have patience with the opera directors and conductors, who are only as good as the artists they are working with. When they're bringing to life the work of living authors, they face the impossible comparison between reality and the sound the authors have in mind. And when they're articulating the work of dead authors, they face the impossible comparison between reality and the idea of the work the audience has in mind.

And have patience with the singing actors, whose livelihoods depend on the successful vibration of tiny muscles in their throats. As if the superhuman demands of their musical craft weren't enough, they are also required to be better actors than Hollywood stars and stay flexible in their understanding of a character, so that they can adapt to the interpretations of directors and conductors.

Have patience with the composer: how awful it must be to chase a sound in your head, try to pin it down on paper, and grapple with so much that *isn't* music, that isn't sound, to articulate and realize that idea. As soon as composers announce they are writing an opera, an imposing gallery of divine geniuses start passing judgment, as if to say, "What temerity to think that you belong in our pantheon . . ."

The poets need our patience, too: their artistic autonomy, like the composers', melts into a collective work. They face the indignity of seeing their name listed under the composer's . . . if it's listed at all.

And the designers—whether shaping the space, clothing the singers, or illuminating the space—face the pressure of a director trying to articulate a concept, invariably in a condition of too-little-time and too-little-money. They, too, see their work subsumed under the name of the director.

As individuals, none of these artists can succeed unless they acknowledge that their pursuit is inextricably linked to each one of their fellow artists. In the limited duration of the rehearsals and performances of an opera, they are bound to one other. And when the next job starts, all the dynamics are reset and reconfigured, for an equally limited time. The whole operation could not be more absurd—nor could the unresolvable paradoxes of life find a more appropriate mirror.

Even more than the emotional dimension, the spiritual dimension of opera, with its core mechanism of collaboration, is essential and ineffable. It would wilt under the heat of too strong a spotlight. And so, rather than fumble for words to encapsulate what can't be expressed, let me instead offer my gratitude for all that is

unreachable
  undefinable
    ambiguous
      indeterminate
        transcendent
          and multitudinous
            in this paradoxical art form, which,
              (despite everything),
                can illuminate our inner lives.

GRATITUDE

I CAN'T SAY WHY MY DAD STARTED TAKING ME TO THE opera. But why he kept taking me even after I showed no enthusiasm for the art form still baffles me. If he had given up instead of pushing through my resistance, who knows where life would have taken me. There would most certainly be no book in your hands.

My dad, Ariel, died suddenly in 2011, never having seen any of my major projects and before The Industry's first full project in 2012. Even as my biggest fan, he admitted needing to see my productions more than once, because the first time was too overwhelming for him to make sense of what was happening. I have yet to do a project since he passed where I don't imagine him in the audience on multiple occasions, imagining the questions he would ask afterward. Since he's passed, my mother, Mali, my sister Yael, my brother Nim, his wife Pam, and their kids Naomi and Skyler all have picked up my dad's mantle and cheer me on wherever I go. I am so grateful to all of them for their support—and I'm sure they would understand why this book is dedicated above all to my dad, whose memory is a blessing for all of us.

// // // // //

SINCE EVERYTHING I DO IS rooted in collaboration, the solitary act of writing has taken some getting used to. Robert Weil at Liveright first approached me to write a book after I wrote a review for the *Los Angeles Review of Books* for a book of Brecht poetry translations that he published. We met in New York the week after *The Magic Flute* opened in Berlin, and from that moment on, the conversations have been rich and rewarding. He's guided this process with care, patience, and honesty. He also connected me to Lynn Nesbit, ostensibly to serve as my literary agent, but probably knowing we were destined to become fast friends. Both of them were indispensable confidantes for me during this process. The rest of the Norton/Liveright team, especially Rebecca Homiski, Julia Druskin, and Ingsu Liu, have all made this process so rewarding. I am also grateful to Sean Burpee for his design of the Time-Curves; Rebecca Karamehmedovic for her help securing photography permissions; and Jacob Bird for last-minute research support.

So many excellent readers have helped me refine and clarify my ideas from their earliest stages. David Levin, whose book *Unsettling Opera* is a kind of North Star for me, convened a reading group for an incomplete manuscript at the University of Chicago's Neubauer Institute for the Humanities. It was intimidating to present the work-in-process to some of the sharpest minds I've encountered—David; Mary Ann Smart, the professor of an opera class I took at UC Berkeley in the late 1990s; Martha Feldman; Elspeth Carruthers; Tara Zahra; and a host of other musicologists and performance scholars from the school. Their feedback and reactions invigorated me in the final leg of writing. My longtime friend Gundula Kreuzer also assembled an excellent group at Yale University to respond to select chapters. My boyfriend, Jeffrey Seller, turned out to be my perfect reader and offered crucial advice. My friends Bernd Feuchtner, Julian Petri, and Alexandre Caruso offered crucial corrections and guidance.

Since my projects are never exclusively mine, I must thank the many collaborators who have worked with me to realize the projects discussed here—the composers, the librettists, the designers, the singers, the dancers, the choreographers, the producers, the artistic administrators, the assistant directors, the stage managers, the stagehands, and on and on. . . . I could fill up another book with the names of people who have made my work possible, so I will limit myself to thanking the individuals who have been involved at the three companies where sustained relationships have been so crucial.

As a "start-up" opera company, The Industry relied on everyone always going "above and beyond." I am most grateful to my first partner at the company, Music Director Marc Lowenstein, who embodies that ethos. My managerial partners have also been model leaders, starting with Laura Kay Swanson as the first Producing Director; our first General Manager, David Mack; our first Executive Director, my friend Elizabeth Cline; and our current Executive Director, Tim Griffin. Ash Fure and Malik Gaines joined me as Artistic Co-Directors in 2021 and have expanded the company's artistic ambition in inspiring ways. Our current staff—Director of Production Tony Shayne; Producer Brian Sea; and Institutional Development Manager Lindsey Schoenholtz—could not be more committed or accomplished. We have had the most loving and supportive board I can imagine, starting with Mary Ann O'Connor as our first board chair, later succeeded by Mark Hoebich, Christine Adams, and our current chair, Ruth Eliel. Along the way, the wonderful individuals of the board have all expended time, money, and love onto every project we have undertaken: Stephanie Barron, Hyon Chough, Kyle Funn, Edgar Garcia, Fariba Ghaffari, Betsy Greenberg, Suzanna Guzman, Chohi Kim, Caroline Mankey, Dr. Erika Marina Nadir, Adam S. Paris, Ed Patuto, Maurice Singer, Debra Vilinsky, and Lucy Yates. We have had many open-hearted and generous individuals who have supported our work and who have since become my friends; I am so grateful to all of them, but our projects would not have been possible without the extraordinary advocacy of Lenore and Bernard Greenberg.

One of my most transformative professional experiences was as an Artist-Collaborator of the Los Angeles Philharmonic from 2016 to 2019. Working on nine projects in three seasons is a daunting proposition for any organization, but the LA Phil team always raised the bar on ambition. The invitation came from the great Deborah Borda, who coined the term "Disrupter in Residence," while Chad Smith encouraged me to always dream bigger. I got to work closest with Meghan Martineau Umber and Taylor Saleeby Comen, who truly were a dream team. And the enthusiasm that Gustavo Dudamel brought to the company impacted all the work I undertook there, regardless of whether or not he was conducting.

Finally, the team at Detroit Opera took a big risk in engaging me as their Artistic Director, knowing that things would no longer be "business as usual." I wrote this book simultaneously with my efforts to realize a new artistic identity for the organization in the wake of Covid-19, and my experiences in Detroit have certainly shaped what this book has become. My friend Gary L. Wasserman first advocated for me to take on this role, and when I accepted the job, he never flagged in his hospitality and love. Other board members—Ethan Davidson, Barbara Kratchman, Ruth Rattner, Mary Kramer, Ankur Rupta, Don Manvel, Fern Espino, Ali Moiin, Naomi André, Bharat Gandhi, and Lisa DiChiera in particular—have been enthusiastic champions for the changes I proposed, and I am grateful to call them all friends. Wayne Brown first brought me on board and navigated the turbulent waters of Covid with grace; his successor as President and CEO of the organization, Patty Isacson Sabee, has been unwavering in her commitment to breaking ever higher ground. I am so grateful to the whole staff of Detroit Opera, especially those navigating the 180-degree change in approach I was pushing for. I want to especially thank my friend Julie Kim for her transformative partnership as the company's Chief Artistic Planning Officer; her successor, Shawn Rieschl Johnson, has taken on the role of Director of Production superbly. And I want to thank the Artistic Department team, who collaborated with me on instituting the highest possible quality without sacrificing care for all our guest artists: Christine Goerke, Associate Artistic Director; Roberto Kalb, Music Director; Elizabeth Anderson, Artistic Administrator and Production Coordinator; Nathalie Doucet, Chief of Music and Director of the Resident Artist Program; Suzanne Acton, Assistant Music Director and Chorusmaster; and Matthew Principe, Director of Innovation.

I finally want to thank the other members of my own team, past and present, starting with my friend Amanda Ameer—if you heard about me at all prior to this book, it's thanks to her tireless advocacy and press savvy. Her partner at First Chair, James Egelhofer, has also been a caring advocate for my work. I am so fortunate to be working with my current manager, Sharon Zhu, who has been tireless in her support; but I'd also like to thank Phillippa Cole and the Askonas Holt team, Matthew Horner and the IMG team, and Scott Levine for all their previous guidance and efforts to help me achieve my potential.

// // // // //

ONE OF THE MOST PROFOUND pleasures I experienced writing this book was rereading the books I consider formative. Returning to texts I had devoured and absorbed in college or just out of school from my position now felt like an archeological study of my mind. So many concepts I've long since claimed as mine are rooted in someone else's explorations. I couldn't help but think of what Susan Sontag wrote about her books: "A library is an archive of longings." Ideas are always links in a chain, stretching back and ideally also stretching a hand forward.

The writings that have had the strongest effect on this book are highlighted as further reading, but simply listing out these cherished books strikes me as an unloving form of acknowledgment. I'd therefore like to close by acknowledging my debt to and gratitude for one of those sources, which shaped me in ways I am still trying to understand, and which offers a perfect expression for what I am feeling at the end of this writing:

> As you read this book, it is already moving out of date.
> It is for me an exercise, now frozen on the page. But
> unlike a book, the theater has one special characteristic.
> It is always possible to start again. In life this is a myth;
> we ourselves can never go back on anything. New leaves
> never turn, clocks never go back, we can never have a
> second chance. In the theater the slate is wiped clean
> all the time.
>
> —PETER BROOK, *The Empty Space*

WORKS CITED

GENERAL REFERENCE

Abbate, Carolyn. *In Search of Opera.* Princeton: Princeton University Press, 2001.

Abbate, Carolyn, and Roger Parker. *A History of Opera: The Last Four Hundred Years.* London: Penguin Books, 2015.

Adams, John. *Hallelujah Junction: Composing an American Life.* New York: Farrar, Straus and Giroux, 2009.

André, Naomi. *Black Opera: History, Power, Engagement.* Urbana: University of Illinois Press, 2018.

Badiou, Alain. *Five Lessons on Wagner.* London: Verso, 2010.

Baker, Evan. *From the Score to the Stage: An Illustrated History of Continental Opera Production and Staging.* Chicago: University of Chicago Press, 2013.

Barenboim, Daniel. *Music Quickens Time.* London: Verso, 2008.

Beckerman, Michael, ed. *Janáček and His World.* Princeton: Princeton University Press, 2003.

Berry, Mark. *After Wagner: Histories of Modernist Music Drama from Parsifal to Nono.* Suffolk: Boydell Press, 2014.

Budden, Julian. *The Operas of Verdi.* Oxford: Oxford University Press, 1979.

Calvino, Italo. *Invisible Cities.* Translated by William Weaver. London: Vintage, 1997.

Cooke, Deryck. *I Saw the World End: A Study of Wagner's Ring.* Oxford: Oxford University Press, 1979.

Heartz, Daniel. *Mozart's Operas.* Edited by Thomas Bauman. Berkeley: University of California Press, 1990.

Kerman, Joseph. *Opera as Drama.* New York: Vintage Books, 1959.

King, Thomas. *The Truth About Stories: A Native Narrative.* Minneapolis: University of Minnesota Press, 2003.

Kreuzer, Gundula. *Curtain, Gong, Steam: Wagnerian Technologies of Nineteenth-Century Opera.* Berkeley: University of California Press, 2018.

Levin, David J. *Unsettling Opera.* Chicago: University of Chicago Press, 2007.

Magee, Bryan. *Wagner and Philosophy.* London: Penguin Books, 2001.

Muller, Ulrich, and Peter Wapnewski, eds. *Wagner Handbook.* Cambridge: Harvard University Press, 1992.

Rancière, Jacques. *The Emancipated Spectator.* London: Verso, 2009.

Ringer, Mark. *Opera's First Master: The Musical Dramas of Claudio Monteverdi.* London: Amadeus Press, LLC, 2006.

Ross, Alex. *Wagnerism: Art and Politics in the Shadow of Music.* New York: Farrar, Straus and Giroux, 2020.

Shawn, Allen. *Arnold Schoenberg's Journey.* New York: Farrar, Straus and Giroux, 2002.

Skelton, Geoffrey. *Wieland Wagner: The Positive Sceptic.* London: St. Martin's Press, 1971.

Smart, Mary Ann. *Mimomania: Music and Gesture in Nineteenth-Century Opera.* Berkeley: University of California Press, 2004.

Sutcliffe, Tom. *Believing in Opera.* Princeton: Princeton University Press, 1996.

Tomlinson, Gary. *Metaphysical Song.* Princeton: Princeton University Press, 1999.

Treadwell, James. *Interpreting Wagner.* New Haven: Yale University Press, 2003.

Waleson, Heidi. *Mad Scenes and Exit Arias: The Death of the New York City Opera and the Future of Opera in America.* New York: Henry Holt and Company, 2018.

Zizek, Slavoj, and Mladen Dolar. *Opera's Second Death.* Oxon: Routledge, 2002.

OVERTURE: AN ART FORM WITHOUT A FUTURE

Burden, Michael. "From Recycled Performances to Repertory: The King's Theatre in London, 1705–1820." In *The Oxford Handbook of the Operatic Canon*, edited by Cormac Newark and William Weber, 115–30. Oxford: Oxford University Press, 2020.

Monteverdi, Claudio. *L'Orfeo: favola in musica in un prologo e cinque atti*. Kassel: Bärenreiter, 2012.

Noiray, Michel, and Franco Piperno. "Foundations: France and Italy in the Eighteenth Century." In *The Oxford Handbook of the Operatic Canon*, edited by Cormac Newark and William Weber, 25–26. Oxford: Oxford University Press, 2020.

Piperno, Franco. "Italian Opera and the Concept of 'Canon' in the Late Eighteenth Century." In *The Oxford Handbook of the Operatic Canon*, edited by Cormac Newark and William Weber, 51–70. Oxford: Oxford University Press, 2020.

CHAPTER ONE: "DON'T YOU GET IT?"

Adorno, Theodor. "The Radio Symphony (1941)." In *Essays on Music*, translated by Susan H. Gillespie, 251–70. Berkeley: University of California Press, 2002.

Beckett, Samuel. *Waiting for Godot*. In *The Complete Dramatic Works*. London: Faber and Faber, 1990.

La bohème. Opera by Giacomo Puccini, composer; Luigi Illica and Giuseppe Giacosa, librettists; Yuval Sharon, director. Detroit Opera, Boston Lyric Opera, and Spoleto Festival USA, 2022. https://www.yuvalsharon.com/la-bohme.

Cage, John. "2 Pages, 122 Words on Music and Dance." In *Silence: Lectures and Writing*, 96–97. Middletown, CT: Wesleyan University Press, 1961.

Marshall, Gary, director. *Pretty Woman*. Touchstone Pictures, Silver Screen Partners IV, Regency International Pictures, 1990. Film.

Wagner, Richard. *Parsifal*. Leipzig: Breitkopf & Härtel, 1914.

——*Siegfried*. Mainz: B. Schott's Söhne, 1901.

CHAPTER TWO: THE FUTURE IN OUR PAST

Aeschylus. *Oresteia*. Edited by Christopher Collard. Oxford: Oxford University Press, 2017.

Beauvoir, Simone de. *The Ethics of Ambiguity*. Translated by Bernard Frechtman. New York: Open Road Integrated Media, 2018.

Böhme, Madelaine, Rüdiger Braun, and Florian Breier. *Ancient Bones: Unearthing the Astonishing New Story of How We Became Human*. Translated by Jane Billinghurst. Vancouver and Berkeley: Greystone Books, 2020.

Eagleton, Terry. *Hope Without Optimism*. Charlottesville: University of Virginia Press, 2015.

Goodman, Alice. *History Is Our Mother: Three Libretti*. New York: New York Review of Books, 2017.

Mozart, Wolfgang Amadeus, and Emanuel Schikaneder. *Die Zauberflöte: eine deutsche Oper in zwei Aufzügen, KV 620*. Kassel: Bärenreiter, 1970.

Ortega y Gasset, José. *Meditations on Quixote*. Translated by Evelyn Rugg and Diego Marín. Urbana: University of Illinois Press, 2000.

Ovid. *Metamorphoses*. Translated by Stephanie McCarter. New York: Penguin, 2022.

Pratchett, Terry. *Maskerade*. London: Corgi, 2005.

Proust, Marcel. *Remembrance of Things Past*. Translated by C. K. Scott Moncrieff and Terence Kilmartin. New York: Vintage Books, 1981.

CHAPTER THREE: "THE POWER PLANT OF FEELINGS"

Caldara, Antonio, and Pietro Metastasio. *Il Temistocle*. Gallica—Open Access, 1780. https://gallica.bnf.fr/ark:/12148/btv1b10074816b/f5.item.

Coppola, Francis Ford, director. *The Godfather Part III*. Paramount Pictures, American Zoetrope, Paramount, Zoetrope Studios, 1991. Film.

Darabont, Frank, director. *The Shawshank Redemption*. Castle Rock Entertainment, Columbia Pictures, 1994. Film.

Descartes, René. "The Passions of the Soul." In *Descartes: Selected Philosophical Writing*. Translated by John Cottingham, Robert Stoothoff, and Dugald Murdoch, 218–38. Cambridge, UK: Cambridge University Press, 1988.

Dylan, Bob. *The Philosophy of Modern Song*. New York: Simon & Schuster, 2022.

Edwards, Jonathan. "7-Eleven Store Owner Uses Classical Music to Drive Away Homeless People." *Washington Post*, January 17, 2023.

Kluge, Alexander, director. *Die Macht der Gefühle*. Kairos, ZDF, 1983. Film, available at https://youtu.be/ToosY-53zB4?si=g_BgRdIBX_InURH2.

Metropolitan Opera. *Aida*. Accessed on April 10, 2024. https://www .metopera.org/season/on-demand/opera/?upc=811357011799.

Monteverdi, Claudio, and Giovanni Francesco Busenello. *L'incoronazione di Poppea*. London: Faber Music, 1968.

Mozart, Wolfgang Amadeus, and Lorenzo da Ponte. *Il dissoluto punito: ossia, il Don Giovanni: dramma giocoso in zwei Akten, KV 527*. Kassel: Bärenreiter, 2005.

———*Le nozze di Figaro: Opera buffa in quattro atti, KV 492*. Kassel: Bärenreiter, 2016.

National Endowment for the Arts. "NEA Opera Honors: Interview with Leontyne Price." Washington, DC, 2008. YouTube video, https:// youtu.be/EqVu_wlxTzM?si=Xt-nBMdjoUlHpf_8.

Proximity. Operas by Daniel Bernard Roumain, Caroline Shaw, John Luther Adams, composers; Anna Deavere Smith, Jocelyn Clarke, John Haines, librettists. Yuval Sharon, director. Lyric Opera of Chicago, 2023. https://www.yuvalsharon.com/proximit-gallery-1/.

Rice, John. "Leopold II, Mozart, and the Return to a Golden Age." In *Opera and the Enlightenment*, edited by Thomas Bauman and Marita Petzoldt McClymonds, 271–96. Cambridge, UK: Cambridge University Press, 1995.

Talk Classical. "Should We Expect Opera Singers to Act?" Accessed April 10, 2024. https://www.talkclassical.com/threads/should-we-expect-opera -singers-to-act.40732/.

Tomlinson, Gary. *Metaphysical Song*. Princeton: Princeton University Press, 1999.

Verdi, Giuseppe, and Antonio Ghislanzoni. *Aida: opera in quattro atti*. Milan: Ricordi, 1913.

Zeami. "A Mirror Held to the Flower (*Kakyō*)." In *On the Art of the Nō*

Drama, translated by J. Thomas Rimer and Yamazaki Masakazu, 74–110. Princeton: Princeton University Press, 1984.

CHAPTER FOUR: A STRANGE FORM OF STORYTELLING

Abbate, Carolyn, and Roger Parker. *A History of Opera: The Last Four Hundred Years*. London: Penguin Books, 2015.

Adams, John, and Peter Sellars. *Doctor Atomic*. New York: Boosey & Hawkes, 2012.

Art Hive. "Pablo Picasso's Quotes on How to Be an Artist, Draw Wildness and Love a Doorknob." Published April 1, 2019. https://arthive .com/publications/1659~Pablo_Picassos_quotes_on_how_to_be _an_artist_draw_wildness_and_love_a_doorknob.

Ashley, Robert. *Private Lives: An Opera*. San Francisco: Burning Books, 1991.

Barthes, Roland. *Image Music Text*. New York: Hill and Wang, 1977.

Bauer, Thomas. *Die Vereindeutigung der Welt: Über den Verlust an Mehr- deutigkeit und Vielfalt*.
Stuttgart: Reclam Universal-Bibliothek, 2021.

Brecht, Bertolt. "The Modern Theatre Is the Epic Theatre." In *Brecht on Theatre: The Development of an Aesthetic*, edited by John Willett, 33–42. New York: Hill and Wang, 1964.

Britten, Benjamin, and Myfanwy Piper. *The Turn of the Screw*. London: Boosey & Hawkes, 2008.

Brook, Peter. *The Empty Space*. New York: Touchstone, 1968.

Budner, Stanley. "Intolerance of Ambiguity as a Personality Variable." *Journal of Personality* 30, Issue 1 (April 2006): 29–50. https://doi .org/10.1111/j.1467-6494.1962.tb02303.x.

Debussy, Claude, and Maurice Maeterlinck. *Pelléas et Mélisande: drame lyrique en 5 actes et 12 tabl*

Eco, Umberto. *The Open Work*. Cambridge: Harvard University Press, 1989.

Eötvös, Peter, and C. H. Henneberg. *Tri Sestri*. Munich: Ricordi, 1997.

Felsenstein, Walter. *The Music Theatre of Walter Felsenstein*. Edited by Peter Paul Fuchs. London: Quartet Books Limited, 1991.

Glass, Philip, and Robert Wilson. *Einstein on the Beach: An Opera in Four Acts*. London: Chester Music, 2006.

Handel, Georg Friederich. *Arminio: opera in tre atti, HWV 36*. Kassel: Bärenreiter, 2011.

James, Henry. *The Turn of the Screw, and Other Stories*. Edited by T. J. Lustig. Oxford: Oxford University Press, 1992.

Janáček, Leoš. *Příhody Lišky Bystroušky: opera o 3 jedáních dle R. Těsnohlídkovy*. London: Universal Edition, 1924.

Jung, Carl Gustav. *The Undiscovered Self*. London: Routledge, 2014.

Lehmann, Hans-Thies. *Postdramatic Theatre*. Oxon: Routledge, 2006.

Messiaen, Olivier. *Saint François d'Assise: scènes franciscaines: opéra en 3 actes et 8 tableaux*. Paris: Leduc, 1991.

Okri, Ben. *Starbook: A Magical Tale of Love and Regeneration*. London: Rider, 2008.

Olson, Brad, host. "The Functions of Rituals." *Pathways with Joseph Campbell*, podcast. May 1, 2021. Accessed on April 10, 2024. https://open .spotify.com/episode/3w27BVluvw5yVmSUEya7kb?si=WvLZMvLlT PiCVdXzQx5fMg.

Rancière, Jacques. *The Emancipated Spectator*. London: Verso, 2009.

Rockwell, John. "Robert Ashley's Video Opera in Debut at Kitchen." *New York Times*, November 18, 1983.

Rodgers, Richard. *Musical Stages: An Autobiography*. New York: Random House, 1975. Quoted in Raymond Knapp, "Canons of the American Musical." In *The Oxford Handbook of the Operatic Canon*, edited by Cormac Newark and William Weber, 475–90. Oxford: Oxford University Press, 2020.

Ross, Alex. "A Grand Tour of Germany's Opera Paradise." *The New Yorker*, June 13, 2022.

Salieri, Antonio. *Prima la musica e poi le parole: divertimento teatrale in un atto*. Kassel: Bärenreiter, 2013.

Saturday Night Live. "Opera Man Cold Opening—SNL." Accessed on April 10, 2024. https://youtu.be/Ta4sbXmeozo?si=qZTrQ2riYgAzW9cG.

Silverman, Mike. "Munich Production Adds New Depth to 'Il Trovatore'" *The Spokesman-Review*, July 5, 2013.

Swafford, Jan. "Learning to Love Mozart." *Slate*, April 10, 2012.

Swed, Mark. "MUSIC: Grand Sitcom: Robert Ashley's Operas Are for TV but Prime Time Isn't Quite Ready for Them Yet So They Are Performed Live." *Los Angeles Times*, March 22, 1992.

Tomlinson, Gary. *Metaphysical Song*. Princeton: Princeton University Press, 1999.

Verdi, Giuseppe, and Salvatore Cammarano. *Il trovatore: dramma lirico in 4 parti di Salvadore Cammarano*. Milan: Ricordi, 1913.

Verdi, Giuseppe, and Luigi Illica. *Tosca: melodramma in tre atti*. Milan: Ricordi, 1963.

CHAPTER FIVE: CASE STUDY: *THE MAGIC FLUTE* IN BERLIN

ATLAS. Opera by Meredith Monk, composer and librettist. Yuval Sharon, director. LA Phil New Music Group, 2019. https://www.yuvalsharon .com/atlas.

Arendt, Hannah. *The Human Condition*. Chicago: University of Chicago Press, 2018.

Aristotle. *Poetics*. Edited by D. W. Lucas. Oxford: Oxford University Press, 2020.

Assmann, Jan. *Die Zauberflöte: Oper und Mysterium*. München: Carl Hanser, 2006.

Bergman, Ingmar, director. *The Hour of the Wolf*. SF-Produktion, 1968. Film.

———*The Magic Flute*. SF-Produktion, Sveriges Radio, Swedish Film Institute, 1975. Film.

Campbell, Joseph, with Bill Moyers. *The Power of Myth*. New York: Doubleday, 1988.

Descartes, René. "The Passions of the Soul." In *Descartes: Selected Philosophical Writing*. Translated by John Cottingham, Robert Stoothoff, and Dugald Murdoch, 218–38. Cambridge, UK: Cambridge University Press, 1988.

Janáček, Leoš, and Kerstin Lücker. *Věc Makropulos: opera ve třech jednáních podle komedie Karla Čapka*. Kassel: Bärenreiter, 2019.

Kleist, Heinrich von. *Über das Marionettentheater (Studienausgabe)*. Stuttgart: Reclams Universal-Bibliothek, 2013.

Mozart, Wolfgang Amadeus, and Caterino Mazzolà. *La clemenza di Tito*. Kassel: Bärenreiter, 2001.

Mozart, Wolfgang Amadeus, and Lorenzo da Ponte. *Così fan tutte: ossia, La scuola degli amanti*. Kassel: Bärenreiter, 1991.

———*Le nozze di Figaro: Opera buffa in quattro atti, KV 492*. Kassel: Bärenreiter, 2016.

Mozart, Wolfgang Amadeus, and Emanuel Schikaneder. *Die Zauberflöte: eine deutsche Oper in zwei Aufzügen, KV 620*. Kassel: Bärenreiter, 1970.

Mozart, Wolfgang Amadeus, and Giambattista Varesco. *Idomeneo: Dramma per musica in tre atti*. Kassel: Bärenreiter, 1972.

Neruda, Pablo. *Book of Questions*. Translated by Sara Lissa Paulson. New York: Enchanted Lion Books, 2022.

Saint-Exupéry, Antoine de. *The Little Prince*. Translated by Irene Testot-Ferry. Ware: Wordsworth Editions, 2018.

Shakespeare, William. *A Midsummer Night's Dream*. Edited by Sukanta Chaudhuri. London: Bloomsbury Publishing, 2017.

———*The Tempest*. Cambridge, UK: Cambridge University Press, 2004.

CHAPTER SIX: THE USE-LESS ART

Artaud, Antonin. *The Theater and Its Double*. Translated by Mary Caroline Richards. New York: Grove Press, 1994.

Carax, Leos, director. *Holy Motors*. Theo Films, Pierre Grise Productions, Pandora Films, Arte France Cinema, WDR/ARTE, 2012. Film.

Hopscotch: A Mobile Opera for 24 Cars. Opera by Veronika Krausas, Marc Lowenstein, Andrew McIntosh, Andrew Norman, Ellen Reid, David Rosenboom, composers; Tom Jacobson, Mandy Kahn, Sarah LaBrie, Jane Stephens Rosenthal, Janine Salinas Schoenberg, Erin Young, librettists. Yuval Sharon, director. The Industry, 2015. https://hopscotchopera.com.

Mazer, Benjamin. "Stop Wasting COVID Tests, People." *Atlantic*, January 3, 2022.

CHAPTER SEVEN: TOWARD AN ANTI-ELITE OPERA

Abbate, Carolyn, and Roger Parker. *A History of Opera: The Last Four Hundred Years*. London: Penguin Books, 2015.

Adorno, Theodor. *Minima Moralia: Reflections on a Damaged Life*. Translated by E. F. N. Jephcott. London and New York: Verso, 2005.

Alexander, Harriet. "Detroit Gives Tragic Classic Opera *La Bohème* a Woke Reboot: City Will Stage Production in REVERSE Order to Avoid Ending Where Main Character Dies So Audience Leaves Feeling 'Hopeful and Optimistic.'" *Mail Online*, March 31, 2022.

Baraka, Amiri. "The Changing Same." In *The LeRoi Jones/Amiri Baraka Reader*, edited by William J. Harris, 186–209. New York: Thunder's Mouth, 1991.

Berg, Alban. *Wozzeck*. Wien: Universal Edition, 2023.

Davis, Anthony, and Thulani Davis. *X: The Life and Times of Malcolm X*. United States: Nani Press, 2022.

Duncan, Aja Couchois, and Douglas Kearney. "Two Writers in Conversation: Aja Couchois Duncan and Douglas Kearney." In *Sweet Land*, 11-2, available at: https://theindustryla.org/wp-content/uploads/2020/02/IND-SweetLand_digitalprogram_20-0320.pdf.

Rabkin, Nick, and E. C. Hedberg. "Arts Education in America: What the Declines Mean for Arts Participation." Accessed on April 12, 2024. Available at: https://www.arts.gov/sites/default/files/2008-SPPA-Arts Learning.pdf.

Reddit. "Why Is Opera Considered Elitist?" Accessed on April 12, 2024. https://www.reddit.com/r/AskReddit/comments/ankwus/why_is_opera_considered_elitist/#.

Rosenblum, Ira. "From Ed Sullivan, 'Rilly Big' Opera Stars." *New York Times*, August 17, 1997.

Schoenberg, Arnold. *Moses und Aron: Oper in drei Akten*. Mainz: B. Schott's Söhne, 1958.

———*Style and Idea: Selected Writings*. Edited by Leonard Stein. Los Angeles: University of California Press, 1986.

Sweet Land. Opera by Raven Chacon, composer; Douglas Kearney, librettist. Yuval Sharon and Cannupa Hanska Luger, director. The Industry, 2020. https://theindustryla.org/projects/sweet-land/.

Weil, Simone. *The Need for Roots*. Oxon: Routledge & Kegan Paul, 1952.

CHAPTER EIGHT: BREAKING THE FRAME

Abbate, Carolyn, and Roger Parker. *A History of Opera: The Last Four Hundred Years*. London: Penguin Books, 2015.

Artaud, Antonin. *The Theater and Its Double*. Translated by Mary Caroline Richards. New York: Grove Press, 1994.

ATLAS. Opera by Meredith Monk, composer and librettist. Yuval Sharon, director. LA Phil New Music Group, 2019. https://www.yuvalsharon.com/atlas.

Beck, Julian. "Mission." Poem. Available at: https://www.livingtheatre.org/about.

Botting, Gary. "The Living Theatre." In *The Theatre of Protest in America*. Edmonton: Harden House, 1972.

Boulez, Pierre. "Sprengt die Opernhäuser in die Luft!" Interview by *Der Spiegel*. *Der Spiegel*, August 24, 1967. https://www.spiegel.de/kultur/sprengt-die-opernhaeuser-in-die-luft-a-ac664ef2-0002-0001-0000-000046353389?context=issue.

Cage, John. *4'33"*. New York: Henmar Press, 1960.

Calvino, Italo. *Invisible Cities*. Translated by William Weaver. London: Vintage, 1997.

Crescent City. Opera by Anne-LeBaron; Douglas Kearney, librettist. Yuval Sharon, director. The Industry, 2012. https://www.yuvalsharon.com/crescent-city.

Field, Andy. "'Site-Specific Theatre'? Please Be More Specific." *Guardian*, February 6, 2008. Goodman, Alice. *History Is Our Mother: Three Libretti*. New York: New York Review of Books, 2017.

Invisible Cities. Opera by Christopher Cerrone, composer and librettist. Yuval Sharon, director. The Industry and LA Dance Project, 2013. https://theindustryla.org/projects/invisible-cities/.

Kaprow, Allan. *Essays on the Blurring of Art and Life*. Edited by Jeff Kelley. Berkeley: University of California Press, 2003.

Miller, Ben. "Renée Fleming Adds a New Role to Her Repertoire: Pat Nixon." *New York Times*, March 24, 2023.

Schechner, Richard, Surekha Sikri, Nissar Allana, and Geeti Sen. "Richard Schechner on Environmental Theatre." *India International Centre Quarterly* 10, Number 2 (June 1983): 237–48. https://www.jstor.org/stable/pdf/23001648.pdf?refreqid=fastly-default%3A32be1e09b25 5821ab56ab67b1b7be5af&ab_segments=&origin=&initiator=&accep tTC=1.

Tommasini, Anthony. "Meddling with Opera's Sacred Human Voice." *New York Times*, August 3, 1999.

Verdi, Giuseppe, and Antonio Ghislanzoni. *Aida: opera in quattro atti.* Milan: Ricordi, 1913.

Verdi, Giuseppe, and Antonio Somma. *Un ballo in maschera: melodramma in tre atti.* Milan: Ricordi, 1914.

Wagner, Richard. *Götterdämmerung.* Mainz: Schott, 1908.

War of the Worlds. Opera by Annie Gosfield, composer; Yuval Sharon, librettist. Yuval Sharon, director. Los Angeles Philharmonic, The Industry, and NOW Art. https://www.yuvalsharon.com/war-of-the-worlds.

CHAPTER NINE: CASE STUDY: *HOPSCOTCH* IN LOS ANGELES

Buñuel, Luis, director. *That Obscure Object of Desire.* Greenwich Film Productions, Les Films Galaxie, 1977. Film.

Cortázar, Julio. *Hopscotch.* New York: Pantheon Books, 1966.

Debord, Guy. "Theory of the Dérive." In *Situationist International Anthology (Revised and Expanded Edition)*, edited by Ken Knabb, 62–66. Berkeley: Bureau of Public Streets, 2006.

Haynes, Todd, director. *I'm Not There.* Endgame Entertainment, Killer Films, John Wells Productions, John Goldwyn Productions, VIP Medienfonds 4, Rising Star, Grey Water Park Productions, 2007. Film.

Hopscotch: A Mobile Opera for 24 Cars. Opera by Veronika Krausas, Marc Lowenstein, Andrew McIntosh, Andrew Norman, Ellen Reid, David Rosenboom, composers; Tom Jacobson, Mandy Kahn, Sarah LaBrie, Jane Stephens Rosenthal, Janine Salinas Schoenberg, Erin Young, librettists. Yuval Sharon, director. The Industry, 2015.

Lepore, Jill. "The VW Bus Took the Sixties on the Road. Now It's Getting a Twenty-First-Century Makeover." *The New Yorker*, July 18, 2022.

Twilight: Gods. Music by Richard Wagner, composer; Richard Wagner, Marsha Music, and avery r. young, librettists. Yuval Sharon, director. Michigan Opera Theatre and Lyric Opera of Chicago. https://www.yuvalsharon.com/twilight-gods.

Virilio, Paul. "The Third Window." In *Global Vision*, edited by Cynthia Schneider and Brian Wallis, 185–97. Cambridge: MIT Press, 1988.

CHAPTER 10: UNRESOLVED PARADOXES

Ashley, Robert. "Biography." Accessed on April 12, 2024. http://www .robertashley.org/.

——"Productions: Perfect Lives." Accessed on April 12, 2024. http:// www.robertashley.org/productions/1977-83-perfectlives.htm.

Boulez, Pierre. "Reflections on *Pelléas et Mélisande*." In *Orientations: Collected Writings*, edited by Jean-Jacques Nattiez, 306–17. Cambridge: Harvard University Press, 1985.

Buber, Martin. *I and Thou*. Translated by Walter Kaufmann. New York: Touchstone, 1996.

Debussy, Claude, and Maurice Maeterlinck. *Pelléas et Mélisande: drame lyrique en 5 actes et 12 tableaux*. Paris: A. Durand & fils, 1907.

Monteverdi, Claudio. *L'incoronazione di Poppea*. London: Faber Music, 1968,

——*L'Orfeo: favola in musica in un prologo e cinque atti*. Kassel: Bärenreiter, 2012.

Okri, Ben. *Astonishing the Gods*. New York: Other Press, 2022.

Ortega y Gasset, José. *Meditations on Quixote*. Urbana: University of Illinois Press, 2000.

Proximity. Operas by Daniel Bernard Roumain, Caroline Shaw, John Luther Adams, composers; Anna Deavere Smith, Jocelyn Clarke, John Haines, librettists. Yuval Sharon, director. Lyric Opera of Chicago, 2023. https://www.yuvalsharon.com/proximit-gallery-1/.

Schoenberg, Arnold. *Moses und Aron: Oper in drei Akten*. Mainz: B. Schott's Söhne, 1958.

——*Verklärte Nacht op. 4; Piano Pieces op. 11 & 19; Five Orchestral Pieces op. 16*. Chicago Symphony Orchestra. Daniel Barenboim, pianist and conductor. Teldec, 1995, compact disc.

Shvetashvatara. *The Thirteen Principal Upanishads*. Translated by Robert Ernest Hume. Oxford: Oxford University Press, 1921.

Tomlinson, Gary. *Metaphysical Song*. Princeton: Princeton University Press, 1999.

Wagner, Richard. *Tristan und Isolde*. Leipzig: Breitkopf & Härtel, 1914.

Wilde, Oscar. "The Decay of Lying." In *Intentions*, 1–56. New York: A. & C. Boni, 1930.

GRATITUDE

Brook, Peter. *The Empty Space*. New York: Touchstone, 1968.

Sontag, Susan. *As Consciousness Is Harnessed to Flesh: Journals and Notebooks, 1964–1980*. New York: Farrar, Straus and Giroux, 2012.

CREDITS

page 248 (above): Leopoldo Metlicovitz
page 248 (below): Emil Stumpp / Deutsches Historisches Museum
page 249 (top left): © 2024 Artists Rights Society; credit: (ARS), New York
page 250 (top right): Wilhelm Höffert
page 253 (bottom left): Franz Hanfstaengl / Bibliothèque Nationale de France
page 253 (bottom right): M. E. de Liphart

INDEX

Page numbers in *italic* refer to illustrations.

immortality of, 30
incomplete, 100
as marionette theater, 132–34, *133*
nonlinear approaches to, 20–23
as popular entertainment, 4, 32, 33, 154, 159,
    183, 201
progressive view of, 39–41
recordings of, 1, 18–21
re-creation of, 4, 40–41, 187
spiritual life of, 260
as suspended time, 256
as symbol of luxury, 14
use-lessness of, 162–63, 171, 173–74
as verb, 194
opera seria, 153
Oppenheimer, Robert, 101, 118
orchestrations, 107, 154, 209
Oresteia, The (Aeschylus), 26, 27, 36–38, 42
Orestes, 36
Orfeo, L' (Monteverdi), 7–10, 31, 38, 63–64,
    67–69, *68,* 97, 154, 262
Orff, Carl, *Carmina Burana,* 217
originalism, 45
original sin, 42
Orpheus, 7–10, 31, 38, 67, 92
Ortega y Gasset, José, 41
    Meditations on Quixote, 263
"O Superman" (Anderson), 156
Otello (Verdi), 44, 153
Ovid, *Metamorphoses,* 45–46
Oxford Handbook of the Operatic Canon, 4

Pacino, Al, 51, 60, 63
painting(s), 86, 97, 180–81, 204–5
Palais Royal (Paris), 152
Palazzo Corsi, 29
Paris, France, 80, 107, 123, 152, 158, 177, 228
Paris Opera, 75, 209
"park and bark," 15, 206
Parker, Roger, *A History of Opera,* 108, 174, 201
Parkinson, John and Donald, 215
Parma, Italy, 32
Parsifal (Wagner), 11–19, 22, 72, 75, 174, 185,
    244, 250, 256
Partch, Harry, 159
    Delusions of the Fury, 158
Pascal, Blaise, 185

Passions of the Soul, The (Descartes), 56
past, the, 2, 35–47, 190, 215, 244
pasticcios, 4
Pathways (podcast), 96
patience, 269–70
patriarchy, 43, 46, 129
Pears, Peter, 245
Pelléas et Mélisande (Debussy), 110–12, 259
Perfect Lives (Ashley), 3, 90–91, 95
performance art, 7, 205
Peri, Jacopo, 30
    Dafne, 29
    Euridice, 29, 31
peripeteia, 131–34, 137, 145
Pesacov, Lewis, 225
Peter Grimes (Britten), 245
Phantom of the Opera, The, 3
Philadelphia, Pa., 23
Philosophy of Modern Song, The (Dylan), 53
Picasso, Pablo, 86, 187
plot-character, 108
poetic readings, 98–100, 110–12, 117, 132, 218
Pollock, Jackson, 204
polyphony, 6, 8, 50
popular culture, 85, 86, 159, 184
popular entertainment, opera as, 4, 32, 33, 154,
    159, 183, 201
"Por un amor" (Reyes), 230, 231
post-dramatic theater, 94, 118
poverty, 163, 176–77
Pratchett, Terry, 36
Prégardien, Julian, *146*
Pretty Woman (film), 14, 15, 20, 21, 173, 183
Price, Leontyne, 61–62, 64, 66, 183
Prima la musica e poi le parole (Salieri), 104–6
production-character, 108
progress, idea of, 25, 36
Prohaska, Anna, *133, 146*
proscenium arch, 32, 128, 196, 201–3, 205, 206,
    210, 212–14, 216, 220, 243, 252
Proust, Marcel, *In Search of Lost Time,* 38–39
Proximity (trio of operas), 69–72, *71,* 225, 266
Public Theater (New York City), 167–68
Puccini, Giacomo, 99, 197
    La bohème, 20–24, 32, 72, 107, 176–77, 182,
        187, 225
    Madama Butterfly, 44, 158